FORDHAM UNIVERSITY LIBRARY
E184.C3 U6 v.31
Becker, Martin Joseph.   000
A history of Catholic life in   010101

0 2015 0428544 0

E
184
.C3U6
V.31

PLEASE DO NOT REMOVE
TRANSACTION SLIP FROM BOOK POCKET
IT IS NEEDED TO CLEAR YOUR RECORD

FORDHAM UNIVERSITY LIBRARY

Duane

This book is due not later than the date on slip. For each book kept overtime there is a fine of 5c for each day.

FACULTY MEMBERS MUST RETURN ALL BOOKS AT THE CLOSE OF THE SPRING SEMESTER

PRINTED IN U.S.A.

MONOGRAPH SERIES
UNITED STATES CATHOLIC HISTORICAL SOCIETY

UNITED STATES CATHOLIC HISTORICAL SOCIETY
**MONOGRAPH SERIES
XXXI**

A HISTORY OF CATHOLIC LIFE IN THE DIOCESE OF ALBANY, 1609-1864

by
MARTIN JOSEPH BECKER

NEW YORK
UNITED STATES CATHOLIC
HISTORICAL SOCIETY
1975

E
184
C3 U6
V. 31

UNITED STATES CATHOLIC HISTORICAL SOCIETY

President
Thomas A. Brennan

Vice President
Rev. Msgr. Florence D. Cohalan

Secretary
Victor L. Ridder

Treasurer
Charles G. Herbermann, Jr.

Editor of Publications
Rev. Thomas J. Shelley

Publications Committee
Joseph G.E. Hopkins
Brother Alexander Thomas   **Victor L. Ridder**

Directors

Richard P. Breaden
George A. Brooks
Rev. Msgr. Eugene V. Clark
Dr. Elisa A. Carrillo
George B. Fargis
Sister Mary Elena Ridder Hanlon, C.S.F.

Joseph G.E. Hopkins
Miss Ethel King
Rev. Msgr. Patrick D. O'Flaherty
Hugo F. Ricca, Jr.
Rev. Thomas J. Shelley
Brother Alexander Thomas
Gaetano L. Vincitorio

TO MY WIFE
AND
TO MY MOTHER

Copyright 1973
by
MARTIN JOSEPH BECKER
and
Copyright 1975
by
UNITED STATES CATHOLIC HISTORICAL SOCiETY

Office of the Secretary
St. Joseph's Seminary, Dunwoodie, Yonkers, N.Y. 10704

A HISTORY OF CATHOLIC LIFE IN THE DIOCESE OF ALBANY
1609 — 1864

By
MARTIN J. BECKER

CONTENTS

Page

MAPS
- DIOCESE OF ALBANY, 1847-1872 xii
- SITES OF CONGREGATIONS, 1847 xiii
- SITES OF CONGREGATIONS, 1864 xiv

PREFACE 15

CHAPTERS
- I. SEED ON A ROCK 17
- II. A BODY WITHOUT A HEAD 31
- III. APOSTACY ON THE FRONTIER 44
- IV. THE NORTH COUNTRY AND THE SOUTHERN FRONTIER 54
- V. FARM, FOREST AND ERIE CANAL 68
- VI. THE LINE OF MELCHIZEDEK 74
- VII. NUMBERS: THE CATHOLIC POPULATION 82
- VIII. IMMIGRATION 88
- IX. A LAND OF MILK AND HONEY 103
- X. LAY TRUSTEEISM IN TROY 115
- XI. THE PROFANATION OF THE TEMPLE IN OSWEGO 122
- XII. THE INTERDICT IN CARTHAGE 132
- XIII. A CROWN OF THORNS IN UTICA 169
- XIV. THE ROOTS OF THE TREE 203

APPENDICES 214
BIBLIOGRAPHY 227

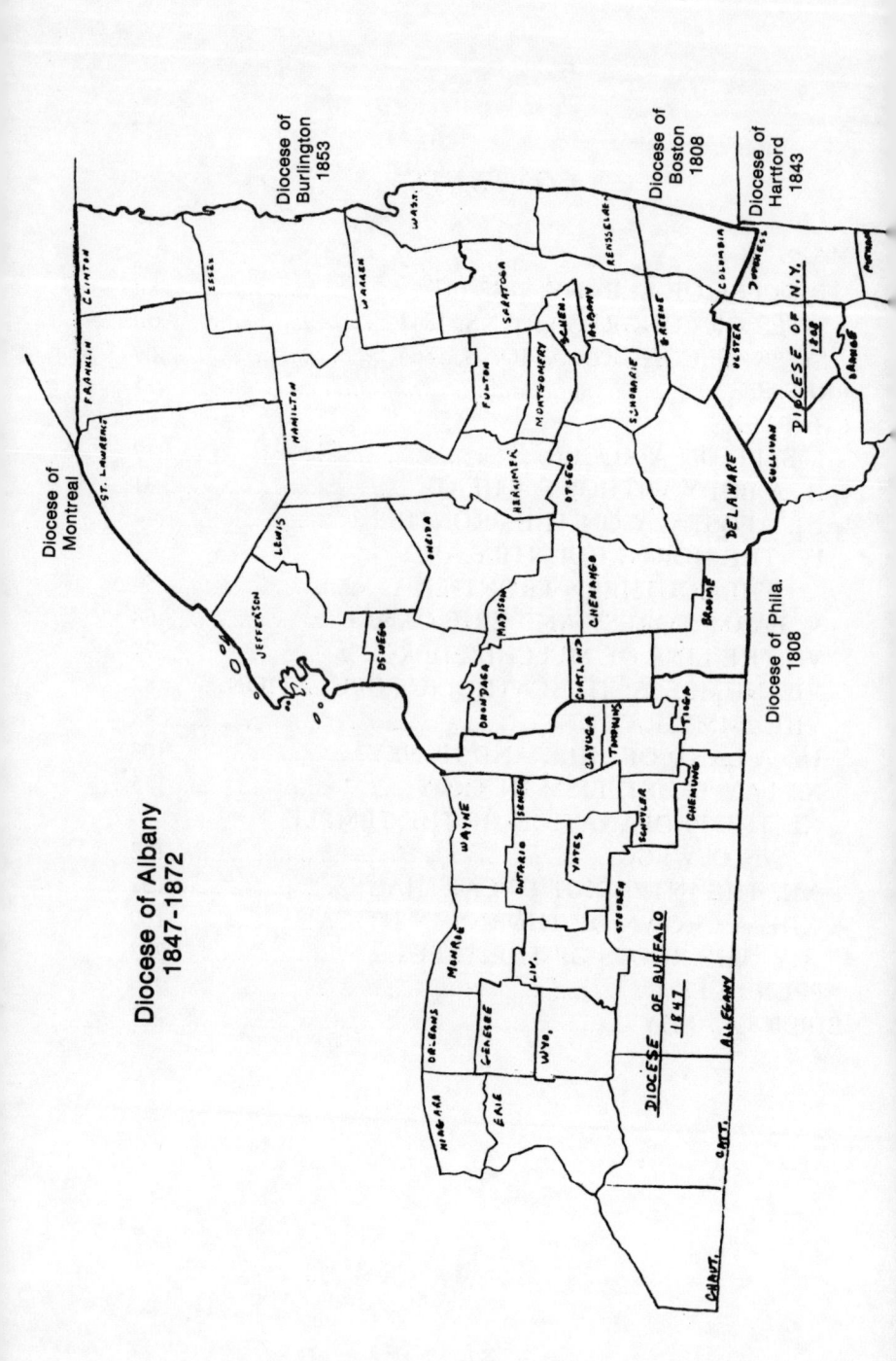

Sites of Churches, Chapels and Mission Stations, Diocese of Albany, 1847. Based on the Catholic Directory for 1848. A Dot is One Congregation.

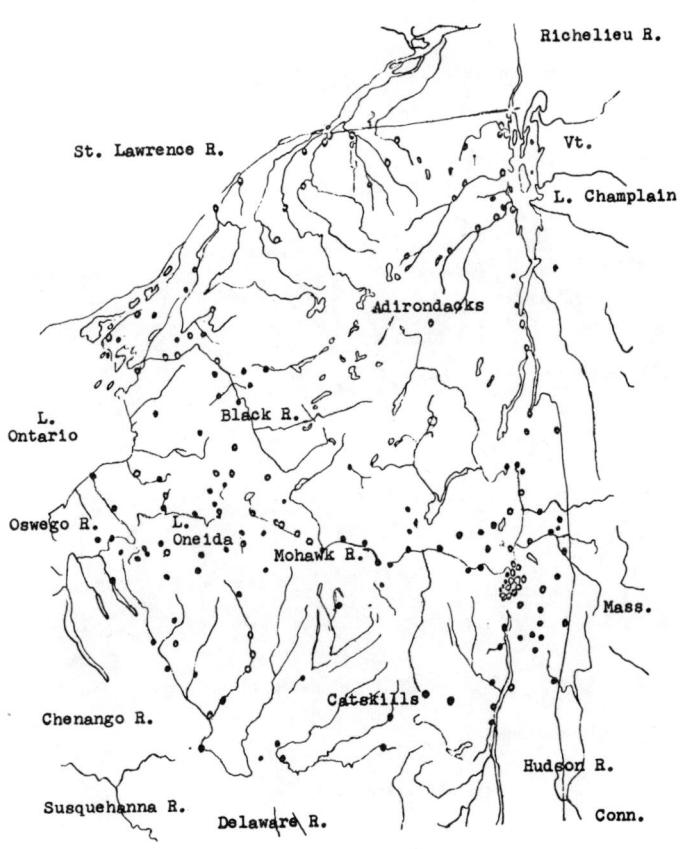

Sites of Churches, Chapels and Mission Stations, Diocese of Albany, 1864. Based on the Catholic Directory for 1865. A Dot is One Congregation.

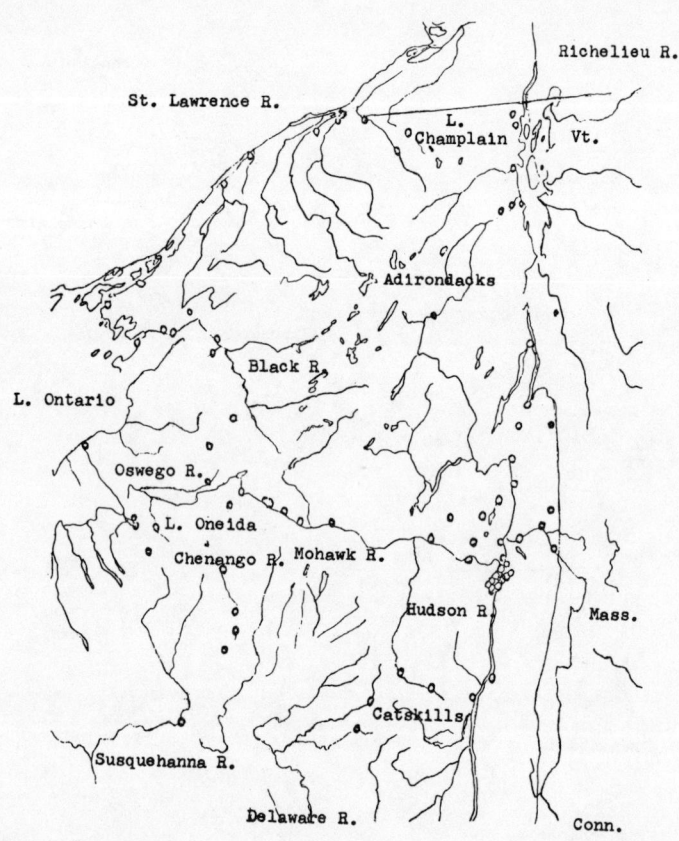

PREFACE

A history teacher knows what it is to hear a student say "the Church" does this, or "the Church" says that. It is the Roman Catholic Church that is always meant, and it is as if Catholics behave as a school of fish. Whatever the reason for this exaggeration of the unity among Catholics, I have tried to come as close as possible to the daily life of the men and women of the Church in the America of long ago and to the differences among them. Whereas most American Catholic historians, who are usually priests, have viewed the Church from the top down, I try, in this study, to look at the Church from the bottom up, that is, from the viewpoint of the laity and their missionary prieests. I peer at the dark side of the moon, not because it is the dark side, but because it is the other side.

In this study of Catholic life in upstate New York from the coming of Samuel de Champlain to the Civil War, there are chapters on early Indian history, natural features, economic activity, apostasy, immigration, ethnic numbers, lay trusteeism and Catholic revivalism, in order to give all of the reasons why the Church prospered in the Diocese of Albany, in spite of the discords that divided its peoples.

To approach the Catholic life of long ago, I have quoted freely and at length from the letters of the Catholics of that time and region and from others as well. Those letters, from clergy and laity alike, are so full of irregularities of spelling, punctuation and grammar, that the use of the word *sic* to indicate an error in the original texts would be impractical. Therefore, I have given the original texts as they are, exactly, without *sic*. In a few cases of obscure meaning, I have interjected a word or two, in brackets, to help the reader, and in every case of a long quotation, I have introduced a paragraphing into the original texts to make them easier to read.

Many people have helped me to write this dissertation. From Ireland, Canada and several of the United States, I have received a cordial assistance. My gratitude goes to Rev. Francis X. Curran, S.J., my mentor at Fordham University, to Mr. Richard Breaden, Rev. Robert B. O'Connor, Msgr. Daniel Flynn and Msgr. George E. Tiffany, for the use of the Archives of the Archdiocese of New York and of the Archbishop Corrigan Memorial Library, at St. Joseph's Seminary, in Yonkers, New York, to Bishop Edwin B. Broderick, Rev. Leo O'Brien, Rev. C. Howard Russell and Mrs. Michael Stanco, for the use of the Archives of the Diocese of Albany, to Rev. Gaston Carriere, O.M.I., of St. Paul's University, in Ottawa, for generously sending me a copy of his history of the Oblate Fathers, to the librarians of the New York Public Library at Forty-Second Street (Reference Division), to the Catholic University of America (Interlibrary Loan), to the Duane Library of Fordham University, to the Catholic Central Union of America, in St. Louis, to Rev. Edmund Halsey, O.S.B., who is the archivist of the American Catholic Historical Society of Philadelphia, to the Misses Mary Vie Cramblitt and Eva L. Reiman of the Library of Pace College Westchester, for several years of kind assistance in making interlibrary loans, to Mr. G. Glyndon Cole and Miss Connie Pope of the North Country Historical Research Center, in Plattsburgh, New York, to Mr. Charles W. McLellan of the Moorsfield Press, in Champlain, New York, to Professor Julian G. Plante of St. John's University, in Collegeville, Minnesota, to Sister Mary Liguori, R.D.C., of the College of White Plains, and Miss Claire Murray of White Plains, New York, for translations from the Latin, and to my wife, Jeanne, for what is beyond words.

CHAPTER I

SEED ON A ROCK

The Catholic Church grew more in the nineteenth century than ever before in history.[1] In the United States, it sprouted as the mustard seed,[2] and at mid-century, the new diocese of Albany, in the state of New York, under its first bishop, John McCloskey, in 1847-1864, shared the lead in America, with older dioceses, in the numbers of churches, priests and worshippers.[3] Somewhere in the life of such a diocese as Albany there lay the roots that fed new life to the tree of Rome, and that nurtured for seventeen years the bishop who was the first American to become a cardinal of the Church.[4]

The diocese of Albany parted from that of New York on April 23, 1847. It ran to the state lines on the north and east, the forty-second parallel on the south, and the western limits of the counties of Broome, Cortland, Onondaga, Oswego and Jefferson on the west.[5] Around it were the sees of Montreal, Burlington, Boston, New York, Philadephia and Buffalo. Twenty-eight counties lay within its borders , and with its 28,129 square miles, it spanned the three regions of the Hudson-Mohawk Corridor, the North Country and the Southern Tier.[6] Here flowed the Hudson, the Mohawk and the Saint Lawrence Rivers, and there stretched Lakes Ontario, George and Champlain, a net of waterways that joined the Atlantic Ocean with the Great Lakes and the Mississippi Watershed. Add the fertile plains, the Adirondack Mountains and three-fourths of the Catskills, and it is no wonder that the region of the diocese has loomed as the key to the struggle of the European powers over North America, the scene of one of the greatest land rushes of all time, and a part of the axis of trade of the United States to this day.[7]

Samuel de Champlain was the first Catholic to enter here.[8] The occasion was his fight with the Iroquois[9] at Lake Champlain in 1609. Today, the schoolbook goes on teaching that, as a result of such early brushes, the Five Nations were cast into the mold of antagonists to th French, like leaden figurines, that the fleur-de-lis was, therefore, not able to make good its later hold on the region of the diocese with its vital military routes, and, by implication, that North America is less Catholic now than it might have been.[10] But the specialist points out that man is ruled in the long run by trade and terrain, not to mention the beliefs of head and heart, and that it is not true that a few musket shots from the father of New France cost the Church a continent.[11]

New York saw few Catholics during the next quarter-century. After the start of a mission for the Hurons at Georgian Bay in Ontario in 1615, the Recollects there longed to take the cross to the lair of the Iroquois. But the beatings and death, which they met at the hands of the tribes around, dashed the hope of such a penetration.[12] Yet, there were the two Portuguese soldiers[13] at Fort Orange[14] in 1626, the *coureurs de bois* in that vicinity before 1634,[15] and the possibility of a young midwife and demirep from Paris at the fort in 1623-1626.[16]

In 1642, the capture of Saint Isaac Jogues by the Mohawks was the beginning of the mission to the Iroquois by the Jesuits of France.[17] It lasted on and off for sixty-seven years. During a truce between the subjects of Louis XIV and the man eaters of the Five Nations, the first Mass in New York was celebrated on November 14, 1655, in a native cabin on Indian Hill, two miles south of present Manlius. The bark hut that was thrown up there four days later was the first Catholic church in the state.[18] While it flourished, the mission drew twenty-five priests and a number of French aids, who performed three thousand baptisms, at a guess, most of which were of dying babes.[19] The price for those souls was three martyr-saints, to wit, Isaac Jogues, René Goupil and Jean de Lalande, and from that vineyard there came one candidate for beatification, an Indian virgin by the name of Kateri Tekakwitha, or the Lily of the Mohawk.[20] In 1709, due to Queen Anne's War, a phase of the struggle between France and Britain over North America, the mission of the French Jesuits in the Mohawk Valley came to an end.[21]

What's more, it left behind a house on sand. Since 1667, there had been a drift of the neophytes from the banks of the Mohawk to the shores of the Saint Lawrence. They fled the rum and malice of red pagan and white trader, as Lot the sins of Sodom. At Caughnawaga and the Lake of the Two Mountains, near Montreal, and at five other reductions[22] in New France, the Praying Indians, in the

SEED ON A ROCK

thousands,[23] worked and worshipped with their missioners. Some died in the odor of sanctity; some slid back to heathenism; and some fought as warriors, first for the French, till the fall of Quebec, then for the British, during the Revolution. Throughout the eighteenth century, the Iroquois of the Faith drew off their kinsmen from the Six Nations[24] of New York to the "seven savage villages of Canada."

Meanwhile, in the Hudson Valley, few "papists" dared the Calvinism of the Dutch, or later enjoyed the toleration of James, the Duke of York and later King of England, and a convert to the Church.[25] Under him, New York had a Catholic governor in 1683-1688, namely Thomas Dongan, a Catholic commandant at the outpost of Albany, the future see, and a mission of three English Jesuits, who were ostensibly in New York City.[26] But Leisler's Rebellion in 1689 ended that. It was a gust of the Protestant wind, which blew from Holland with William and Mary. For the "Romanists" of the province, a darkness fell on the land. "Jesuits, priests and popish missionaries" were outlawed in 1700, and were priced at $113 apiece for the Indians who would turn them in. But not till 1709 did the Iroquois make to play the Judas, and then, finally, the last of the French Jesuits left the Mohawk Valley. Afterwards, till the Revolution, New York seemed not to wear "the least face of popery."[27]

It is not generally known, but while Father Thomas Harvey stayed in New York City, his fellows, Fathers Henry Harrison and Charles Gage, were on a secret mission for ten years all told, in 1684-1700, on the Susquehanna River in the Southern Tier of New York and in northern Pennsylvania. Governor Dongan had sent them there in a new English policy of wresting from France the hold on the Indians of New York and eventually on the continent of North America. After the Orange or Protestant coups in New York and Maryland in 1689, which began in a century of "crypto-Catholicism" in those provinces and a hue and cry after Catholics as fifth-columnists, so to speak, the English Jesuits had to dodge and double with such aliases, disguises and enigmatic messages[28] that a historian of the Society of Jesus itself did not discover the secret till nineteen years ago. Some of the facts are that Harrison, a linguist, took diplomatic trips to Montreal and Albany, that he and Gage fled their mission in 1690, that Harrison sailed to Europe, fell into the hands of pirates, was released, took his last vows, and returned to America, that he was finally able to go back to the mission in 1697, alone, for a second stint, during which he had to live in the wigwams "without a shirt," that he died, or was killed by hostile Indians in 1700, and went into an unknown grave, that an Indian runner later brought in his priestly goods, and that the Susquehannas kept the Faith for long years after.[29]

In spite of all of this, Catholics continued to blow into upper New York before the winds of chance. They were among the hundreds of Palatines in the valleys of the Schoharie after 1712 and the Mohawk after 1721, at such places as Middleburgh, Stone Arabia, Herkimer, German Flats and Palatine Bridge.[30] But under the load of mixed marriage, a lack of priests, and Protestant proselytism, their old religion crumbled.[31] The Reverend John Frederic Haeger, a *landsmann,* who shepherded them across the sea, as a missioner of the Society for Propagating the Gospel in Foreign Parts, wrote in October of 1710, soon after landing in New York: "I instructed fifty-two in the fundamentals of our religion according to the Church Catechism; among them were thirteen Papists."[32]

The Acadians too appeared, like tumbleweed. Thrust from their forest primeval, during the last and fiercest of the intercolonial wars, for refusing to bend the knee to George II, seven-thousand of them were strewn along the Saint Lawrence River and the Atlantic Coast to the Great Lakes and the mouth of the Mississippi. A band of seventy-eight of them in 1756 were sent to Georgia, whence they were sent to South Carolina, whence they sailed to Long Island, where they were seized and scattered inland, where the magistrates were directed to employ the able-bodied, and to bind out the children to such persons as would make them "useful good subjects," which meant Protestants, of course.[33] All told, 229 of them were shipped to New York, of whom 77 were farmed out in Orange and Westchester Counties.[34] "Scorpions in the bowels of the country," they writhed among their captors.[35] They tried to flee to the French fortress at Crown Point in 1757, but were caught near Fort Edward, on the upper Hudson. When the French took Fort William Henry at Lake George, the British at once clapped all of the Acadians into jail. In 1764, the Governor of Martinique sent to fetch them, but the arm of New York would not let them go.[36] In time, their broken families melted into the Protestant land.

Another happening of Catholics took place at Johnstown, in Fulton County, for about twenty years after 1773. They were 220 or so at the start, and they had a priest of their own.[37] Though some were Irish or German, most of them had just arrived from the Scottish Highlands with Gaelic still on tongue. It took Father John MacKenna three languages to look after them. He was the first

Catholic missioner in those parts after the French Jesuits. Born in Ireland, educated at Louvain, ordained in Scotland, he had emigrated with his congregation of three hundred clansmen and some Irishmen in 1773. Eighty of them died at sea in thirteen weeks.[38] After landing penniless in New York City, and receiving the charity of seventy pounds in money from the Old Presbyterian Church, they settled on the lands of Sir William Johnson in the Mohawk Valley. They did that, without the gift of a church building from their landlord, who was an apostate from Ireland and a patron of the other denominations.[39] When the Revolution broke out, the priest and most of his flock, who were sworn to George III, made the trek to Canada, in small and separate parties, between October of 1775 and June of 1776, via the Lakes, or through the Adirondack Mountains. The distance between Johnstown and the Saint Lawrence River, as the crow flies north, is about 160 miles. One band of fugitives lived on wild plants and the flesh of their dogs for ten days.[40] In Montreal, they took up arms against their Protestant and militant ex-neighbors, whose ill will they had fled. Father MacKenna, a goliath of a man, chaplained many a raid into the Mohawk Valley. "It is extremely difficult for me to offer Mass every day because of the fighting but nothing is more important."[41] At the Battle of Oriskany, in 1777, he lost missal and vestments. The Highlanders who stayed on the Mohawk kept faith with their king, and refused to muster with the rebels.[42] After the war, little by little, they drifted off to Canada, although some were still in the Valley in 1791. Father MacKenna went back to Ireland, where he died in 1789; the Highlanders of the Mohawk found a home on king's land in Glengarry County, in Ontario, across the river from Ogdensburg; and if any of the Catholics, of Irish and German stock, clung to central New York, the Revolution covered their footsteps.

The Champlain valley belonged to New France until 1759.[43] From the time of the erection of a trading post at the head of the lake in the early 1600's, and especially after the construction of Fort Saint-Frédéric[44] at Crown Point in 1730-1731, throne, altar and seigneurs pushed the settlement of the river mouths along the lake at a dozen separated spots. Military duty, farming, fur trading and smuggling were the occupations. In 1731-1759, thirteen chaplain-pastors, mostly Recollects, registered 243 baptisms, 31 marriages and 198 deaths (75 in one battle in 1756). Toward the end of that period, eight hundred men, women and children dwelt at Crown Point and at Chimney Point on the opposite shore, and, in 1889, the traces of their houses, streets and orchards were still visible. When the French struck flags in 1759, they blew up forts, chapels and their hope for the Faith on Lake Champlain.[45]

At the same time, the Jesuits and the Sulpicians each planted a new reduction for the Iroquois in the North Country. Father Antoine Gordan, a Jesuit, set down a community in 1754 at the mouth of the St. Regis River.[46] Father Francois Picquet, a Sulpician, laid out a village in 1749 at the mouth of the Oswegatchie.[47] On the south shore of the St. Lawrence, away from Montreal and toward central New York, the two missions were twins of purpose. The Mohawks at Canajoharie and Fort Hunter were seeking a haven from the land grabbers, and resented the failure of the British to send them preachers of the Word. At Caughnawaga and the Lake of the Two Mountains, the soil was giving out, ill will was brewing between the half-breeds and the full-bloods, and the brandy and barrack life of the city of Montreal were rotting the soul of the Indian. Politics were in it too. As the British, the French were at the old game of wooing the Six Nations, and so, of tilting to themselves the balance of power in America.

Aquasasne, the Indians called St. Regis, "the land where the partridge drums." Its pioneers were a band of the Six Nations from New York and thirty families of Caughnawagas, with relics of the Lily of the Mohawk. Chief Karekowa came with his kin. Spear-side, they were the issue of the white children of New England, who had been kidnapped by the Iroquois of Canada during Queen Anne's War, and who, years later, at home in the longhouse and the Church, would not go back to their parents. Blood of cannibal and blood of Puritan mixed in the veins of Karekowa.

Life in a reduction, free of Whites, was sober and industrious. When the braves were not away to war, they hunted and fished, traded in furs, and won fame for their paddles in shooting the rapids of the St. Lawrence. The squaws tended the corn, the cows and the chickens, and were likened to the Ladies of Mercy in piety. Sometimes, their asceticisms had to be softened. In 1783, St. Regis had 380 inhabitants. It straddled the border, the Catholics in Quebec, the others in New York, a cleft that boded ill.

Father Gordan shone with the light of one who was sent. When his church burned down, he built another. When the French left, he turned British. When 1763 brought hard times, and Louis XV cut off an annuity, and George III begrudged a pound, and the Jesuits were suppressed, and the Revolution hurt the villagers from both sides, the missioner kept his register, and saw his people through.[48] The Americans who invaded Canada in 1775 labeled him "an old Jesuit...an arch Villain and a Tory."[49] But he died at Montreal in 1779, after thirty years among the Iroquois, "a very great loss to Government."[50]

At Oswegatchie, where Ogdensburg sits at present, the Abbé Picquet named his village La Présentation. There, in 1750-1760, were the pastor and five assistant priests, one at a time, a storekeeper or fur trader, a soldiery of Whites, three-thousand Indians, a chapel, shrines, a Way of the Cross, one episcopal visitation, schooling, catechism, an "orchestra," 56 weddings, 409 baptisms, 120 confirmations, and so on. The residents, though still in savagery, had to swear off liquor and satyrics, and some were sent away for breaking the rule. Yet, there was a bond between pastor and people. Wrote the abbe, during an outbreak of smallpox: "I buried an Iroquois, who died in my room." On his leaving for France to get help, the Indians cried: "Father, my soul is dark!" "You have inflicted death on me!" "Your children will not see the first fall of snow!"[51]

There was no separating trade and politics from religion on the missions of North America in the eighteenth century. That fact, plus something in the man himself, made the abbe play a role, during the intercolonial wars, that was a confusion of service to God, Mars and Mammon. La Présentation, his brainchild, was designed to be a fort and a trading post as well as a mission. It was a parry to the thrust, that is, to Fort Oswego, which the British made from the Mohawk Valley into Lake Ontario, and which threatened to cut New France in two. In 1752, the missioner wrote:[52]

> I have succeeded in establishing within three years, one of the most flourishing missions of Canada. I am now in a position to extend the empire of Jesus Christ and of the King, my two good masters, to the extremity of the New World...and do more than England and France could do with several millions and all their troops.

Under his regime, during the French and Indian War, La Présentation was a listening post, a supply depot, a little Hague or Geneva, and a military base. Spies and scouts came and went; the sawmill turned out lumber for fortifications; and the tribes of New York and the Old Northwest were feted or threatened in order to clutch them to France. Whenever the pastor was there, he himself drilled his red commandos. Montcalm visited the mission in 1756, and his aide-de-camp wrote:[53]

In the morning, the Indians of La Présentation sang their war song; a whole cow and a barrel of wine were given to them for their war banquet. We left at eight-thirty in the morning, the Iroquois forming a hedgerow under arms, French fashion, one of them beating the march skillfully, and all saluting the general with three volleys of musketry.

The Abbé Picquet, who was "an excellent priest and a perfect missionary" to his bishop, was as much a diplomat and a soldier. "I have sent a plan of attack to our generals," he wrote. In regard to an alliance with the Indians, Montcalm said: "The Patriarch of the Five Nations has his plan...His propositions must be accepted."[54] As a leader of the Oswegatchies and other Indians, the abbe was in all of the big battles in 1745-1760 from the Ohio Valley to Lake Champlain. He slogged. He slept on snow. To set an example, he first forded creeks. With other chaplains, he said Masses, heard confessions, and gave general absolutions. He exhorted the Indians before the battle of Fort Carillon: "Children, cheer up! Have hope! The good God and His Divine Mother will protect you!"[55] After victories, he led *Te Deums* before tall crosses. He tried to stop the western savages from butchering the captives, and drinking their blood. Among the Indians, who were the third force in America, there were Sir William Johnson for the British. But the French had the abbe. A Sulpician, he was to the enemy "the great Jesuit of the West." They tried to bribe him; they put a price on his head; but to no avail. Governor Duquesne avowed: "The Abbé Picquet is worth more then ten regiments."[56]

But France had to let go of its "few acres of snow." While William Pitt was making the lion roar with troops and suppies to America, and New France was pleading for help, Versailles sent word: "When the house is burning, no attention is paid to the stables." Quebec replied: "No one will say that you talk like a horse."[57] The Abbé Picquet and his Oswegatchies retreated from La Présentation, a military target, in July of 1759. The British renamed it Fort Oswegatchie, and, under the indecisive treaty with the United States in 1783, held it till 1796. When Montreal fell in 1760, many begged the abbé to stay, to take the oath to George III. But gone was his dream of an Indian republic under the fleur-de-lis, and he fled to New Orleans to avoid capture. The last of the great French missioners to New York in the eighteenth century died in France in 1781, honored by his two good masters, the crown and the triple tiara.

Most of the Oswegatchies settled at Caughnawaga and the Lake of the Two Mountains, near Montreal. A remnant, however, stayed in their old home, without a priest and in contact with a British garrison. They became a costly nuisance to Government, and went the way of all flesh. During the Revolution, they clung to neutrality, except for a few on either side. Afterwards, the British moved them to Indian Point, on the St.Lawrence River, three miles below Ogdensburg. There, a village was built for them, on land that was sold and resold under them, and there they lived, twenty-four families, under a French squaw man of a sachem. In 1806-1807, they were evicted, and scattered to the reservations at St.Regis and Onondaga, not much of their Faith remaining.

In New York today, in the dioceses of Albany, Syracuse and Ogdensburg,[58] what is left of the Church of that time, from the coming of Champlain to the Declaration of Independence? What remains of Isaac Jogues, René Goupil, Jean de Lalande and Henry Harrison, of the longhouse of the Lily of the Mohawk, of Father Gordan and the Abbé Picquet, of the French, the Germans, the Irish and the Highlanders, of Father MacKenna's missal, of the Jesuits, the Recollects and the Suplicians, of Karekowa's kin, of the soldiers, the smugglers, the explorers and the *coureurs de bois,* of that first bark chapel, of the uncounted holy sacraments, of the cannibal converts, and of the tall crosses of victory? Lo, the Sower sowed on rock.[59]

[1] Kenneth Scott Latourette, *A History of the Expansion of Christianity,* Vol. IV: *The Great Century A.D. 1800 — A.D. 1914* (7 vols.: New York; Harper, 1937-1945), pp. 4, 22, 32, 461.

[2] In 1841-1850, Whites increased by 37 percent, Catholics among them by 142 percent. Bishop Gerald Shaughnessy, *Has the Immigrant Kept the Faith* (New York: Macmillan, 1925), p. 134.

[3] Among the 30 dioceses in the U.S. in 1849, Albany, though sharing with Cleveland and Buffalo the 28th to 30th places in order of age, was 4th in churches and mission stations, 8th in priests, and 6th in communicants. Rev. Paul P. Ciangetti, "A Diocesan Chronology of the Catholic Church in the United States," *Catholic Historical Review,* XXVIII, No. 1 (April, 1942), 57-70; *Catholic Directory for 1850,* p. 231.

[4] In 1875.

[5] Donald C. Shearer, *Pontificia Americana: A Documentary History of the Catholic Church in the United States (1784-1884)* (Wash., D.C.: Cath. Univ. Amer., 1933), p. 241.

[6] The state then had 59 counties and an area of 47,939 sq. m., of which

Albany diocese contained 59 percent. Buffalo diocese, erected with Albany, had 19 counties, and N.Y. diocese, dating from 1808, had 12 counties in N.Y. State, plus seven counties in northern N.J. I divide the 28 counties of the diocese of Albany as follows: the Hudson-Mohawk Corridor contains Albany, Columbia, Fulton, Hamilton, Herkimer, Madison, Montgomery, Oneida, Onondaga, Oswego, Rensselaer, Saratoga, Schenectady, Warren and Washington; the North Country contains Clinton, Essex, Franklin, Jefferson, Lewis and St. Lawrence; the Southern Tier contains Broome, Chenango, Cortland, Delaware, Greene, Otsego and Schoharie. See map p. xii.

[7] John H. Thompson (ed.), *Geography of New York State* (Syracuse: Syracuse Univ. Press, 1966), pp. 3, 143, and map at back; Albert Perry Brigham, *Geographic influences in American History* (Chautauqua: Chautaugua Press, 1903), pp. 4, 12, 22-25, 32.

[8] Nellis M. Crouse, "The White Man's Discoveries and Explorations," *History of the State of New York*, ed. Alexander C. Flick (10 vols. in 5; Port Washington, N.Y.: Ira J. Friedman, 1962, originally 1933-1935), I, chap. V.

[9] Iroquois was their French name, five Nations their English name. Severally, they were the Mohawks, Oneidas, Onondagas, Cayugas and Senacas. The Mohawks dwelt where Schoharie Creek runs into the Mohawk River, and the others to the west, at the lakes now bearing their names.

[10] Oscar T. Barck, Jr., and Hugh T. Lefler, *Colonial America* (New York: Macmillan, 1959, reprint 1964), p.175.

[11] George T. Hunt, *The Wars of the Iroquois* (Madison: Univ. of Wisconsin Press, 1940), p. 69.

[12] John Gilmary Shea, *History of the Catholic Missions among the Indian Tribes of the United States, 1529-1854* (New York: P.J. Kenedy, 1854), pp. 169-170, 205-206.

[13] John Gilmary Shea, *The History of the Catholic Church in the United States* (4 vols.; New York: Author, 1886-1892). I, 86.

[14] It was built by the Dutch as a fur trading post in 1617 at the head of navigation on the Hudson River. The English renamed it Albany in 1664, when they conquered the New Netherlands.

[15] Hunt, p. 69.

[16] E.B. O'Callaghan (ed.), *The Documentary History of the State of New York* (4 vols.; Albany: Weed, Parsons, 1849-1851), III, 49-51. Hunt, pp. 28-30, calls the two documents in O'Callaghan a forgery by Gov. Dongan to fortify the English claim to New York.

[17] Shea, *Missions*, pp. 205-331, 550: Rev. Thomas Hughes, S.J., *History of the Society of Jesus in North America: Text* (2 vols.; New York; Longmans, Green, 1908-1917), II, chaps. XII-XV.

[18] A stone shaft marks the site of the Mass. Rev. Arthur A. Weiss, S.J.,

"Jesuit Mission Years in New York State, 1654-1879," *The Woodstock Letters*, LXXV, No. 1 (March 1946), 7-9. The church was probably dedicated to St. John Baptist. Shea, *Church*, I, 252.

[19] In 1668-1678, the zenith of the mission, there were a reported 2,221 baptisms. Before and after that period, the numbers of such were small. Shea, *Missions*, pp. 288-289, 293. The Iroquois in 1660 were about 11,000. Allen W. Trelease, *Indian Affairs in Colonial New York: The Seventeenth Century* (Ithaca: Cornell Univ. Press, 1960), p. 16.

[20] *New Catholic Encyclopedia* (1967), VII, 906, XIII, 181, 978-979.

[21] Later, the French Jesuits, disguised as Indians, tried in vain to steal back to their children in Christ, Weiss, pp. 17-18.

[22] Reduction was the term for a mission village because it was meant to *lead back* the Indian from idolatry. Caughnawaga was the largest of the Jesuit reductions. The Lake of the Two Mountains belonged to the Sulpicians, but received catechumens from the Jesuit mission of New York. Hughes, II, map in front, "Jesuit Missions: Canada."

[23] In 1766, the Canadian reductions had 3,150 Iroquois and others, including 900 braves. That total dropped to 2,874 in 1783, after their fighting in the Revolution. In New York the Iroquois were 11,000 in 1660, but 1,960 in 1763. War, disease and exodus, balanced by adoption, shrank the Five Nations of New York, and made a lasting split between the Iroquois of Canada, who were Catholic, and those of New York, who either remained pagan, or became Protestant. *Ibid.*, II, chap. XV.

[24] The five Nations became six when the Tuscaroras joined in 1712.

[25] Rev. John Tracy Ellis, *Catholics in Colonial America* (Baltimore: Helicon, 1965), chaps. VII, XIII, Rev. Francis X. Curran, S.J., *Catholics in Colonial Law* (Chicago: Loyola Univ. Press, 1963), gives the texts of the laws on religion in the New Netherlands and New York.

[26] Hughes, II, chaps. XIV-XV, esp. pp. 140-147. Also, see below, pp. 8-9.
[27] The Rev. Andrew Burnaby of England was in New York City in 1759. He reported "a few Roman Catholics" there among the Anglicans and many Dissenters, esp. Presbyterians. Rev. Joseph PauL Ryan, "Travel Literature as Source Material for American Catholic History," *Illinois Catholic Historical Review*, X, No. 3 (Jan. 1928), 199. For an alleged plot of Catholics in 1741 with Spanish Negroes, who had been captured, and sold into slavery in New York, see William Harper Bennett, *Catholic Footsteps in Old New York* (New York: Kirwin and Fauss, 1909), chaps. XII-XV.

[28] "Disguises and Aliases of Early Missionaries," *Woodstock Letters*, XV, No. 1 (1886), 72-74.

[29] Rev.Robert A. Parson, S.J., "Father Henry Harrison," ibid., LXXXII, NO. 2 (May, 1953), 118-147.

[30] Walter Allen Knittle, *Early Eighteenth Century Palatine Emigration*

(Phila.: Dorrance, 1937), chap. VIII, passim.

[31] Rev. Lambert Schrott, *Pioneer German Catholics in the American Colonies (1734-1784)* (New York: U.S. Cath. Hist. Soc., 1933), chap. III.

[32] Bennett, chap. XI, esp. p. 228. Over 5,600 persons, or about one-third of the Palatines who had crossed to London to be emigrated by the British government to North America were returned to the Rhineland in 1709-1714, because they were Catholics who would not apostatize. Knittle, pp. 8, 63, 66, 78-79.

[33] E.B. O'Callaghan (ed.) *Documents Relative to the Colonial History of the State of New York* (Albany: Weed, Parsons, 1856-1858), VII, 125. An act of the legislature, July 6, 1756, empowered the justices of the peace to bind out those under 21. Arthur George Doughty, *The Acadian Exiles* (Toronto: Glasgow, Brook, 1922), pp. 145-146, 156-157.

[34] Bennett, chap. XVI. Those who were deposited in Westchester and Orange Counties, in August of 1756, numbered 35 men, 11 women and 31 children. The others were scattered among Staten Island, Rye, New Rochelle and the villages between Flatbush and East Hampton. Rev. John K. Sharp, "The Acadian Confessors on Long Island", U.S. Cath. Hist. Soc., *Historical Records and Studies,* XXXIII (1944), 57-63.

[35] Rev. Peter Guilday, *The Life and Times of John Carroll* (Westminster, Md.: Newman Press, 1954, originally 1922), p. 68, quoting the gov. of Penn.

[36] Shea, *Church,* I, 429-433.

[37] Rev. Mr. Richard K. MacMaster, S.J., "Parish in Arms: A Study of Father John McKenna and the Mohawk Valley Loyalists, 1773-1778," U.S. Cath. Hist. Soc., *Historical Records and Studies,* XLV (1957), 107-125, esp. p. 109. MacMaster says that they were "four or five hundred Celts," but he misreads his source, "Letterbook of Captain Alexander McDonald, of the Royal Highland Emigrants, 1775-1779," New York Historical Society, *Collections for the Year 1882* (Vol. XV), pp. 224, 354.

[38] Eugene R. Fingerhut, "Immigrants in Colonial New York, 1770-1775," (Unpub. M.A. thesis, Columbia Univ., 1957), pp. 25.26.

[39] James Thomas Flexner, *Mohawk Baronet: Sir William Johnson of New York* (New York: Harper & Row, 1959), pp. 25.26.

[40] "Letterbook," p. 357.

[41] MacMaster, p. 122.

[42] George Clinton, *Public Papers of George Clinton, first Governor of New York, 1777-1795-1801-1804* (10 vols.: Albany: State Printers, 1899-1914), V. 538.

[43] Guy Omeron Coolidge, "The French Occupation of the Champlain Valley from 1609 to 1759," Vermont Historical Society, *Proceedings* (New Series) VI, No. 3 (Sept., 1938), *passim.*

[44] It had a well built chapel, with morning and evening prayer everyday, Henry DeCourcy, *The Catholic Church in the United States,* trans. and enlarged by John Gilmary Shea (New York: Edward Dunigan and Bros., 1856), p. 458, n.

[45] Coolidge, "French Occupation," pp. 300-308: Winslow C. Watson, *The Military and Civil History of the County of Essex, New York* (Albany: J. Munsell, 1869), chap. VIII; W.J. Eccles, *The Canadian Frontier, 1534-1760* (New York: Holt, Rinehart and Winston, 1969), p. 145: Rev. John Talbot Smith, *A History of the Diocese of Ogdensburg* (New York: John W. Lovell, 1884), p. 11.

[46] Hughes, II, 353, n. 3, 418, n. 10. Shea, *Missions,* pp. 339-342, 501, names him Mark Anthony Gordon. See also Smith, *Ogdensburg,* pp. 285-294.

[47] Rev. Philias S. Garand, *The History of the City of Ogdensburg* (Ogdensburg: Rev. Manuel J. Belleville, 1927), Part I, chaps. I-X, Part II, chap. I; Shea, *Missions,* chap. XVIII.

[48] After 1763, the villagers scraped along on the produce of a farm of 120 acres and an alms of 20 pounds a year from the Catholics of London. Ewen J. Macdonald, "Father Roderick Macdonell, Missionary at St. Regis and the Glengarry Catholics," *The Catholic Historical Review,* XIX, No. 3 (Oct., 1933), 270.

[49] Martin I.J. Griffin, *Catholics and the American Revolution* (3 vols.: Ridley Park, Penn.: Author, 1907-1911), I, 110-112. The Society of Jesus was suppressed in 1773-1814, but the Jesuits continued their identity in many ways. Rev. Thomas J. Campbell, S.J., *The Jesuits, 1534-1921* (2 vols.; New York: Encyclopedia Press, 1921), II, 601.

[50] Hughes, II, 421, n. 10, Shea, *Missions,* pp. 341, 501, dates his death in 1777. Smith, p. 287, says he retired to Montreal in 1775 for reason of health. But there is the possibility that it was due to the American invasion.

[51] Garand, pp. 45, 58.

[52] *Ibid.,* p. 37.

[53] Garand, p. 70.

[54] *Ibid.,* p. 83.

[55] *Ibid.,* p. 112.

[56] *Ibid.,* p. 52.

[57] *Ibid.,* p. 127.

[58] Ogdensburg was separated from Albany in 1872, Syracuse in 1886.

[59] Ellis, pp. 164-166. In 1927, there were about a dozen Catholic Iroquois families in Ogdensburg. Garand, p. 154. In Canada, in January of 1962, on six Indian reservations, there were 16,282 Catholic Iroquois. Nora Story *The Oxford Companion to Canadian History and Literature* (New York:

Oxford Univ. Press, 1967), p. 384. The best known monument of Catholicism there is the Shrine of the North American Martyrs in Auriesville, N.Y.

CHAPTER II

A BODY WITHOUT A HEAD

The Revolution harrowed New York for the rooting of the Church. While war was trampling out the thin lines of life upstate, the bars to the Faith were lowered. The French and Indian War, which had brought down Catholic scalping knives upon the frontier, had become a crusade against "popery." After the Peace of 1763, anti-Catholicism had ebbed. It had flowed again in 1774, when the Quebec Act had thrust a wall between the Protestants of the east and the lands of the west, and the froth of rebellion had paired Clement XIV with George III in "No King, No Popery!" But the wish of the rebels to win over the Canadians, the prudence of being civil to the Frenchman and the Spaniard, the need to make one nation of many, and the ideals of the revolt, all brought on a springtime for the Church.[1] "There is no more remarkable intellectual revolution in American history than the *volte-face* not merely toward the French but towards the Catholics wrought in that struggle."[2] In 1782, the Abbé Robin, a French chaplain, landed at Boston, marched west and south with his army, and wrote letters along the way.[3]

> Notwithstanding the fact that I was a Frenchman and a Catholic priest, I was continually receiving new civilities from several of the best families in the town; but the people in general retain their old prejudices.

In New York, the Constitution of 1777 made every religion free and equal. Yet, it was worded to shut the door to Catholics by forcing the would-be citizen to swear away allegiance to all but the State. In 1801, this requirement was narrowed to the holder of civil and military office. The ban on priests was lifted in 1784. In 1806, as the result of an agitation, which was political and religious, and which was marked by violence between Catholics and Protestants and by the killing of a constable, in and about the one Catholic church, the test oath of 1801 was repealed, and a Francis Cooper became the first Catholic in 123 years to sit in the Assembly.[4] The Catholic cup began to fill.

During the war, Catholics trafficked upper New York. They were in the British and Continental armies and particularly in the two American regiments of Colonels Hazen and Livingston, which the Congress had willed to be recruited in Canada and the United States, and which was called Congress' Own. While fighting up and down the Champlain Road,[5] and seeing its riches, each side had a Catholic chaplain. The Abbé Louis de Lotbinière, in disobedience to the Bishop of Quebec, served as chaplain to Congress' Own. With the Westphalians, among the regiments of the king, there was a Father Theobald. He was captured, and in 1779 wrote from prison to General Washington. The letter, which was evidently not delivered, asked for a parole in order to enable the priest to become a pastor at Albany. One opinion is that the invitation to do so had come from Congress' Own while in that city and not from any civilians.[6]

After the British army evacuated New York in 1783, and the first capital of the United States was located there a year later, the city swarmed with merchants, diplomats and military men from France, Ireland, Spain and Portugal.[7] Travelers too came from those Catholic lands. They had a yen for the wilderness, and their letters may be supposed to have pollinated their co-religionists with the idea of immigration. Offhand, there was Chastellux, who toured in 1780-1782, La Rochefoucault-Liancourt, in 1795-1797, and Castiglioni, in 1785-1787.[8] The Italian attended a Mass in New York City in 1785, in a *camera poco decente*.[9] Vivid among the travelers were the Marquis de Moustier and his sister, the Marquise de Brehon. In January of 1784, they arrived on His Most Christian Majesty's ship, the forty-gun *D'Aigrette,* he as Minister to the United States, she in his entourage, with others of their family. Their hauteur aside, he wore earrings and red-heeled pumps to the fetes and balls, and she kept a Negro child by her side, and fondled a monkey. The pair of them journeyed up the Mohawk in September of 1784 to see the Indians and the federal commissioners make the Second Treaty of Fort Stanwix, which opened more of the state to the Whites.[10]

After the Peace of 1783, the pioneer trod upstate New York for the first time in numbers.[11] He was usually a New Englander,[12] and he hated the Church as the "Mother of Harlots."[13] Since the immigrants then were largely Protestant,[14] there were few Catholics about. One was a Doctor Joseph Whelan, who was living at Johnstown, on a farm, with his family, in 1786. Two years before, he had come from Ireland with two brothers, one the Capuchin Father

Charles Whelan. The friar became the first pastor of St. Peter's, which was the first congregation of Catholics to be incorporated in New York City and New York State. He was, therefore, the first priest in eighty-four years in the province and state, under cover of law.[15] At odds with a rival, who was also an Irish Capuchin, and with the lay trustees of the Church, he left in February of 1786. He stayed with his brother at Johnstown for some time, and then with the Jesuits in Maryland until the spring of 1787, when he went to Kentucky. In 1790, he was at his brother's again for a while.[16] It is probable that "old fr. Whelen" ministered at times in Albany.[17]

The Lynch family were other Irish Catholics then in the Mohawk Valley. Dominick Lynch, a rich merchant from Galway, who was settled in New York City, began to buy land at Fort Stanwix in 1786. Four years later, he owned two-thousand acres there. He laid out the village of Lynchville, now Rome, in Oneida County, put in improvements, and attracted settlers. Though he built a summer home near the fort, he spent most of his time in New York City. His son James was admitted to the bar in 1799, practiced in Rome, later in Utica, then moved to New York City, where he died in 1853. In time, the family gave land and money to Catholic congregations. One fact remains to be said about the family of Dominick Lynch. They were thirteen children. Ater a Catholic upbringing, most of them left the Church, on account of mixed marriages.[18]

When Fort Saint-Frédéric was built at Crown Point in 1731, the Champlain Valley beckoned to the *habitant,* or farmer of Quebec. But war stood in the way.[19] With peace in 1760, the families of Montey and the two Laframboise brothers and their farm hands became the first to settle there. They located at Chazy and Coopersville, in Clinton County, and other *Canadiens* dotted the northern rim of the state as far west as Waddington.[20] Driven off by Burgoyne's army in 1777, some of them enlisted in Congress' Own. After the Revolution, they were among the Canadian and Nova Scotian Refugees, who were mustered out, and who waited in New York City and Fishkill, in Dutchess County, during 1781-1786, for recompense from state and nation. It was they, whom the Jesuit missioner, Father Ferdinand Steinmeyer, alias Farmer, began to visit in stealth, in 1781, from his haven in Philadelphia.[21] In 1784, the state awarded them a tract of land on Lake Champlain, and two years later, the Congress gave them provisions for fifteen months and their transportation back to Clinton County.[22] There, they became known as the Canadian Settlement, and there, in 1790, the first Catholic church arose in the state, north of New York City, after the Revolution, and was burnt to the ground two years later, it is suspected, by some of its own congregation.[23] In 1790, the Settlement had 170 *Canadiens* in 40 families and 408 persons with British names in 87 families.[24] Among the latter were James Murdock McPherson, a justice of the peace, and Pliny Moore, the founder of the village of Champlain. The *Canadiens* included Francois Montey, Jean Baptiste Laframboise and Jacques Rouse. Rouse was the "warden" of the Catholic church and a captain of militia till 1802. Around 1793, he moved to Rouses Point. Attainted and excommunicated in Canada for rebellion,[25] he and his compatriots took the land and citizenship, which New York gave them for their service,[26] and in 1786, they hewed out a string of log shanties along the lake from Point au Roche to the Great Chazy River.[27]

At the turn of the century, the *habitant* of Quebec was not the peasant of France.[28] *Habitant* he called himself, because it did not clank of servility. Bred with the Indian and the *coureur de bois,* he had some of the wild ways of the forest. Nature indulged him in his slovenly tillage, and on the farm of his ancestors, in bare feet, a red sash around his waist, he was a Prodigal Son. Under a government that took no tax, and under a *seigneur,* or semi-feudal landlord, who was as likely to be interested in social standing as in the piling up of wealth, the rent and the *corvée* were trifles. The *habitant* was courteous enough under his roof, but soldiering had made him a scrapper. According to one of his bishops, he made more noise in an hour than an American did in a half-day.[29] *Je me souviens* (I remember), he was wont to say, and he clung to the past with inertia. He could not be driven, but he might follow. Cast into a phenomenal rate of increase by early marriage, he was big, strong, self-willed, impulsive, illiterate, "ignorant, lazy, dirty and stupid beyond belief." Furthermore, there was a difference between the Montrealers and those of downriver. The latter were called sheep for their relative docility. But the Montrealers, who had to grapple with raw nature to the west, had the name of wolves. In time, more "wolves" than "sheep" came to the North Country.

The Church was the backbone of Canada, but the Faith of the *Canadien* was skin-deep. Said Peter Kalm, the Swedish traveler on the St. Lawrence in 1750: "Religion here appears to consist solely in exterior practices."[30] It was the chase of pleasure that sometimes made the *habitant* forget his devoirs to altar and pulpit. He might troop into church with his dogs, or step out to a tavern as soon as the cure began to preach, or brawl at the door during the service. His wife went to mass in coiffure and décolletage, and the two of them were not above the *mariage à la gaumine,* or as Mason Wade puts it, a "do-it-yourself" wedding. Another matter was the tithe. The king had to eke it out, because the *habitant* could not be made to pay enough to support his cure. Yet, the *habitant* liked the priest, by and large, and lived at peace with him.[31]

In 1775-1783, crisis came to Canada, and schism rose on the St. Lawrence. "Perhaps no event has exercised so much influence upon Quebec, directly or indirectly, as the American Revolution," says Gustave Lanctot.[32] One-hundred-thousand[33] *Canadiens* were torn between duty to England and nostalgia for France. On one side, they were adjured by their bishop to support Great Britain, becaust it protected them in their Faith. On the other side, they were propagandized by the Continental Congress to become the fourteenth state. But flanked by threats and menaces, they took the view that it was a fight within the British family, they clung to neutrality, and they waited to see which side would win. A thousand or so of them, however, who lived in the path of the invading Americans, south of Quebec City and Montreal, and in the Richelieu Valley near Lake Champlain, in 1775-1776, collaborated with the *Bostonnais*. They sold supplies, or gave information, or even took up guns against their own countrymen. A few went so far as to shoot at, and to lay violent hands on, some of their priests, and to turn them over to the Americans as prisoners of war. One declared that he knew "neither the authority of the bishop nor that of the vicar general," and threatened to put them into the hands of the invaders at Three Rivers.[34] Another shouted in church at the cure: "You are an Englishman, and you wamt to force us to submit and to become English too!"[35]

It was Bishop Briand who gripped the *Canadiens* in neutrality, or pushed them into the fight for their God-given king. He pleaded that the Quebec Act had saved their laws, their customs and their holy Faith. He asserted that the *Bostonnais* would show their Church no mercy. He argued that they, the *Canadiens,* had enjoyed more prosperity under England than under Frnace and more religious liberty under Anglicanism than under Gallicanism. He admonished that God and common sense demanded their loyalty to King George. He interdicted. He excommunicated. He laid on penances *à la* Canossa. Obeying, the *Canadiens* emerged from the Revolution, nevertheless, with a streak of republicanism and anticlericalism.[36] And the bishop cried: "How little faith there is in Canada, although the outer shell of religion still remains.!"[37]

At Chazy, the Refugees, who were excommunicated, huddled in their shanties on Sundays for hymns and prayers, without a priest. The Bishop of Quebec played the Hound of Heaven. Again and again, he urged two of his cures to visit them, but nothing seems to have come of it.[38] If they had done so, was it likely that those French Canadian stiffnecks would have performed the penance of kneeling at a church door, with a lighted candle, in public, to beg forgiveness? In the end, of course, some of them fell away. But at long last, in May of 1790, there came along an erst-while cure of theirs, a rebel priest, a deported priest, the "first American tramping priest,"[39] the Abbé Pierre Huet de la Valinière.[40] A Breton and a Sulpician, he was brought to Canada in 1754 by the Abbé Picquet as a recruit for the mission. He was ordained a year later, at the age of twenty-three or four. Till 1759, he served as chaplain of the hospital in Montreal, where he learned English from the British prisoners, he later said, the better to serve his king. He was then pastor of a number of parishes nearby, one after the other, until 1777. He must have spent some time in the company of the Abbé Picquet, his brother Sulpician, who was in and out of Montreal until 1760. In any case, the two of them had the same devotion to France.

The Revolution undid the Abbé de la Valinière. Before 1777, he enjoyed the pick of the parishes around Montreal, and he showed his energy in rescuing two English women from an Indian stake, in writing a litany for the Sisters of Charity, and in taking the pains to learn to speak English in order to serve his native land. But after-events revealed him as quarrelsome, litigious, disobedient and footloose. Among the handful of priests on the St. Lawrence who were suspected of giving aid and comfort to the rebels, the Abbé de la Valinière was looked upon by his superiors as "among the most guilty and the least converted."[41] After the signing of the alliance between France and America in February of 1778, when many in Canada hoped for a French fleet beneath the Plains of Abraham, as for the Second Coming, the bishop moved the abbé to a poorer parish near Quebec City. It was because he was urging the return of Canada to France, and because the Montrealers were lending him an ear. The abbe tried to sue the bishop for usurping the royal *jus patronatus* and for harming him in name, health and property, but not a lawyer would touch the case. The priest was out of step. He was a Gallican in ultramontane Quebec. He was a Frenchman in British Canada. "Alas," he wrote, "how sad it is for a priest, so far from home and under English domination, to defend his right against a Bishop of their naming and according to their taste."[42]

The abbe was deported from Canada, and thereafter, as Cain, the brother of Abel, he wandered in exile for twenty years. He was condemned by church and state. "A perfect rebel in his heart," said the Governor-General.[43] "I no more looked upon him as a member of our house," said the Superior of the Sulpicians in Montreal.[44] And the bishop of Quebec wrote:[45]

> What shall we do, my dear Vicar General, with this poor man?...He asks me for a certificate of good standing and behavior so as to go wherever the Lord calls him. Can I give him one as long as he will hold a conduct so much opposed to my orders? I have forbidden him...to say Mass publickly until he has made arrangements with the government, and he has nevertheless officiated without having complied....

The Sulpicians offered him a pension if he would live in Paris, but he turned it down. Instead, as he wrote later:[46]

> I go wandering throughout all America, through New York and Boston. I travel by every dangerous route. I visit nearly every district. I start again from Pennsylvania and arrive at Fort Pitt. I sail all the way down the Ohio, the Kentucky and the Mississippi, without any sleep, traveling on foot or in a canoe. Five times I cross the Gulf of Mexico and try to return to Canada. Havana, Spanish Florida, Charlestown (Charleston, South Carolina), Stonington (Connecticut) and New York offer me nothing new.

After eight months on board an English prison ship, he was freed for want of evidence of treason. He was shipwrecked off Belgium, stricken by yellow fever in Santo Domingo, was robbed, lost his baggage, walked from Ostend to Paris, walked from the coast of Massachusetts to Montreal, and walked from Philadelphia to the fork of the Ohio. In the United States, he was welcomed by Father John Carroll, the Prefect Apostolic, who used his services at first among the French and the French Canadian Refugees in New York City, and later sent him to the Illinois country as his *grand vicaire*. But everywhere the abbé quarreled or found a rub. He printed a self-defense in which he spoke of "having suffered great persecution for the cause of America in the last war and having been obliged to take refuge in the United States."[47] In 1798, Canada opened the door to him again, and he was received with a pension at the house of the

Sulpicians in Montreal, on condition that he live there quietly. He died in 1806 in a fall from a wagon.

During 1790-1792, the abbé alighted at Chazy, as if a bird of passage. The Refugees, who had known him as their cure in Canada and in New York City, Newburgh and Fishkill, where they had been waiting for a few years for their military bounty lands, at first made him welcome. With him, they shared the work of building a priest's house and a log church.

Clement Gosselin was among them. As a major in Hazen's regiment, he had spied in Canada, and been wounded at Yorktown. He and the other Refugees, after the war, received scrips for land on Lake Champlain and in 1789, he sold one-thousand acres to Jacques Rouse, another of Congress' Own. In 1791, at Chazy, Gosselin married Marie Catherine Montey, whose family had sent eight men to fight for the Americans. McPherson performed the ceremony, as justice of the peace, but a year later, by dispensation, the union was blessed in the church at St. Hyacinthe, in Quebec, Gosselin died at Chazy in 1816.[48]

Soon after arriving at Chazy, the abbe had a falling out with his flock. He agreed with the Laframboises, for the spring and summer of 1790, to farm with his own hands and side by side with them. Jean Baptiste and his two sons had belonged to Hazen's regiment. When the missioner came, the wolf was at the family's door. They had nothing to eat but some corn and a day's supply of potatoes.[49] The abbé, who had a little money, fed them from planting time to harvest home. But then they quarreled over the sharing of the crop. Maybe it was this that was in the missioner's mind when he complained to Pliny Moore that someone had robbed him, but that the judge had taken the other person's word in the dispute. Another rasp was Gosselin's civil wedding. Concubinage, the cure called it. He berated the participants for a sneaking ceremony, and he wrote to Pliny Moore: "I'am afraid of these bad fellows for the common report is, they may burn me in my house or kill me with a gun."[50] Sure enough, someone, whoever it was, or whatever the reason, burnt down the buildings of the church,[51] probably in 1792, and the missioner dusted Clinton County off his feet.

But that did not end the trouble at Chazy. In October of 1792 and again in 1794, the civil law looked into one or more fights between Jacques Rouse and Lorant Olivier, on one side, and Peter Dubree and Peter Jonqueray, on the other.[52] Why did the 250 *Canadiens* there in 1786[53] dwindle to 170 four years later?[54] And why did they leave so few gravestones there in time?[55] Was there an omen in the words of Rouse to Dubree: "I am full of grief that, so few Frenchmen as we are here, we cannot live in peace together"?[56]

Elsewhere in New York and America, the Catholics were no different.[57] In fact, it is moot whether they were a Church. Wrote Father Ferdinand Farmer in 1785: "I cannot conceive how we could be a body without a bishop for a head."[58] Without such a head until 1789,[59] and then without a visitation from that head for years, without priests, or too few, and rogues among them, without churches and sacraments, without the comfort of each other's company, due to a separation by tongue and wilderness, with apostasy on every side among an aggressive, Protestant population, with lewdness in Irish servants, and falseness in French intellectuals, it is to be doubted that the Catholics of America in that day were one, holy, catholic and apostolic. Disorder lived with them. Confusion dwelt among them. There was distrust between Rome and the new see of Baltimore, between bishop and priest, between priest and layman, between regular and secular, between Frenchman and Irishman and Irishman and German. There was even friction within the religious orders, God save the mark![60] Used to a legal and financial niche in Europe and Canada, many Catholics floated free in America, as if weightless in the void of non-establishment. "It's very expensive to observe one's religion in the States," the *Canadien* complained.[61] Perhaps the Catholics were their own worst enemies. A half-century later, a partisan Catholic historian wrote: "We must avow that nothing is more sad than the commencement of the Church in New York. Disobedent priests, rebellious and usurping laymen!"[62]

---

[1] John Tracy Ellis, chap. XIV; Rev. Charles H. Metzger, S.J., *Catholics and the American Revolution* (Chicago: Loyola Univ. Press, 1962), chaps. I-III, VI.
[2] Howard Mumford Jones, *America and French Culture, 1750-1848* (Chapel Hill, N. Car.: Univ. N. Car. Press, 1927), p. 352.
[3] Ryan, "Travel Literature," X, No. 3 (Jan., 1928), p. 207.
[4] John Tracy Ellis, pp. 369-370, 405, 434; Curran, pp. 116-117; Leo Raymond Ryan, *Old St. Peter's* (New York: U.S. Cath. Hist. Soc., 1935), pp. 16, 83-86; John Webb Pratt, *Religion, Politics, and Diversity* (Ithaca: Cornell Univ. Press, 1967), pp. 121-129.
[5] The chain of waterways between the Hudson and the St. Lawrence Rivers. It was the route of Father John Carroll and the other American commissioners to and from Montreal in the spring of 1776 in the vain attempt to ask the Canadians to join in the Revolution. Guilday, p. 102.

[6] Griffin, I, 41-74, 114-126, 174-175.
[7] Bennett, chaps. XVIII-XIX.
[8] Ryan, "Travel Literature," X, No. 3 (Jan., 1928), 180-185. Nearly 70 Frenchmen published works on their travels and sojourns in America in 1780-1800. J.I. Wyer, "Later French Settlements in New York State, 1783-1800," New York State Historical Assoc., *Proceedings,* XV (1916), 177.
[9] Archbishop James Roosevelt Bayley, *History of the Catholic Church on the Island of New York* (New York: Cath. Pub. Soc., 1870), p. 54.
[10] Bennett, pp. 386-387, 407-408; Ruth L. Higgins, *Expansion in New York* (Columbus, Ohio: Ohio State Univ., 1931), p. 103.
[11] David M. Ellis and Others. *A Short History of New York State* (Ithaca: Cornell Univ. Press, 1957), chap. 13.
[12] David M. Ellis, "The Yankee Invasion of New York, 1783-1850," *New York History,* XXXII, No. 1 (Jan.,1951), pp. 3-17.
[13] Metzger, chaps. I-II, pp. 56-59.
[14] *Ibid.,* chap. VIII.
[15] Possibly, Mass had been said *sub rosa* in New York City in 1775, 1776 and 1784, and possibly a Catholic chapel had been destroyed there by fire in 1776. It is certain that an Abbé de la Motte, who had been the chaplain of a French warship, had been captured and paroled in the city, had said a Mass there in 1778, and had been jailed for it by the British. Ryan, *Old St. Peter's,* pp. 33-37; Bennett, pp. 338, 378.
[16] Ryan, *Old St. Peter's,* pp. 51, 60, n. 68; Rev. Norbert H. Miller, "Pioneer Capuchin Missionaries in the United States (1784-1816)," U.S. Cath. Hist. Soc., *Historical Records and Studies,* XXI (1932), 190, 198, n. 67, 201. Bayley, p. 183, lists Father Whelan with the Johnstown address, among the subscribers to Carey's Bible, which was published in 1790. See also Guilday, pp. 248-256.
[17] "The Church in Albany," *Records of the American Catholic Historical Society of Philadelphia,*XXIII (1912), 176.
[18] Rev. Thomas F. O'Connor, "Catholicism in the Fort Stanwix Country," *Records of the American Catholic Historical Society of Philadelphia,* LX, No. 1 (March, 1949), 83 text and n. 12; Thomas F. Meehan, "Some Pioneer Catholic Laymen in New York — Dominick Lynch and Cornelius Heeney" U.S. Cath. Hist. Soc., *Historical Records and Studies,* IV (Oct., 1906), 285-292; Bennett, pp. 392-393.
[19] Mason Wade, *The French Canadians, 1760-1945* (Toronto: Macmillan, 1955), p. 36. In 1789, The Marquis de Chartier de Lotbinière, a French Canadian then living in New York City, laid claim to two tracts of land on either side of the stream that joins Lakes George and Champlain, which tracts were then in the possession of the state of New York, and which, he declared, had been granted to him by the King of France as seignories before 1760, and had been confirmed to him by the Treaties of 1763 and 1783. William Ray Manning (ed.), *Diplomatic Correspondence of the United States: Canadian Relations, 1784-1860,* Vol. I: *1784-1820* (3 vols.; Wash., D.C.: Carnegie Endowment for International Peace, 1940-1943), 360-364. The Marquis had been a liaison between France and the Thirteen Colonies during the Revolution. Griffin, I, 69-74.
[20] Smith, pp. 12-13, 157-158.

²¹Louise H. Zimm, and Others (eds.) *Southeastern New York* (3 vols.; New York: Lewis Historical Pub. Co., 1946), I, 310. On Oct. 5-7, he baptized 14 children at Fishkill, the oldest of whom was five, and all of whom had French names. See also Schrott, p. 70.
²²Sister Mary Christine Taylor, S.S.J., "A History of the Foundations of Catholicism in Northern New York" (Unpublished Ph.D. Dissertation Dept. of American Studies, St. Louis University, 1967), p. 83; Manning, I, 357-358; Shea, *Church*, II, 268.
²³Hugh and Charles W. McLellan, "Pierre Huet de la Valinière, Priest on Lake Champlain, 1790-1791," *The Moorsfield Antiquarian*, I, No. 4 (Feb., 1938), 239-255.
²⁴The entire population of the town, or township, of Champlain was 127 families, or 578 persons, of whom three persons were slaves. Some indeterminate family names make the ethnic division approximate. U.S., Census Bureau, *Heads of Families...Census.....1790*, New York (Wash.; Govt. Print, Office, 1908), pp. 9, 56. Many of Congress' Own were recruited south of the border. Griffin, I, 115-126.
²⁵See below, p. 33.
²⁶Manning, I, 357-358.
²⁷McLellan, "de la Valinière," pp. 239-255. The Little Chazy is a few miles south of the Great Chazy River.
²⁸Wade, chaps. I-II; W.J. Eccles, chap. V; R.L. Jones, "French Canadian Agriculture in the St. Lawrence Valley, 1815-1850," *Approaches to Canadian Economic History*, ed. W.T. Easterbrook and M.H. Watkins (Toronto: McClelland & Stewart, 1967), pp. 110-126.
²⁹Bishop Joseph-Octave Plessis, *Journal des Visites Pastorales de 1815 et 1816* (Quebec: Imprimerie Franciscaine Missionaire, 1903), pp. 157-158.
³⁰Quoted in Gustave Lanctot: *Canada and the American Revolution, 1774-1783* (Cambridge: Harvard Univ. Press, 1967), p. 5.
³¹Lanctot, chap. I; Eccles, chap. V; Wade, *passim*.
³²*Quoted in Wade*, p. 74
³³The population of Quebec was 91,500 in 1775, and 119,000 in 1785. M.C. Urquhart, *Historical Statistics of Canada* (Cambridge: Univ. Press, 1965), p. 54.
³⁴Lanctot, p. 121.
³⁵*Ibid.*, p. 84.
³⁶Wade, *passim;* Lanctot, *passim;* Griffin, I, 114-125, 177-180, II, *passim,* III, *passim*. For the text of an excommunication, see Shea, *Church,* II, 109-110.
³⁷Lanctot, p. 69.
³⁸Taylor, p. 84.
³⁹Griffin, I, 75.
⁴⁰*Ibid.*, I, 75-91; Bennett, pp. 376-377; McLellan, "de la Valinière," pp. 239-242.
⁴¹Griffin, I, 78.
⁴²*Ibid.*, I, 86.
⁴³*Ibid.*, I, 75.
⁴⁴*Ibid.*, I, 78.
⁴⁵*Ibid*, I, 87-88.

⁴⁶Bennett, pp. 376-377.
⁴⁷Shea, *Church,* II, 431, n. 4.
⁴⁸Griffin, I, 135-137.
⁴⁹In August of 1787, Lorant Olivier and Clement Gosselin, Majors, petitioned Congress on behalf of the Canadian Settlement to continue the allowance of provisions that had been made to them for fifteen months. They were hard up. Having waited two years for a subdivision of the state's grant of land, they were now prevented from farming it, partly by the British who held a post in the northern part of it, and partly by a faulty survey that had cost each of them the pledge of one-half of their lands and that had failed to give them a valid title. Manning, I, 357-358.
⁵⁰McLellan, "de la Valinière," p. 246.
⁵¹Where *ibid.,* p. 241, simply says arson, Smith, p. 32, says the Catholics did it to get rid of the pastor.
⁵²Hugh and Charles W. McLellan, "Peter Dubree & Peter Jonqueray *ads.* Jacques Rouse," *The Moorsfield Antiquarian,* I, No. 2 (Aug., 1937), 129-134.
⁵³Shea, *Church,* II, 268-269.
⁵⁴Above, p. 30.
⁵⁵Hugh and Charles W. McLellan, "Index of Names: Inscriptions from Old Graveyards," *The Moorsfield Antiquarian,* I, No. 4 (Feb., 1938), 325-328, II, No. 4 (Feb., 1939), 347-359. Smith, p. 32: "as if in punishment of their wanton act (arson) all trace of them has disappeared from that neighborhood."
⁵⁶McLellan, "Peter Dubree," p. 130.
⁵⁷Rev. Thomas T. McAvoy, *A History of the Catholic Church in The United States* (Notre Dame, Ind.: Notre Dame Press, 1969), chaps. III-IV; John Tracy Ellis, chaps. XIV-XV.
⁵⁸Guilday, p. 207.
⁵⁹John Carroll became Superior in 1784 and Prefect Apostolic in 1785, but did not have the powers of an ordinary till 1789. *Ibid.,* chaps. XIV-XIX.
⁶⁰Rev. Francis X. Curran, S.J., "The Jesuit Colony in New York, 1808-1817, U.S. Cath. Hist. Soc., *Historical Records and Studies,* XLII (1954), 51-97. The bickering was Churchwide. In 1799, Sir John Hippisley, M.P., a negotiator in Rome, wrote: "The disunion between the Secular and Regular clergy, even in Rome, is surpassed only by the squabbles existing between the several subdivisions of orders among the Monks and Friars themselves. Quoted in Rev. Vincent Reginald Hughes, O.P., *The Right Rev. Richard Luke Concanen, O.P., first Bishop of New York (1747-1810)* (Freiburg: Studia Friburgensia, 1926), p. 51.
⁶¹Mason Wade, "The French Parish and *Survivance* in Nineteenth Century New England," *Catholic Historical Review,* XXXVI, No. 2 (July, 1950), 168.
⁶²DeCourcy-Shea, p. 352. On the harm to all organized religion in New York City, due to the American Revolution, see Ryan, *Old St. Peter's,* chaps. II-IV. One of the oddities of that period of crisis for Catholics in America was the intrigue to establish an Oneida bishopric, in central New York. What began as trade between some Frenchmen in Philadelphia and the tribe of the Oneidas swelled into a dream to Catholicize all of the Indians of North

America, and to ally them to Spain for the security of Florida, Louisiana and the island of Cuba. Guilday, 392-417; E.B. O'Callaghan (ed.), *Documents Relating to the Colonial History of the State of New York*, VII, 43, 582, VIII, 122, 551, n. 1, 631, n. 1.

CHAPTER III

APOSTACY ON THE FRONTIER

How many Catholics were there in upstate New York between 1790 and 1847, when the diocese of Albany arose? Who were they, and where did they live? How many fish were there in the Sea of Galilee, when Jesus walked the water? Where did they swim, and what were their species? The apostles found out by casting a net. But few were the Catholic fishers of men on the frontier.

The Census of 1790 is mum on religion. But there is evidence, which is ambiguous, that besides the 170 Catholics in that year at Chazy and Coopersville, there were another 2,300 in the Mohawk Valley.[1] In 1790, the entire country had about 35,000, most of whom came after the Peace of 1783.[2] It has been estimated that their number, in 1790-1850, went from 35,000 to 1,606,000.[3] The gain was 1,571,000 and 70% of them were immigrants and their American issue. Among those Catholic immigrants, the Irish had the majority. They were 65% in 1790-1820, and 76% in 1840-1850. Contrariwise, the Germans were as nil in 1790-1820 and about 15% in 1840-1850. Another group, and smaller yet, were the Canadians. From the Maritime Provinces as well as Quebec, they were 1% of the Catholic immigration after 1830, though they seemed to be more in New York State, because they bunched in the North Country. The French of Europe and the West Indies were in a class by themselves. Arriving in two waves of exiles, the one from the revolutions in France and Santo Domingo in the early nineties, and the other after the fall of Napoleon in 1815, most of the first wave went home in the late nineties, and most of the second wave after 1830.[4] The French were 10% to 14% of the foreign-born Catholics in 1790-1840, but only 3% in 1840-1850.

The fall-out of aliens, and so of Catholics, was heavy in the Hudson-Mohawk Corridor, medium in the North Country, and light in the Southern Tier. In 1835, for instance, the Corridor, with 59% of the entire population of the future diocese, drew 62% of the "male aliens not naturalized." The figures for the North Country, in the same order, were 17% and 27% and for the Southern Tier, 24% and 11%.[5]

Transit made the difference. The Southern Tier did not compare with the other two in their contact with the ports of Quebec and New York. Before the War of 1812, the North Country had the advantage of steamboats on Lake Champlain and on the Hudson and St. Lawrence Rivers, while the Hudson-Mohawk Corridor was one of the best natural routes to the west, even before the coming of the Erie Canal and the railroads in the 1820s and 1830s quickened the flow of people along that route.[6] The opening of the Champlain and St. Lawrence Railroad in 1836 gave the North Country another edge.[7] As a matter of fact, that region, during 1821-1826, had its own port of entry, to wit, Ogdensburg, alias Oswegatchie, alias Frenchman's Bay. It tallied the arrival in that period of 517 immigrants, including 207 Irishmen.[8] As for the number of Catholics in 1790-1847 in the diocese-to-be, guesswork steps in where methodology fears to tread. One historian says, with reluctance, that in the early twenties, while there were perhaps 15,000 Catholics in New York City, more or less, not counting the ones who floated free of congregations, and who were only presumptive, therefore, the diocese of New York, including all of that state plus the seven counties of northern New Jersey,[9] had maybe 50,000 Catholics, half of them unorganized.[10] Fewer than 1,000 were in the city of Albany.[11] More than this we dare not say, except to point out that the vortex of the population of the state, outside New York City, lay in the Mohawk Valley.[12] In 1847, Bishop John Hughes thought that his diocese of New York had 230,000 Catholics.[13] The entire population of the state was then nearly 3,000,000.[14]

However many of the Catholics, and wherever, the fact is that apostates were everywhere among them. Not all were like Doctor Richard Collins, who immigrated to New Jersey in 1765. Of his three sons, he once said: "I have raised one Methodist, one Quaker, and one Universalist." He himself died a Methodist in 1808.[15] But what could one expect of the Catholic immigrant, who was used to following the lead of someone else, when the most prominent Catholic layman in New York City at that time was Hector St. John de Crevecoeur, a deist, whose wedding had been performed, and whose children had been baptized, by a Huguenot minister.[16]

Apostasy was a hard word, once upon a time. To the Catholic, it was the sin of sins against the King of Kings. To the Irishman and the French Canadian, who mixed politics with religion in a blend of nationalism, it was also treason.[17] If the word conjures up a Judas Iscariot or a Henry VIII, it will be unfair to the memory of the Catholics who were here when the United States was young. Let charity say simply that many of them lapsed or fell away. After all, they were not like Benedict Calvert, the fourth Lord Baltimore, who became a Protestant in 1713, because he thought that his barony in Maryland was worth more than a Mass.[17] Nor were they like Père Potencien, the Superior of the Recollects at Trois Rivières, who became an Anglican minister in New Jersey in 1847, with wife and children.[18] Nor were they like the Jesuit Father Charles Wharton, who did the same in New York in 1784.[19] In fact, most of the Catholics of America, then and later, never heard of them, or needed such Judas sheep to go astray. There were reasons enough in the daily life of the eighteenth and nineteenth centuries for people to leave the Church in America.

"From its very nature, the life of a colonist presents manifold temptations to neglect the interests of the soul." Those were the words of an American Presbyterian minister in 1844.[20] To speak of the United States, in general, and of upstate New York, in particular, it was worse for Catholics. Not a priest, not even a drop of holy water as a reminder, did they have, many of them, for years at a time, in those early days. As immigrants, their life was topsy-turvy, in a psychic and cultural way. The men were single, like as not, surrounded by Protestant women. Ethnicity divided them, and poverty, drink and swinking toil ground them down.[21] On top of that, the Revolution left a wake of disaffection. Was it not himself, the future Bishop of Baltimore, John Carroll, who wrote in 1784: "No authority derived from Propaganda will ever be admitted here."[22]

True, there were Catholic heroes in those days. Take the Irishman, whom John Francis Maguire, M.P., author and traveler, met somewhere in Ontario in the 1860's. On his arrival, thirty years before, the nameless immigrant had gone to work on the public roads, breaking stone.[23]

Between Saturday evening, when his week's work was over, and the Monday morning, when another week of labour commenced, this devoted Catholic would constantly walk a distance of between forty and fifty miles, to attend Mass and perform the duties enjoined by his church. And when his children grew in strength, he would make them the companions of his journey.

He was the sort of man who said: I came with nothing but my own four bones, a sharp axe, and the help of the Lord."[24]

And take the missioners. Father Joseph Mosley, S.J., covered ten counties in Maryland, Virginia and Delaware, before the Revolution. In 1764, he wrote: "Between 3 or 400 mile was my last Mass fare, on one horse."[25] Father Ferdinand Farmer, S.J., was another chip off that rock of ages. After years of making the circuit of eastern Pennsylvania, New Jersey and New York, he died in 1786. When he rode out on his last rounds in 1785, Father Robert Molyneux said: "He is no more fit to take that journey than I am to fast forty days and nights like St. Stylites."[26]

But many Catholics were not so true.[27] If apathy slew a thousand, mixed marriage smote ten thousand.[28] Catholics vanished among Protestants, and few of them surfaced again, as did William Mooney and John Leary, who attended Trinity Episcopal Church in New York City, until St. Peter's Catholic Church arose in 1785. Before that, the people scoffed: "John Leary goes to Philadelphia once a year to get absolution."[29] Catholics then were more like James O'Neill of Liverpool, in Onondaga County, in the early 1800's, who fell away, and earned the name of "Yankee Jim."[30] Or they were like the Irishwoman at Binghamton, in Broome County, in the 1830's, who walked into the Episcopal church one Sunday morn to have her child baptized.[31] Or they were like those French Canadians of the North Country, who are recalled by the superstition of the *loup-garou:* he who fails in his Easter duty for seven years will turn into a werewolf.[32]

In that first half-century, the French of Europe and the West Indies stood out among the immigrants.[33] Refugees all, from the ex-king Joseph Bonaparte to the slave Pierre Toussaint, most of them were aristocrats, or bourgeoisie, or planters, and used to high living. Yet, some had fled with the clothes on their backs alone, and here for a few years, they ate the crumbs under the table. The United States was a way station for them until they returned home. Grimly, they tried to transplant the salon and the chateau. When a young lady talked during a contra-dance, the master of ceremonies scolded: "Do you think you are here for your own pleasure?"[34]

French fashions swept the country. Even the Iroquois were said to have their dancing master. Having dreamt of *égalité* in the New World, the French shrank, nevertheless, from the hard facts of democracy in America. Brotherhood was one thing, but mob rule was another. They brought their intra-Gallic hates with them. When one met his enemy in the street, he spat on the sidewalk. "Consider that your face!"[35] Bourbonists plotted to rescue Louis; Bonapartists conspired to free Napoleon; but to no avail. On balance, the French won favor, but some of them gave umbrage. One profiteered. Another played the flute on Sunday in Connecticut. Queer to them was the mixture of religion and daily life in America.

The future diocese of Albany, in the first forty years of the nineteenth century, was sprinkled with Frenchmen.[36] Singly, and in groups, they turned up at Johnstown, Cooperstown, Plattsburgh, Saratoga and at Albany. Titles of nobility clustered in the last named place as they did in New York City.[37] At Oneida Lake in Oneida County, at Greene on the Chenango River in Chenango County, at Morris and New Lisbon on Butternut Creek in Otsego County, and at Castorland on the Black River in Jefferson County,[38] they "lived among us, looked down on us and left us, leaving scarcely a trace of influence upon us."[39]

However it was, the local histories still sparkle with their vignettes: the veterans of Napoleon who turned out at Rosiere, in Jefferson County, in 1832, to welcome Bishop Dubois, in uniform and with a volleyof gunfire;[40] the baby who was born to a couple of the *haute bourgeoisie* at Verona, in Oneida County. It died in 1797, and was buried in its cradle. A year or so later, after the parents had left, apparently, and when a canal was being dug at the portage between Rome and Oneida Lake, the workmen shoveled up the tiny corpse, and, we hope, tucked it back into the bosom of mother earth.[41]

In name, the *émigré* was ordinarily a Catholic. But that was a canopy that stretched from the Sulpicians, who opened the first seminary for priests in America, to Talleyrand, the schismatic, who arched the eyebrows of Philadelphia by playing the man about town with a Negress.There were the Roman bishops of the United States, many of whom at first were Frenchmen.[42] There was Toussaint, a hairdresser in New York City, who went to Mass everyday for sixty years, and died in the odor of sanctity.[43] And there was the American branch of the Bonaparte family. Charles Joseph Bonaparte, 1851-1921, a resident of Maryland, a grand-nephew of Napoleon I, a graduate of Harvard, and a trust-busting Attorney General to Theodore Roosevelt, lived and died in the Church.[44]

On the other hand, take the Franchots of Butternut Creek, in

Otsego County, in New York State. They fled France around 1790, rich and bourgeois, a widower and his four sons, but whether Catholic or not, we cannot tell. In any case, the youngest son, Pascal Franchot, wedded two wives of Dutch Yorker stock, endowed the land with eleven children and thirty-five grandchildren, organized a Masonic lodge and an Episcopal church, and in a century, became the Abraham of more than a hundred Americans.[45]

How much of the Creed can have stuck to the émigrés after they had breathed the same stormy air for years with a Noah's ark of freethinkers? In 1789, the Prefect Apostolic John Carroll wrote:[46]

> They are everywhere a scandal to religion, with very few exceptions. Not only that, but they disseminate, as much as they can, all the principles of irreligion, of contempt for the church and disregard for the duties which both command.

It took the death of a little daughter to bring the Marquise de la Tour du Pin "a religious awakening denied her in the disordered society of her youth."[47] She and her husband farmed with slaves on the road between Schenectady and Watervliet in the nineties, and they worshipped at St. Mary's in Albany.

The French immigrants in America had three effects on religion. They gave, or discarded, priests to the Church; they fed the infidelism of the Jeffersonian Democrats; and they infuriated those Federalists and Protestants who kept the flame of Calvin. It was the last group, which damned Jew with Jesuit, Rome with Robespierre, and Catholics with the enemies of Christ. Did not Bishop Dubourg of New Orleans own a set of Diderot's *Encyclopédie?* From such a potpourri of Gallic beliefs, there came both vim to the Faith and the rage that would kill Catholics and burn their churches.

Frenchmen, Irishmen, Germans, they left the Church in numbers. in 1860, the Austrian Jesuit Father, Francis Xavier Weninger, was in New Jersey on one of his well-known missions.[48]

> Here in Elizabethtown, I came upon a remarkable state of affairs. At least half of the parish seemed to have lapsed from the Faith, or apostatized, and of the other half, at least half of them were in mixed marriages, so that the education of the children was largely in the hands of the Protestant part.

Father Weninger had come from Austria in 1848, and had a mission of preaching from state to state. He used to say: "America! America! You are a dangerous land for me."[49]

[1]*Shea, Church,* II, 432, citing a letter from an old missioner in Mass., Father Francis A. Matignon, to Bp. Carroll, July 23, 1798, says that at sometime in the 1790's "a Rev. Mr. Finn had a little flock of seventy Catholic families at Fort Stanwix, on the Mohawk, and it was said that there were four hundred Catholic families between that place and Albany. "Did the 400 include those at Albany and Ft.Stanwix? In 1790, the average family in New York State and in the U.S. had 5.7 persons. U.S. Bureau of the Census, *A Century of Population Growth* (Wash.: Govt. Print Off. 1909, reprint, 1966), p. 96, So, the 400 families amount to 2,280 persons. O'Connor p. 83, doubts the item about Rev. Flinn, whom he identifies as an Irish Capuchin, Thomas Flynn, See Miller, p. 226, on Flynn.

[2]John Tracy, Ellis p. 459.

[3]Shaughnessy, chaps. IV, VIII and p. 251.

[4]There were 200 on the Susquehanna River, in northern Penn., in the nineties. T. Wood Clarke, *Emigrés in the Wilderness* (Port Washington, N.Y.: Ira J. Friedman, 1967, originally, 1941), pp. v-vi, and chaps. VIII-IX. In 1790-1794, about 10,000 of them came from the troubled French West Indies to New York City and Phila. There were 4,000 in N.Y.C. in the fall of 1793. Wyer, p. 185. As early as 1769, perhaps, there were Catholics on the lower Susquehanna in Penn. Shea, *Church,* II, 292. The Delaware and Susquehanna Valleys were corridors from Penn. to the Southern Tier of N.Y.

[5]New York, *Census of the State of New York for 1835* (Albany: Croswell, Van Benthuysen and Burt, 1836), table of "Recapitulation," back of book, unpaged.

[6]G.P. deT. Glazebrook, *A History of Transportation in Canada* (2 vols.; Toronto: McClelland and Stewart, 1964), I, 67-71; Champlain Transportation Co., *The Steamboats on Lake Champlain, 1809-1930* (Albany: Champlain Transp. Co., 1930), passim; David Lear Buckman, *Old Steamboat Days on the Hudson River* (New York: Grafton Press, 1907), chap. I.

[7]Glazebrook, I, 45.

[8]U.S., Scty. of State, Annual "Report of Passenger Arrivals," for the years 1821-1827, in *U.S. Govt. Documents Serial Set,* Vols. 69, 83, 103, 118, 140 and 154. The count of passenger arrivals began in the U.S. on Oct. 1, 1819, and was reported by quarter-years. In the period of Oct. 1, 1819-Sept. 30, 1826, there were 28 quarters. Oswegatchie reported for only 8 of them. Since some of the arrivals were in the winter, we cannot explain away the gaps by saying that the passengers came only in warm weather. So much for the accuracy of those early statistics. Chances are that many more immigrants landed at Oswegatchie than were reported, or at the other many steamboat landings on the St. Lawrence between St. Regis and Sackets Harbor.

[9]A glance at a map will show why the official documents speak of northern N.J. as eastern N.J. Shearer, p. 192.

[10]Charles G. Herbermann, "The Rt. Rev. John Dubois, D.D., Third Bishop of New York," U.S. Cath. Hist. Soc., *Historical Records and Studies,* I, Part II (Jan. 1900), 348-355, discusses the several estimates of the Catholic population in 1790-1833. Bp. John Dubois reported in 1836 that the state of N.Y. with 47,000 sq. m., had 180,000 Catholics, and the seven counties of N.J., with 4,300 sq. m. had 20,000 Catholics. Bp. Dubois to the Abp. of

Vienna, New York, March 15, 1836, *Berichte der Leopoldinen-Stiftung,* X (1837), 7-8. But, Herbermann, p. 348, rejects that estimate and others as not trustworthy.

[11] A recent historian estimates the number of practicing Catholics among the Irish in Albany in 1820 as 300, or 2% of the population of that city, and in 1830 as between 1,000 and 2,000, or between 5% and 10% of the population. He bases his "reasonable guess" on some Albany newspapers and on the *Souvenir of Centennial Celebration and Historical Sketch of St. Mary's Parish.* William Esmond Rowley, "Albany: A Tale of Two Cities, 1820-1880" (unpublished Ph.D. dissertation, Dept. of History, Harvard Univ., 1967), pp. 132-133. Shea, *Church,* III, 497, n. 3, and Herbermann, p. 354, estimate 2,000 Catholics in Albany in 1828-1829. That figure evidently included Germans and others.

[12] If we view the state of New York in 1820 as divided, not into counties, but into the two later (not yet existing) dioceses of Albany, Buffalo, together with the (already existing) diocese of N.Y. as the three diocese were in late 1847, then the diocese of Albany (in 1820) had a whole population of 685,-100, that of Buffalo 320,500, and that of N.Y. 367,200. The proportions were about the same in 1825 and 1830. Albany diocese was the biggest in area and counties. N.Y., State Dept., "Report of the Secretary of State Giving the Census of the Several Congressional Districts in 1820, 1825 and 1830," New York State *Senate Documents,* 55th Session (1832), Vo. I, Doc. No. 65, p. 12.

[13] *Catholic Directory for 1848,* p. 273.

[14] New York State, Supt. of the Census, *Census of the State of New York for 1875* (Albany: Weed, Parsons, 1877), p. 2.

[15] Thomas Hobbs Maginnis, *The Irish Contribution to America's Independence* (Phila.: Doire, 1913), p. 73.

[16] Ryan, *Old St. Peter's,* p. 45; Thomas Philbrick, *St. John de Crevecoeur* (New York: Twayne, 1970), pp. 18-19, 33-34, 44. Stephen Girard, the rich Philadelphian who died in 1831, was another non-practicing Catholic, F.E.T. (trans. and ed.), *Diary and Visitation Record of the Rt. Rev. Francis Patrick Kenrick, Administrator and Bishop of Philadelphia, 1830-1851* (Lancaster, Penn.: Wickershaw Print. Co. 1916), p. 66.

[17] J. Moss Ives, *The Ark and the Dove* (New York: Longmans, Green, 1936), pp. 268-270.

[18] Bennett, pp. 289-292.

[19] Guilday, chap. IX.

[20] Rev. Robert Baird, *Religion in America* (New York: Harper, 1844), p. 39, and Book I, chaps. XIII-XVI, for a discussion.

[21] Above, pp. 37-38. Below, pp. 68-71.

[22] John Tracy Ellis, pp. 426-427. Note the parallel between Carroll's opposition to Propaganda and his allegiance to the Pope, on the one hand, and on the other, the Continental Congress's attitude to Parliament and the King before July 4, 1776. Carroll's opposition to Propaganda ceased when he accepted an appointment from it as Prefect Apostolic a few months later.

[23] John Francis Maguire, *The Irish in America* (New York: D & J. Sadlier, 1868), p. 128.

[24] *Ibid.,* p. 44.

²⁵Rev. Edward I. Devitt, S.J. (ed.), "Letters of Father Joseph Mosley, 1757-1786," *Woodstock Letters,* XXXV, No. 1 (1906), 45.
²⁶Rev. John M. Daley, S.J., "Pioneer Missionary, Ferdinand Farmer, S.J.: 1720-1786," *ibid.,* LXXV, No. 4 (Dec. 1946), 319.
²⁷Of Catholics outside Maryland before the Revolution, McAvoy, p. 24, says "most" fell away, and John Tracy Ellis, p. 380, says "many" fell away.
²⁸Almost every account by visiting or domestic priests or bishops in those days makes frequent reference to mixed marriage as the chief reason for leakage from the Church. There must be 50 letters or more from the priests of the diocese of Albany among the papers of Cardinal McCloskey, which say the same thing.
²⁹Ryan, *Old St. Peter's,* pp. 15-16.
³⁰Theresa Bannan, M.D., *Pioneer Irish of Onondaga* (New York: G.P. Putnam's Sons, 1911), p. 67.
³¹Sister Mary Teresa White, "Reminiscences," *Records of the American Catholic Historical Society of Philadelphia,* XII (1901), 62.
³²Harold W. Thompson, *Body, Boots and Britches* (New York: J.B. Lippincott, 1940), pp. 115-117. This bit of lore was collected at Mooers, in Clinton Co.
³³Frances Sergeant Childs, *French Refugee Life in the United States, 1790-1800* (Baltimore: John Hopkins Press, 1940), *passim;* Howard Mumford Jones, chaps. V, VIII, X-XIII.
³⁴*Ibid.,* p. 235.
³⁵*Ibid.,* p. 138, n. 85.
³⁶Clarke, *passim;* Wyer, pp. 178-188; John Warner Barber and Henry Howe, *Historical Collections of the State of New York* (New York: S. Tuttle, 1845), 173, 446; Francis Whiting Halsey, *The Old New York Frontier* (New York: Scribner's Sons, 1901),pp. 359, 370-371; Daniel E. Wager (ed.), *Our County and Its People* (2 vols.; n.p.: Boston Hist. Co. 1896), I, 139, 165; James Arthur Frost, *Life on the Upper Susquehanna, 1783-1860* (New York: King's Crown Press, Columbia Univ., 1951), p. 14; Childs, p. 72. In 1793 or later, Chancellor Robert E. Livingston found the Count St. Hilary and his wife, the Countess of Clermont, living at Oneida Lake. He took a fancy to them, and they became long-term guests on his estate in Columbia Co. That explains the name of the most famous steamboat in America. Franklin Ellis *History of the Columbia County* (Phila.: Everts & Ensign, 1878), p. 128, note.
³⁷Howard Mumford Jones, p. 138.
³⁸In the early 1790's, an Abbé Nicholas Perrot was among the French settlers on the Black River for a few years. Taylor, pp. 94-95; Guilday, p. 408.
³⁹Clarke, pp. ix-x.
⁴⁰Taylor, pp. 125-126.
⁴¹Wager, I, 581.
⁴²Rev. Joseph Bernard Code, *Dictionary of the American Hierarchy* (New York: Longmans, Green, 1940), pp. 367, 407, for lists of dates of appointment with countries of birth.
⁴³Ryan, *Old St. Peter's,* pp. 210-215.
⁴⁴*Dictionary of American Biography,* I, 427-428.

[45]Clarke, pp. 102-108.
[46]Quoted in John Tracy Ellis, p. 442.
[47]Childs, p. 27, DeCourcy-Shea, p. 470, says that the la Tour du Pins were charter members of St. Mary's.
[48]Franz Xavier Weninger, Missionär der Gesellschaft Jesu, *Erinnerungen aus Meinem Leben in Europa und Amerika durch Achtzig Jahre — 1805 bis 1885* (Columbus, Ohio: J.J. Lessing, 1886), p. 228.
[49]Quoted in Rev. Ernst Anthony Reiter, S.J., *Schematismus der katholischen deutschen Geistlichkeit in den Ver. Staaten Nord-Amerika's* (New York: Friedrich Puster, 1869), p. 6.

CHAPTER IV

THE NORTH COUNTRY AND
THE SOUTHERN TIER

The wilderness of the future diocese of Albany was hinged to the see of Baltimore in 1784-1808,[1] then to the see of New York until 1847.[2] But geography decreed for a while that the grace of God would come to the Catholics of the Southern Tier from Philadelphia and to those of the North Country from Quebec. The Southern Tier and the North Country are mostly mountainous. At first, lumbering and the other industries of the woodland, as tanning, and the making of barrels and of potash, overshadowed farming in those two regions, and the dearth of transportation in the Southern Tier made of it a region of Protestant nativism.[3]

In the thirties, as many as five missioners made their way up the Susquehanna Valley at different times to Binghamton, in Broom County.[4] Bishop Francis Patrick Kenrick, the Coadjutor of Philadelphia, included the village in four of his visitations, the last time in 1849, almost two years after Albany became a see.[5] Father Michael Hurley, an Augustinian, was the first to appear. He found a few Catholic families there in 1834.[6] Sixty-seven years later, a Visitation nun, Sister Mary Teresa White, put pen to paper about her childhood in Binghamton and about her family who blazed the Catholic trail there.[7] She remembered the coming of the priests through the dark forest and the wildcats that killed the sheep.

> I see now the little wooden chapel embowered in forest trees, and recall how one time two little brothers and one little sister of mine were benighted four miles from home and hurried through the forest, scarcely daring to breathe, the brothers holding the little sister between them, and now and then the howl of a wolf in the distance.

In January of 1835, the Jesuit father Stephen Dubuisson fought his way to them. (It was he who once levitated at the altar, according

to report.)[8] The nun reminisced in 1901:[9]
> The snow was so deep that a horse could not be allowed to break the way for the priest's sleigh, as there would be danger of the animal breaking its legs; so my father and brothers walked before the sleigh and broke the road for the horse and his precious burden...the Lord's Anointed.

This remembrance lays bare another side to Catholic life on the frontier. Before St. John's of Binghamton was built in 1838, the home of the Whites was church and rectory. One happening there was unforgettable. The day after a wedding, the bride came back alone to ask the name of her husband. It turned out that the match had been made in haste by friends, on account of the brief and unexpected visit of a priest, and the young lady had been too flustered at the ceremony to get the name of the stranger she married.[10]

Of the 408 priests and bishops[11] who left a trace of service in 1790-1864 in the region of the diocese of Albany, 94 of them came from Canada.[12] Their faculties issued first from Baltimore, then New York City, then from the see of Albany. Henri-Marie de Pontbriand was the first prelate to visit from Quebec, but that was in 1752, when his own crozier reached into the North Country.[13] In 1771-1773, Bishop Joseph-Olivier Briand turned down a request of Propaganda to bring Confirmation to the Thirteen Colonies. It was the eve of the Revolution, and he had learned that, as a bishop, he would be as popular there as a publican in Judea, or as welcome as a collector of the Stamp Tax, and that, as a Roman bishop, he would loose a storm on Catholics.[14] In 1801, however, Monseigneur Pierre Denaut had the blessing of the see of Baltimore when he called at St. Regis and Oswegatchie.[15] It then became the usage of the bishops of Canada and New York to link arms across the border. In order to oversee their subjects, who migrated from one diocese to another, back and forth with the seasons, like reindeer, each bishop made the other his vicar general.[16]

There was a lapse of that exchange in 1815-1816, due to a vacancy in the see of New York and the disorder that marked it.[17] In 1815, Bishop Joseph-Olivier Plessis happened to be passing through New York City. He noted that "the faithful of the diocese are put out by the delay in the arrival of their new bishop. Some are beginning to say that they can do without him, if he does not come."[18] Maybe the lack of faculties for New York was one of the reasons why the Canadian prelate did no more than stop off for tea in Burlington and for lunch at Rouses Point, although he must have known that the Canadian and other Catholics along the Champlain Road had never, or not for an age, laid eyes upon a bishop.[19]

Next year, Monseigneur Plessis set out on the upper St. Lawrence to tour his own missions in the west. The pastor of St. Regis, meanwhile, Father Joseph Marcoux, readied the children for Confirmation. They were Indians and Whites, some Canadian, and some from New York. But the Yorkers were out of luck. When the bishop returned from the Great Lakes, they learned that neither he nor the missioner had the right to serve them in ordinary case. A few weeks before, in fact, a Catholic murderer in Ogdensburg had had to go to his hanging, while Father Marcoux had been stopped from giving him anything more than words without shrift. The bishop later found the faculties from New York in the mail at Montreal, and forwarded them to St. Regis.[20] In the spring of 1816, John Connolly became the first ordinary of New York to visit upstate,[21] and thereafter, the Catholics of that region saw their chief shepherd every few years.[22]

Four Catholic missions grew up in the North Country in the early 1800's, to wit, Carthage in Jefferson County, Ogdensburg in St. Lawrence County, St. Regis in Franklin County, and Coopersville in Clinton County.[23] From the Indian reservation, the see of Quebec sent the Word into Franklin, St. Lawrence and Clinton Counties, between Massena on the west and Churubusco on the east, a span of forty-five miles. There, a half-dozen rivers tumbled to the St. Lawrence, and the trees stood tall and thick as the Lord God had made them. In 1818, a surveyor beheld "one vast and entire wilderness inhabited by no human being, except a few savages, and, in one spot, a few Frenchmen."[24]

The *Canadiens* came first. Before the Revolution, they logged on the Salmon and St. Regis Rivers, and floated the masts to Montreal. But they were few among the Protestants from Vermont at the turn of the century. After the War of 1812, the torch of the Faith there passed to the Irish, who began to trickle in by way of Quebec. They came to grips with the frigid earth at Hogansburg, Chateaugay, and Brasher Falls, at Trout River and Fort Covington, at Bombay, Brushton, Malone and Massena, where the farming was hard, and forestry fed mankind.[25]

Consider the reduction or reservation of St. Regis again for a while. After 1785, it nearly always had a pastor,[26] and the Catholic Indians increased. They were 270 among a total of 600 in 1801, and 190 of them were confirmed.[27] Though the church was on the Canadian side of the reservation, most of the tribe were under the protection of the United States.[28] A half-century later, when the population was 1,482, with 413 on the American side, now, and 1,069 on the Canadian side, there were 338 Catholics among the Americans and 978 among the Canadians.[29]

Father Roderick Macdonell was the first pastor at St. Regis to become permanent after Father Gordan. He had studied at Scots College, in Valladolid, in Spain, and had been ordained, at his own request, not only for the mission among his clansmen in Ontario, but also for the Indians nearby. For twenty-one years, after he immigrated in 1785, he lived at St. Regis, serving as well the Scots across the St. Lawrence River and whomever else he could reach in the North Country of New York. He mastered the Iroquois tongue, built churches of stone, with walls that were four feet thick, and won the love of his Indians. When he died in 1806, at the age of fifty, the tribe had to threaten the Highlanders with bloody war in order to get this body for burial under the church that he had built for them. He was, said his bishop, "a good and pious man — learned and of great physical strength."[30]

During the strain between Great Britain and the United States over the Canadian boundary and other matters, before the Webster-Ashburton Treaty of 1842,[31] the site of the reservation of St. Regis, smack on the border, was a well of trouble for the tribe and for the Catholics among them. American troops attacked the village in October of 1812 in a misunderstanding over its neutrality, and Father Jean Baptiste Roupe, the pastor since 1807, together with forty Indians, was placed under arrest. Already under the suspicion of the British of taking bribes from the Americans in the form of rations, the priest and the Indians were marched off by the Americans to Plattsburgh.[32]

It seems that Father Roupe was soon freed, because he spent the next eight months at Quebec in teaching the Iroquois language to a native of that city by the name of Joseph Marcoux. The young man was so quick at it, and at his studies for the priesthood, that he was ordained at the age of twenty-two, by dispensation, on June 12, 1813, and five days later, he was assigned to St. Regis. For six years, he labored there, until he fell victim to the dissension. Somebody denounced him as an "American" priest, and the government forced Bishop Plessis to shift him to Caughnawaga, near Montreal.[33]

In 1827, St. Regis boiled over.[34] The trouble with the tribe and with the Catholic congregation was that it was torn by allegiances. Since the Revolution and the War of 1812, the St. Regis Indians had split apart under the shields of Britain and the United States. A survey of the border in 1817, pursuant to the Treaty of Ghent, had drawn eyes to the fact that the church and the village of the reservation lay in Canada.[35] The American Indians had become trespassers. At that time, they were in the majority. "A petty warfare" came to a head on June 14, 1827, the day of the *grande fête de Dieu,* or Corpus Christi. Traditionally, the tribe had turned out with guns, flags, fifes and drums to parade through the village and to the church for services. Some of the Indians had the privilege of wearing an alb, or carrying a candle, or doing something else in the ritual, which they clutched as an honor, and passed from father to son.[36]

According to the Indian Agent in Canada, the tribe gathered as usual on that day, but the American chiefs took the van. Then, "brandishing swords," and lofting the American flag with its "Spread Eagle," they processioned to the church. The Americans were bent on entering so; the British objected; the Americans pressed on; the British blocked the doorway with their bodies; a fight broke out; and the pastor, Father Joseph Vallée, shut the church, and postponed the fete. The Americans left. They threatened that, unless they had a hand in the doings, they would stop the salary of the priest, strip the church of half its furnishings, and they dared the king himself to stand in the way. The British asked for the protection of the Canadian militia, and the Agent reported to the government.

In the version of Bishop John Dubois of New York, who first visited the North Country soon afterward, the Americans simply wanted to plant their flag alongside the Union Jack at the church, albeit on British soil. They laid their grievance before the bishop, and asked for a church and a priest of their own. The bishop pointed out the peril of such a separation, and wiped away their scowls with the help of an old sachem, who said at one point in the discussion: "My father, we are no longer Christians since we lack charity."[37] At the episcopal Mass that followed, a dozen Indians wore surplices cut from blankets, and the tribe chanted in Iroquoisan and Gregorian, as the Blackrobes had taught them. Many received the sacraments of the Eucharist and Confirmation.

In Washington, the British Minister put it to Henry Clay, the Secretary of State, that the Americans at St. Regis were "intruders." He asked that the boundary line on the reservation be marked by a stone or a flagstaff, and that the Americans be moved to the south of it, in order to avert bloodshed. Clay replied with the details of an arrangement, which he had received from the American

Agent to the Six Nations, and in 1828 peace settled on St. Regis.[38]

The North Country lies open to Canada at Lake Champlain and along the upper St. Lawrence. In 1820, the Irish[39] Catholics first appeared in Franklin and St. Lawrence Counties at Hogansburg, Bombay, Malone and Massena. The Dalys, the Walshes and others were few and scattered, but whenever possible, they trekked from their farms to St. Regis. There, Celt and Iroquois knelt together to eat the Crucified Christ, and left their Irish and Indian names in the registers, in a hodgepodge, for a priest-historian to wonder at sixty-four years later. In 1884, Father John Talbot Smith talked to some of the oldtimers of that mission of long ago, who recalled the Easters and Christmases before they had a priest of their own, when some of them trudged twenty-five miles to the Indian church, as the snow crunched underfoot, and the night was bright with stars.[40]

"I lift up mine eyes unto Quebec, whence cometh deliverance." So might the Psalmist have sung as a Catholic in the North Country. Father Vallée, alone at St. Regis, and with a pidgin English at best, shouldered the burden of a growing Irish flock for seven or eight years. Time and again, the Auxiliary at Montreal begged the Ordinaries at Quebec and New York for an English-speaking assistant for that mission. "The Irish are now as numerous as the Canadians," he wrote in 1824.[41] But the only response was a priest on the fly, and rarely at that. In the end, Father Vallée collapsed, and was replaced by Father Francis Xavier Marcoux. *Clear Sky,* the Indians called him, for his blue eyes, rosy cheeks and yellow hair. That first year of 1832 tried him terribly. Cholera and ship fever stole up the St. Lawrence with the immigrants, and killed 134 of his Indians. But he was young and tough, and stuck it out for a half-century, living the loneliness of a White man on an Indian reservation.[42]

Among the dozen stations of the mission of St. Regis, in the parts of three counties and a thousand square miles of frontier in New York, where Protestant preachers roamed, seeking souls to acquire, in the year of 1830, the Catholics numbered maybe 2,000.[43] There were 500 at Bombay in 1824, 600 at Hogansburg in 1828, and the rest were scattered small. Except for a smidgin of Germans, they were Irish and French Canadians. The Irish abounded at such places as *Irish Ridge* on the Little Salmon River and the *Irish Settlement* at Hogansburg. Elsewhere, dwelt the *Canadiens.* Bishop Dubois wrote in 1830:[44]

> I could not end if I spoke of all the people I found in abandonment along the lakes and the St. Lawrence. At least half of the

inhabitants of those villages are French of Canada, who have settled on the fringe of New York.

While the Irish steadily increased throughout the state, the *Canadiens* began to swarm into the North Country in the late thirties, due to a depression and a rebellion in Canada in 1837-1838.[45] Alexander Leclair came to work in a cement factory at Massena, where a Mass was celebrated in his home, probably in 1837.[46] By 1854, the *Canadiens* in the mission of Corbeau, or Coopersville, amounted to four thousand. They were mostly farmers there, but elsewhere they worked in the lumber camps and at the iron forges along the rivers of the Adirondacks.[47]

In the fall of 1834, the Catholics of Hogansburg formed the congregation of St. Patrick's, and with the help of land and materials from William Hogan, the land promoter, they began to build a church.[48] It was a small, stone box, only forty feet by sixty,[49] but it showed that the sap was rising. Finally, in 1836, that mission saw its first permanent pastor from the see of New York. Father John McNulty had been born in County Mayo, Ireland, in 1805, had grown up there, had immigrated to Canada, had studied at the seminary in Montreal, had been ordained there in May of 1835 by Bishop Dubois, who had stationed him at first in Albany for the rest of the year, and then had sent him to Franklin County.[50] He was to learn the Indian language from Father Vallée at St. Regis, to teach him English in return, and to serve the English-speaking Catholics. Between the missions of Ogdensburg on the west and Coopersville on the east, Father McNulty became the shepherd of the new mission of Hogansburg. It would litter ten parishes someday. Likable and energetic, the young missioner plunged into the spreading of the Faith. He pushed the buying of parcels of land before the prices rose, and he saw to the building of churches.[51] Above all, for five years or so, he brought the grace of God, on horseback, wagon and foot, to a scattering of souls.[52]

There is no reason to suppose that "Siberia of New York" was any easier on the priest than it was on the Reverend James Erwin, a Methodist circuit rider, who must have crossed his path at many points.[53] In fact, the Catholic missioner had a harder time of it, probably, on account of fewer and smaller congregations and a leaner base of support. Reverend Erwin had two assistants when he came to the Chateaugay Methodist mission in 1835. Together, the three Protestant preachers had to cover an area with a circumference of four hundred miles every six weeks. Each one had a horse, saddle, saddlebags and a book or two. (The priest had to carry vestments and altar things in addition.) The Methodist rider usually rode fifteen to thirty miles on a Sunday, and "spent from six to eight hours in meetings." People came from as far as fifty miles away, and the local residents lodged them, some families taking in as many as twenty or thirty persons each. Even then, since the population was sparse, some of the visitors had to stop more than several miles away from the "quarterly meeting" sometimes in barns. When a schoolhouse or other public building was too small for the crowd of Protestants, the services moved into any big barn. At times, the temperature in the "church" fell below zero, the pulpit was a carpenter's bench, and the "pews" were in the stable and barn, on the floor and in the hayloft. Reverend Erwin slept wherever he could, in a straw bunk, in a trundlebed with any children who were there, shivering with the cold, with chickens roosting overhead, and pigs and calves at his feet, later breakfasting in overcoat and muffler, with hands that were numb. At places in Canada on his circuit, he had to travel with an armed escort, with firebrand and rifle, to guard against the wolves, the bears and the panthers. Even so, the Methodist preacher sang hymns as he rode, and held prayer meetings in the snow.

Like cymbals, they clashed, priest and preacher, Protestants and Catholics. Nativism became American in the thirties. Anti-Catholicism and xenophobia began to disturb the nineteenth century (although its noise was muffled in the hinterland)[54]. In the *Malone Palladium,* the Reverend Ashbel Parmelee attacked "Romanism," and Father McNulty rushed to its defense. "The Friends of the Reformation in Northern New York" appeared upon the scene.[55] In a gale of zealotry, Father McNulty was convicted of seduction, which the tenor of his life belied, according to the priest-historian of the North Country.[56] He was fined and imprisoned, but escaped to Canada, probably in 1841. [57]Forty-two years, he lived there on the mission, until he died in a home he had built for the homeless.

At Lake Champlain, in the mission of Coopersville, or Corbeau, as the locals still call it, after the Abbé Valinière left, there was no priest for fourteen years. Then, in 1806-1812, the Abbe Joseph Signay, the curé of Chambly, near Montreal, came two or three times a year for a few weeks at a time, until the War of 1812 and a lapse of faculties put an end to his visits. During that period, his plan to build a church there hit a snag. Not only were the Canadian-Americans poor, but they had come from a country where it was

Government that bore the cost of religion. And, they shied away from buying a church lot, because they distrusted the land titles there. When Father Signay sent his news to Quebec, Monseigneur Plessis, a fox in shepherd's clothing, advised them to begin with a cemetery. "When even as many as twenty bodies are buried there, no one will think of regaining possession."[58]

The Northeastern Boundary Dispute lay behind that distrust. From the Treaty of Paris in 1783 to the Webster-Ashburton Treaty of 1842, the line between the United States and British North America was in contention. Some of the land titles in the North Country were uncertain, as a result. Till 1796, the British occupied Point au fer, which was an American spit, near the mouth of the Great Chazy River, a few miles south of Rouses Point, and which guarded the entrance to Lake Champlain.[59] The Canadian-Americans nearby, in 1787, prayed the Congress to continue its aid to them.[60] They were grateful to the national government for an earlier grant of provisions for fifteen months, and to the state of New York for the gifts of citizenship and a tract of land. But they remained in need. The British at Point au fer would not let them farm in the vicinity of that post, and the division of the tract had been faulty, and now had to be made all over again.

> By some unhappy means in carrying the kind intentions of the public into execution the blessing designed us is like to prove otherwise...We therefore pray your honours to take our case into your wise consideration (More than forty families on the faith as well as the kind incouragement of the public bewildered! not a foot of land and no way to support our families but by culti vating land) truely deplorable! and grant a continuation of provisions for such and for such only as have continued and are determined to continue on the land and promote the settlement.

In 1793, war broke out between Britain and France, and the sky darkened over Clinton County. As a result of the propaganda of Citizen Genet, there was a cabal of European Frenchmen in September of 1796 at Rouses Point, bent on raising a rebellion in Canada. But the *Canadiens* wanted no part of Jacobinism, and the plot aborted.[61] Even before that, in 1794, the British Minister to the United States protested that Americans were trespassing on British-held places along the border.[62] They, he wrote

> erect buildings within the posts now occupied by his Majesty's forces, imprison or compel to fly persons settled under the

authority of his Majesty's officers, and last summer held their judicial courts *surrounded by armed men,* at the distance of five miles within the post of Point au fer.

The British troops withdrew from the North Country in 1796 as a result of the Jay Treaty, but the boundary line, like a fallen live wire, continued to sparkle. In 1818, it was discovered that the section of the border at Rouses Point lay, not along the forty-fifth parallel where it belonged, but forty-two hundred feet to the north of it.[63] This periled the property of the American farmers to the north of the parallel, as well as Fort Montgomery, later dubbed "Fort Blunder," which the United States had built at Rouses Point at a cost of a million dollars. For a while, officials kept the mistake under their hats, lest the local farmers go on a rampage. But in 1842, the Webster-Ashburton Treaty fixed the line once and for all, leaving it where it ran in the North Country, with forty square miles around Rouses Point inside New York. So ended a period of fifty-nine years, during which the Catholics of that mission had to think twice about buying land and building churches.

[1]Father John Carroll, S.J. who was on the mission in Maryland, was appointed Superior of the Mission in the U.S. on June 9, 1784. Four months later, apparently in October, he became Prefect Apostolic, and on Nov. 6, 1789, the Bishop of Baltimore. Guilday, pp. 203, 214-219, 360.
[2]The see of New York was established on April 8, 1808. Shearer, pp. 99-100.
[3]Thompson, *Geography,* pp. 26, 31-33, 149 150, *passim;* Frost, pp. 14-16, 82-84, *passim.*
[4]White, pp. 61-66.
[5]F.E.T., pp. 129, 159, 195, 255.
[6]Most Rev. Michael Augustus Corrigan, "Register of the Clergy Laboring in the Archdiocese of New York From Early Missionary Times to 1885," U.S. Cath. Hist. Soc., *Historical Records and Studies,* I, Part II (Jan., 1900), 205-206. For a slightly different account, see Wm. Foote Seward (ed.), *Binghamton and Broome County: A History* (3 vols.; New York: Lewis Historical Publ. Co., 1924), I, chap. XI.
[7]White, p. 61. For details on the White family, see F.E.T., p. 101, n. 124.
[8]Rev. P.A. Jordan, S.J., "St. Joseph's Church, Philadelphia," *Woodstock Letters,* III, No. 2 (1847), 94-98; Rev. Jeremiah Kelly, S.J., "Gonzaga College," *ibid.,* XIX, No. 2 (1890), 167-178.
[9]White, p. 61.
[10]*Ibid.,* p. 65. Bp. John Hughes of New York in a pastoral in 1842, hit at the hasty marriages that were then common, and ordered the banns four days before every wedding. Lawrence Kehoe (ed.), *Complete Works of the Most Rev. John Hughes* (2 vols. in one; New York: Cath. Publ. House, 1864), I, 317-318.
[11]John Carroll, 1784-1808; Richard Luke Concanen, 1808-1810; John Con-

nolly, 1814-1825; John Dubois, 1826-1842; John Joseph Hughes, 1837-1847; John McCloskey, 1843-1864. The dates are of their episcopates not their ordinariates. Carroll traversed northern N.Y. only in 1775.

[12] I have put together a catalogue of index cards, one for each priest and bishop who ever officiated in the region of the diocese of Albany before 1865. Chief sources for this information are the *Catholic Directory* for the years 1822-1865, Most Rev. Michael Augustus Corrigan, "Register of the Clergy Laboring in the Archdiocese of New York from Early Missionary Times to 1885," U.S. Cath. Hist. Soc., *Historical Records and Studies*, Vols. I-XI (1899-1916), serially; l'Abbé J.-B.-A. Allaire, *Dictionnaire biographique du Clergé-canadien* (6 vols.; Montreal: various publishers, 1908-1934); and the papers of John Cardinal McCloskey, Archives of the Archdiocese of New York and of the Diocese of Albany.

[13] He visited La Présentation, or Oswegatchie. Garand, pp. 37-38.

[14] Guilday, pp. 158-161.

[15] Taylor, p. 92. Some spell it "Denaut," others "Denault."

[16] Shea, *Church*, II, 442; Taylor, chap. IV; Bp. John Connolly to Bp. Plessis, New York, June 7, 1816, and the text of the faculties from Connolly to Plessis, New York, June 6, 1816, in the *United States Catholic Historical Magazine*, IV, Nos. 1-2 (1891-1892), 188-189, 197-198; text of faculties, dated Quebec, Oct. 10, 1850, from Abp. P.F. Turgeon of Quebec to Bp. John Hughes and 12 other bishops, including John McCloskey of Albany, Archives of the Archdiocese of Quebec; Bp. Ignace Bourget to Bp. John McCloskey, Montreal, Jan. 13, 1857, Archives of the Archdiocese of Montreal. The ordinaries of the U.S., amongst themselves, did the same thing. Of his visit to Binghamton, N.Y., in 1836, Bp. Kenrick of Phila. wrote: "The Bishops...in the last Provincial Council of Baltimore (1833), granted to each other the right to exercise faculties, when traveling (outside their respective dioceses), this right extending also to the priests traveling with them. The Sacrament of Confirmation, however, I administered, presuming the permission of the Bishop (Dubois of N.Y.); for, to the present time, he has not been able to reach this part of his diocese. Moreover, I have written to him informing him of what I did." The brackets are the editor's. F.E.T., pp. 129-130. The mutual grant at the Council of 1833 must have been verbal, because the only express matter of faculties related to priests. Rev. Peter Guilday, *A History of the Councils of Baltimore (1791-1884)* (New York: Macmillan, 1932), pp. 76, 92, 107, 179, 258.

[17] Guilday, *John Carroll*, pp. 639-642; Rev. Francis X. Curran, S.J., "The Jesuit Colony in New York, 1808-1817," U.S. Cath. Hist. Soc., *Historical Records and Studies* XLII (1954), 51-97.

[18] Plessis, *Journal*, de 1815, p. 161.

[19] He was hasting home to his duties, *Ibid.*, chap. VIII. In 1815, Burlington had about 100 French Canadians, most of whom were recent arrivals, apparently. Wade, "Survivance," pp. 164-166.

[20] Plessis, *Journal*, de 1816, pp. 4-11, 70-71.

[21] Shea, *Church*, III, 177. Richard Luke Concanen, the first ordinary of New York, 1808-1810, never reached America, owing to the Napoleonic blockade. The see was administered for him by Father Anthony Kohlmann, S.J. Bp. Connolly was consecrated the second ordinary of New York on

THE NORTH COUNTRY AND THE SOUTHERN TIER 65

Nov. 6, 1814, but the War of 1812 was on and he would have been an enemy alien in America, as a British subject. He did not land in New York City until Nov. 24, 1815, after the war ended. Guilday, *John Carroll,* chap. XXXI; Hughes, *Concanen,* Part III.

[22] Outside bishops came on occasion after that. Toward 1830, Bp.Alexander Macdonell of Kingston, or Upper Canada, spent a month at the spa in Massena, in St. Lawrence Co., for his health. He found a few Irish families there, who had come a few years before, and collecting them at the court house, he said the first mass in that village, and gave instruction in Faith. Presumably, he had faculties. Smith, pp. 272-273; Taylor, p. 123, n. 49. He was probably that Canadian Bishop who visited about the same time with Chancellor Reuben H. Walworth in Saratoga Springs. He was dressed in knee breeches, large buckled shoes, and was a zealot for temperance. William Leete Stone, *Reminiscences of Saratoga and Ballston* (New York: Worthington Co., 1890), p. 341. On another occasion, in 1854, Bp. de Goesbriand of Burlington blessed the cornerstone of St. Peter's, the church of the Oblate Fathers, in Plattsburgh, at the request of Bp. McCloskey of Albany. Wade, "Survivance," p. 172, n. 45.

[23] I follow Smith, *passim.* Ogdensburg was also called Oswegatchie, and Coopersville was Corbeau.

[24] John Bassett Moore, *History and Digest of the International Arbitrations to Which the United States Has Been a Party* (6 vol.: Wash., D.C.: Govt. Print. Off., 1898), I, 77, and for maps, VI, nos. 1-5. The surveyor was speaking of the region along the Canadian border between the St.Croix and St. Lawrence Rivers. The Frenchmen were at the Canadian Settlement on Lake Champlain. In 1820, the population of the six counties of the North Country was 87,500. N.Y., *Census for 1875,* p. 2.

[25] Ulysses Prentiss Hedrick, *A History of Agriculture in the State of New York* (New York:Hill and Wang, 1966, originally, 1933), *passim,* esp. chap. VII, "Sustaining Industries"; William P. Munger, *Historical Atlas of New York State* (Phoenix, N.Y.: Frank E. Richards, 1941), *passim;* William Reed, Life on the Border, Sixty Years Ago (Fall River: Adams, 1882).

[26] Shea, *Missions,* p. 501.

[27] Taylor, p. 92, Bp. Denaut of Quebec visited then.

[28] Below, pp. 57-58.

[29] The American Indians also included 48 Methodists and 8 Episcopalians. New York, *Census of the State of New York for 1855,* (Albany: Weed, Parson, 1856), pp. 500-501 and notes. In 1836, Bp. Dubois had reported 1,000-1,200 Catholic Indians at St. Regis, and, elsewhere in his diocese, 2,000 Indians, who were pagan or "half corrupted by the sectarians." Bp. Dubois to the Abp. of Vienna, New York, March 15, 1836, *Berichte der Leopoldinen-Stiftung,* X (1837), 6.

[30] Ewen J. Macdonald, "Father Roderick Macdonell, Missionary at St. Regis and the Glengarry Catholics," *Catholic Historical Review,* XIX, No. 3 (Oct., 1933), 265-274. In 1806, the Rev. Alexander Macdonell, a young kinsman of Father Roderick, and fresh from Scotland, ministered at Oswegatchie, apparently, while on the mission in Ontario. Taylor, p.73. quotes a letter from Bp. Plessis of Quebec to Father A. Macdonell, dated Montreal, Feb. 7, 1806, advising the missioner to pay off the cost of a

priest's house at Oswegatchie by using the salary which the government had paid him for his services at Oswegatchie. But it is not clear to me why the British government paid for a mission to Catholics on American soil, unless it was not to the Whites at Ogdensburg, but to the Oswegatchie Indians, whom the British kept under their thumb after the Peace of 1783 at Indian Point, near Ogdensburg, until 1796. See above, p. 25.

[31] Hugh L. Keenleyside and Gerald S.Brown, *Canada and the United States* (New York: Alfred A. Knopf, 1952), chap. V.

[32] Taylor, pp. 101-102. Shea, *Missions,* p. 501, says that Roupe was a Sulpician.

[33] John Gilmary Shea, "Caughnawaga, and the Rev. Joseph Marcoux, Its Late Missionary," *The Metropolitan* (Baltimore), III, No. 10 (Nov. 1855), 589-594. Taylor, p. 102, gives his date of assignment.

[34] Letters dated June, 1827-March, 1828 in Manning, I, 166-167, 662-663.

[35] To clarify the picture, we must distinguish the reservation from the village on the reservation. Shea, *Missions,* p. 346, errs in saying that the border cuts through the village. The fact is, the line crosses the reservation south of the village. There is no U.S. Post Office on the part of the reservation that juts into Franklin Co., N.Y. Munger, p. 55; U.S. Postal Service, *Director of Post Offices* (Wash., D.C.: Govt. Print. Off., 1971),p. 125.

[36] Smith, pp. 292-293.

[37] Bp. Dubois to the Society for the Propagation of the Faith, Lyons, March 16, 1830, *Annales de L'Association de la Propagation de la Foi* (Lyons and Paris), IV, No. 22 (Oct., 1830), 458.

[38] In the absence of particulars, it is a guess that the Americans chose to change their civil allegiance rather than their domiciles. That can explain why, in 1855, the ratio of Americans to Britishers on the reservation was the reverse of what it was in 1827. See above p. 56.

[39] See below, p. 59.

[40] Smith, Part V.

[41] Quoted in Taylor, p. 109.

[42] Smith, pp. 290-291.

[43] The total population of the six counties of the North Country was then 149,900. *Census of New York for 1875,* p. 2. The 2,000 is my estimate based on Smith, Part V, Taylor, chap. IV, and the report of Bp. Dubois to the Society for the Propagation of the Faith, in the *Annales,* 1830, as cited above, n.37.

[44] *Ibid.* p. 459.

[45] Marcus Lee Hansen, *The Mingling of the Canadian and American Peoples* (New Haven: Yale Univ. Press, 1940), chap. VI; Roswell A. Hogue, *Centennial, 1853-1953; St. Peter's Roman Catholic Church, Plattsburgh, N.Y.* (Plattsburgh: St. Peter's Church, 1953), Preface and chap. I.

[46] Smith, p. 274.

[47] DeCourcy-Shea, p. 464. Many of the fugitives were of the middle-class, and had to go elsewhere to make a living. One was the doctor, Edmund Bailey O'Callaghan, who turned historian, and edited the multi-volumed *Documents Relating to the Colonial History of the State of New York* Another was Theophile Gautier, who became the grandfather of Arthur S. Hogue, a well known lawyer of Plattsburgh. Rev. William Lucey, S.J., "The

Diocese of Burlington, Vermont; 1853," *Records of the American Catholic Historical Society of Philadelphia,* LXIV, No. 3 (Sept., 1953), 136n. 28. Also, Hogue, p. 10.

[48]Taylor, pp. 122-123.

[49]Smith, p. 236.

[50]Corrigan, "Register," II, Part II (1901), 75-76; Bp. John Dubois to the Abp. of Vienna New York, March 15, 1836, *Berichte der Leopoldinen-Stiftung,* X (1837), 6. There is an English translation of this letter in U.S. Cath. Hist. Soc., *Historical Records and Studies,* X, (Jan., 1917), 124-129.

[51]Franklin B. Hough, *A History of St.Lawrence and Franklin Counties, New York* (Albany: Little & Co., 1853),p. 521, credits him with St. Peter's of Massena, St. Joseph's of Malone, St. Mary's of Fort Covington and St. Mary's (St. Patrick's) of Hogansburg. But St. Patrick's was built before he arrived. Above, p. 60.

[52]Smith, pp. 235-236; *Catholic Directory* for 1836-1841, pages for the diocese of New York.

[53]Frederick J. Seaver, *Historical Sketches of Franklin County* (Albany: J.B. Lyon, 1918), pp. 167, 246-251.

[54]Rowley, chap. VII, "The Nativist Reaction."

[55]Taylor, pp. 124-125; Seaver, p. 191.

[56]*Ibid.;* Smith, *Ogdensburg,* p. 237.

[57]Father McNulty was reported as at Hogansburg in December of 1840, but not listed in the diocese of New York in December of 1841. In December of 1860, he was listed as at a new church in Caledonia, dio., of Hamilton, Ont. *Catholic Directory for 1841,* p. 188; *for 1842,* pp. 148-151; *for 1860,* p. 285. The *Directory* for every year received its information from the bishops in the previous December.

[58]Quoted by Taylor, p. 90. According to an unidentified newspaper of Sept. 13, 1815, some nuns had recently lived in a two-story house in Plattsburgh.Hogue, p. 15.

[59]Map entitled "Places Held by British Forces in Northeastern United States at the Close of the Revolutionary War," Alfred Leroy Burt, *The United States, Great Britain and British North America* (New Haven: Yale Univ. Press, 1940), p. 22.

[60]Lorant Olivier and Clement Gosselin, Majors, to Congress, Lake Champlain, Canadian Settlement, Aug. 13, 1787, Manning, I, 357-358.

[61]Burt, pp. 166-175.

[62]Manning, I, 409-410.

[63]Moore, I, map facing p. 149, and text on p. 80. There was more to the troubles than that. Canadians and Americans, officials and private citizens, clashed over the possession of Carleton and Barnharts Islands between Cape Vincent and Clayton in the St. Lawrence, over the right to navigate the St. Lawrence, and over the collection of port fees at the Canadian landings on that river. More, the Papineau Rebellion in Montreal in 1837 attracted American filibusterers, who invaded Canada from Champlain and Rouses Point in 1837-1838. In retaliation, Canadian militia bands invaded the U.S. at Mooers and Perrysville and Rouses Point, arresting Americans, and burning barns and haystacks. All of the American complainants had French names, and most of them were no doubt Catholic. Manning, II, 6, 36-37, 67, 319, 412-413, 418, 421, 422, 934, III, 44-49, 70-73, 703.

CHAPTER V

FARM, FOREST AND ERIE CANAL

After the Napoleonic Wars, the Europeans flocked to America as never before. The post of Quebec received 587,000 of them in 1816-1846, and New York City 896,000 of them in 1822-1846.[1] A "mania" drove the Irish.[2] Their homeland was a showcase of Malthusianism, of what happens to a people who outnumber the bounties of nature. Life was "a continual scuffle between the magistrates and the multitude."[3] Under the names of Whiteboys and Ribbonmen, terror reared its dragon heads. Government tried to bleed off the paupers and troublemakers in the twenties and thirties by paying for their emigration. The Catholics had preference.

In 1823-1824, nine ships were dispatched to Quebec at different times, with two thousand and more of certified paupers from County Cork. All, or most, were Catholics and small farmers who had been dispossessed, and had begged Government for help to flee the "Slavery of Rents, Tythes and Leases," the "murders and houseburnings," and the "stalking Starvation in this our native land."[4] On last legs, they boarded vessels, which proved to be worse than slavers. One ship in 1841 carried 175 passengers in a hold that the law had marked for 32. In 1823-1824, the paupers rioted at sea. Some died in mid-ocean, or on arrival, or in a year or two. Some entered the North Country and the Southern Tier. Knowing only how to spade potatoes, they had to learn to survive with a strange axe in an alien forest.

To clear the land was the first step for the famer.[5] But how to feed the family before the potatoes were big in the ground? One way was to burn the debris of the forest, stir the ashes with lye in a caldron, and boil it down to a residue, which was called *pot ash* or *potash,* and which was an ingredient of soap. Thirty cords of wood make a sixth of a ton of potash, or less of the finer pearlash. A cord of wood was a pile that was eight feet long and four feet high and wide. It was a one-man or a one-family operation, with the need only of muscle and a big, iron pot. The stuff was packed into barrels, which were another product of the woodland, and rafted to Montreal from the North Country, and to Philadelphia from the Southern Tier, or after the coming of the Erie Canal system, to the Hudson River at Albany and Troy. Oddly, Catholicism was sometimes behind the chopping down of trees, as Sister Mary Teresa White once recollected.[6]

They found that a priest from Philadelphia would come for a brief visit if his expenses could be paid. Dr. Robert Rose, the proprietor of these immense lands, had offered a sum of money to any one who would clear a certain amount of forest. My oldest brother, afterwards Judge White of New York, started out, axe in hand, and worked day after day felling trees until he earned the priest's expenses.

That was before the famine rush of 1847, when Irish immigrants did make it on farms, countrary to popular belief. Behold Minerva Padden.[7] In 1834, she landed in New York City, took service with the Beekmans, of elegant name, saved her wages, left a year later, and married Timothy Donovan. They bought a farm at Hull's Cross Roads, in the town of Hannibal, in Oswego County. It was a section of squatters and shaky land titles, and the Donovans knew the risk. For seven years, they slaved on their fifty acres, for which they had paid a dollar an acre, clearing the land, and improving it, and turning down an offer of $220 for the property.

One month after that offer, misfortune hit. A prior title showed up, and the Donovans were out, with their five children, a cow and a few sheep. "We were too poor," Mrs. Donovan wrote to the Beekmans, "to hire a farm for we had no team to work with so we commenced again in the woods." They bought another piece of land, of eleven acres, for seventy-seven dollars, and God only knows where they got the eleven dollars for a down payment. Now ill luck began to dog them. Though Mr. Donovan was sober and steady, he had no head for business; Mrs. Donovan ailed for a year; the snow was six feet deep in March; they had to sell the cow; and they could not make the payments.

But after a night of tribulation, the sun shone. Neighbors helped them to build a log cabin; their landlord, Gerrit Smith,[8] game them a period of grace; and the Beekmans sent them twenty dollars for another cow. Oh! the lovely milk money. Writing to Mr. Beekman in 1846, Mrs. Donovan sent the gratitude of herself and her husband, who was illiterate.[9]

That the Lord would bless and prosper you and yours is Sir the prayer of your unworthy servant...I forgot to mention that the land we bought now we will get a State Deed for when we get it Paid for, then no body can turn us out doors.

The Erie Canal was another come-hither for the Irish. In the first years of its digging, from 1817 on, west of Utica, only one of four of the navvies was an immigrant,[10] but that ratio soon reversed itself. Bogtrotters from the west of Ireland were preferred, because they worked best in, or were the only ones willing to work in, the muck and quicksands. Almost naked, with only the tools that the circumstances would allow, as spade and wheelbarrow, in rain and flood, kneedeep in the mire, they dug that ditch through the forest. A Stakhanovite would have marvelled at the three Irishmen in 1817 who shovelled out a section that was fifty feet long, forty feet wide and four feet deep in five-and-a-half days. At the rate of twelve-and-a-half cents a cubic yard, each of them earned "the very liberal wage of one dollar and eighty cents per day."[11] That particular rate probably did not carry the fringe benefit of food, or "found," as they called it in those days, but it was eked out with doses of whiskey to ward off the ague and with the shelter of a box of boards called a "shanty." Whatever the pay, the bogtrotters outconsumed all other laborers in victuals, drink, clothing and health. If the Erie was like the Wabash and Erie, which was dug in Indiana in 1833, it claimed a corpse for every six feet.[12]

In the early forties, during the season of navigation, there were about 25,000 people at work on the canals of New York State.[13] One historian suspects, in view of the ease with which they were hired and fired every year, that there was a lot of hidden unemployment upstate then.[14] Over five thousand of the canallers were boys, half of whom were orphans, many Irish Catholics. The boys were "drivers," that is, they drove the tow horses for the canal boats. Redemptioners in practical slavery, some of them, they were usually paid ten dollars a month with keep, were commonly cheated of their pay, and often ended up behind bars, sick, vagrant, or criminal. Two sixteen-year-old boys walked into a police court in a canal town in December of 1860. They asked to be sent to the penitentiary till spring, when the canal would open again for navigation. Drivers since May, they had been done out of their wages, and had no place else to go. They were sent up for six months for vagrancy.[15] In general, life on the canals was swinish. The Erie, which was lined with Irish shanties, was the "Big Ditch of Iniquity," and the stretch of it between Watervliet and

Schenectady was the "Barbary Coast of the East."[16]

The "Last Judgment" by Michelangelo on the altar-wall of the Sistine Chapel shows the escape of some souls from hell. It reminds one of the few Irish Catholics on the Erie Canal who rose from rags to riches. The family of Thomas Moran was among them.[17] In Killara, County West Meath, after the famine of 1847, Thomas read the letters from his in-laws in Frankfort, in Herkimer County, on the Erie Canal. They urged him to come over. The canal would give him a good living in his craft as a stone mason. At the age of sixty-one, he left his native village with his wife and seven children, aged twenty-four to five, in the fall of 1850, and sailed for America.

> Oh! Cursed be the power that to fury could drive thee,[18] And forced thee to leave thy loved isle of the west, Thrice cursed be the wretch who dared to deprive thee, And turn thee from Erin, the home thou lov'st best.

Mary Moran, the wife and mother, died at sea, and with a lay burial service, was dropped into the ocean. After forty-five days on the Atlantic, the widower and his children landed in the port of New York, spent the night there with friends, and then made their way for two days by railroad, steamboat and wagon to Frankfort, where they settled in their first home in America, a canal shanty.

A boatman's logbook in 1842 recorded a description of the Irish shanties that lined the canals of the state.[19]

> They are of pine boards, the roof at a sharp angle, with the ends of the boards projecting over front and rear, forming a sort of piazza to shelter the women from the rays of an American sun; the sides are not more than five feet high, the chimney of rough stone is on the outside and hardly extends to the peak of the roof, it is sometimes elongated by a headless flour barrel.

Welcomed by relatives and friends from the home they loved best, the father and his seven motherless children put their agonies behind them. Frankfort was a bustling lockport with small factories, and Thomas went to work repairing the stone locks between Utica and Little Falls. At an average per diem of $1.75 before the Civil War, as a stone mason, he made about one-and-three quarter times as much as a common laborer, for twelve hours a day in summer and ten in winter.[20] The children turned to their new life with a will. The older girls kept house, and worked in the village; the boys became drivers, and in the winter, did other jobs, and went to school.

Michael, 17, is the one to watch. As a driver, at fifty cents a day plus found, he walked the eighty miles to Troy, back and forth, six hours on, six off, for about 220 days a year, from April to December.[21] He rose to steersman, saved his money, and after five years, bought his own boat. In those days, a canalboat cost a few thousand dollars. It was usually bought for a down payment of, say, five hundred dollars, with installments to come. But two or three good seasons could pay off the debt.[22] In a life that was probably like that of a trucker today, Michael prospered. People said the he could "handle men as well as mules." By 1860, he was operating a fleet between Buffalo and New York, at the age of 27. In 1857, he became a citizen, and in 1862 married Margaret Haggerty of Albany, an immigrant like himself, in St. Mary's there. Seeing the changes in the marine traffic in the harbor of New York and the coming of the Civil War, Michael moved his base to Brooklyn in 1860, and branched into steam tugboating. He became known as the "Commodore of the Irish Navy." A century later, one of his five sons, Eugene F. Moran, who told this in his eighties, was the vice chairman of the Port Authority of New York and the chairman of the Moran Towing and Transportation Company. The diocese of Albany did not have many Catholics like Michael Moran.[23]

[1]See below, p. 83.
[2]Helen I. Cowan, *British Emigration to British North America* (rev. and enlarged, Toronto: Univ. Toronto Press, 1961, originally 1928), chaps. II-IV.
[3]*Ibid.*, p. 65, quoting Charles Stewart Parnell, the Irish nationalist.
[4]*Ibid.*, p. 67.
[5]Historians speak of the virgin woods of New York State as a "timber and potash frontier." Philip L. White, "Patterns of American Community Development: The Rural East" (unpubished typescript, 1964, copy at the North Country Historical Research Center, State University College, Plattsburgh, N.Y.), p. 11.
[6]Sister M.T. White, p. 62.
[7]Philip L. White (ed.), "An Irish Immigrant Housewife on the New York Frontier," *New York History,* XLVIII, No. 2 (April, 1967), 182-188.
[8]Famous in history as a reformer in the antebellum ferment, he was also one of the biggest landowners in New York State. He sold much land to Irish immigrants on easy terms and in small parcels. Charles M. Snyder, *Oswego: From Buckskins to Bustles* (Port Washington, N.Y.: Ira J. Friedman, 1968), p. 102. Contrary to popular belief, the absentee landlords of the New York frontier, especially before 1830, did not oppress their tenants, generally speaking, and in fact were lenient to them and often victimized by them. Philip L. White, "Patterns of American Community Development," *passim.* White is talking about Beekmantown, in Clinton County.

[9] Philip L. White, "Irish Immigrant Housewife," p. 186 Philip L. White, "Patterns of American Community Development," p. 9, estimates on the basis of the *N.Y. Census for 1855* that in 1855, in Clinton County, illiteracy was 38% among the French Canadians, 21% among the Irish, and only 2% among the American-born.
[10] New York, Canal Commissioners, *Annual Report for 1819*, p. 10.
[11] New York, Canal Commissioners, *Annual Report for 1818*, p. 13.
[12] New York, Canal Commissioners, *Annual Report for 1820*, p. 6; Madeline Sadler Waggoner, *The Long Haul West: The Great Canal Era, 1817-1850* (New York: G.P. Putnam's Sons, 1958), pp. 234-235.
[13] Deacon M. Eaton, Missionary of the American Bethel Society, *Five Years on the Erie Canal* (Utica: Bennett, Backus & Hawley, 1845),p. 32.
[14] Walter B. Smith, "Wage Rates on the Erie Canal, 1828-1881," *Journal of Economic History*, XXIII (Sept.., 1963), p. 306.
[15] *Bottoming Out*, I, Nos. 3-4 (July, 1957), 14, does not identify the source.
[16] Ronald E.Shaw, *Erie Water West: A History of th Erie Canal, 1792-1854* (Lexington, Ky: Univ. Ky. Press, 1966), chap. XII, Alvin F. Harlow, *Old Towpaths* (New york: D. Appleton, 1926), *passim; Bottoming Out, passim*, for pictures and a miscellany of canal lore. The last named was a semi-annual publication of the Canal Society of New York State, and appeared in 1956-1965 only.
[17] Eugene F. Moran and Louis Reid, *Tugboat, The Moran Story* (New York; Chas. Scribner's Sons, 1956), chap. I; Eugene F. Moran, Sr., "THe Erie Canal as I Have Known It," *Bottoming Out*, III, No. 2 (1959), 2-18.
[18] One of six stanzas from "The Emigrant," author unknown, in *The Freeman's Journal and Catholic Register*, Jan. 24, 1846.
[19] *Bottoming Out*, III, No. 13 (sic) (1959), 6-7.
[20] Moran, "The Erie Canal," pp. 2-6, says $4.00 a day, but he was 86 in 1959, when he wrote the article.I use Smith, "Wage Rates," p. 304, who saw the actual payrolls.
[21] *Bottoming Out*, II, No. 1 (Oct., 1957), 16.
[22] *Bottoming Out*, II, Nos. 3-4 (July, 1958), 12.
[23] I chose to tell about the Morans, rather than the Devereuxs and others, because the Morans are not mentioned in American Catholic histories.

CHAPTER VI

THE LINE OF MELCHIZEDEK

In upstate New York, during the first half of the nineteenth century, a priest was rare, a good priest was worth his weight in offerings, and a good priest who could speak French or German as well as English was like the coin in the parable that was lost and found.[1] Athirst as Bishop McCloskey was for clergymen, he was determined to use only those without a taint.[2] Nonetheless, he and his predecessors had to make do.

In the 402 priests and six bishops[3] who served at one time or another in the region of the diocese of Albany between the Revolution and the Civil War, there was virtue and vice, there was prudence and folly. Think of Bishop Dubois. When he was a young missioner in Maryland and Virginia at the turn of the century, a sick call once drew him from the confessional. It was a Saturday evening. For fifty miles, he rode a horse through woods, rain and the blackness of night, twice fording a swollen river, and returning in the morning to say Mass and to preach, without food or rest. A quarter-of-a-century later, as a bishop, in his sixties, worn with work and crippled by rheumatism, he traveled three thousand miles on one tour of his diocese. He made many such visitations as a sick, old man, by horseback, stagecoach, canalboat, dogsled and foot, at times on crutches, at times alone.[4]

But, dovelike as he was in the sacraments, he lacked the guile of the serpent in guarding the property of the Church. The Sulpicians, of whom he was one, parted company with him in 1826, just before he was mitered, on account of what has been imputed to him as a rashness in piling up debt. "Our good old prelate means well, but unfortunately never does anything right," said his vicar general in 1834.[5] After a series of strokes invalided him in body and mind, Rome took away the administration of his diocese in 1839. "What wrong have I done," he cried.⁶ However, to use his own words, "he obeyed the bit, but not till he had covered it with foam.⁷ Then, with his young coadjutor, John Hughes, in charge, the old shepherd spent the last three of his fifty-one years on the mission in America in preparing for death. It came for him in 1842.

Between Bishop Dubois, at one end of the range of priestliness, and a few reverend rogues at the other end, there was a spectrum of devotion and peccadillo under lifetimes of service. Consider Fathers Jeremiah O'Callaghan, James Hourigan, John Farnan, Charles Pascal and Pierre-Marie Mignault. Father O'Callaghan, of the diocese of Boston, was an apostle on Lake Champlain in 1830-1845, in New York as well as Vermont.⁸ In that day of soaring nationalism, the Irish and the *Canadiens* were combustible, whenever they had to pray together. What made it worse (such were the accidents of British imperialism) was that the Irish were used to supporting their Church and the *Canadiens* were not. As a result, the French Canadian priest jested that God might separate the two nationalities in heaven, and the Irish one said amen to it, tongue in cheek, of course. At Christmas, Father Jeremiah would enter the pulpit, and read out the names of the contributors to the collection, in this way: "Frank Leclaire of Winooski. Frank is a Frenchman, but not like the rest; he is a gentleman. Thank you, Frank. God bless you.⁹

Father James F. Hourigan was born in County Tipperary in 1815.¹⁰ As other Irishmen, he probably had to work for a few years before he could heed the call. He did his theology at St. Joseph's Seminary, which was then at Fordham, near New York City, and was ordained by Bishop McCloskey in 1847 at age thrirty-two. After an assistancy of a few months in the city, he went to Binghamton.¹¹

Rev. James Hourigan/Dear Sir/You are by these presents duly appointed Pastor of the Catholic congregation of Binghamton. The circuit of your mission will embrace the three counties of Broome, Chenango and Delaware. The ordinary faculties and jurisdiction granted to Pastors in this Diocese are likewise hereby communicated to you and confirmed./Given by order of the Bishop of New York and attested by the Seal of the Diocese, this 19th day of July, 1847./(signed) John (McCloskey) Bp. of Axiere/Coadjutor of N. York.

Father Hourigan lived in the saddle. Outside Binghamton, he made the rounds of Norwich, Oxford, Sherburne, French Creek,

Deposit, Forks, Summit and Upper Lisle.[12] Edward White, a lawyer and a farmer, who had emigrated from Ireland to become one of the first Catholics at Binghamton, and who was the father of the later Sister Mary Teresa White, wrote to Bishop McCloskey in 1850: "Our church affairs are prospering under the ministry of one of the most amiable, most generous, & kindest of Pastors.[13] When the priest came to Binghamton, St. John's Church, which was nine years old, lay under leaden debt. But, in spite of the poverty of the people, and on account of their loyalty, Father Hourigan became a "builder." He bought land, and added cemeteries, a school, a convent and a rectory. Not only did he pay off the mortgage on St. John's, but in 1873, he built St. Patrick's at a cost of $170,000.[14]

Among a people who were plagued by *shebeens,* or whiskey shops, and by a clannishness that came from Ireland, that was sharpened by a rivalry for jobs, and that divided the Irish into "Far Ups," "Far Downs," and a number of other factions, Father Hourigan was the keeper of the peace. In fact, they said that he was better than a posse of constables. He patrolled the towpaths of the Chenango Canal on a horse, and the tracks of the Erie Railroad on a handcar, on the lookout for the work of the Lord, or trouble. If trouble, and words failed him, he was usually able to arbitrate the matter with a blackthorn club.[15] Sister Mary Teresa White recalled his telling her father once about a brawl that had been shaping up between two gangs who were separated by a bridge. "What did you do?" asked Mr. White. Father Hourigan replied: "I took the bridge, sir".[16]

Father John Farnan was one of the first priests in America to go into schism.[17] Born in Ireland in 1788, and educated at a seminary in Paris, he was ordained by the Archbishop of Dublin in 1812, and he probably spent the next few years in that jurisdiction. He came to New York City in 1818 at the invitation of Bishop Connolly, and was soon sent to Utica. From the St. Lawrence River, 120 miles to the north, and from Lake Erie, 190 miles to the west, to the village of Utica on the Mohawk River and to somewhere east and south of that spot, all of western New York was his care.[18] It was a howling wilderness, mostly, where bounties were paid for wolves, and where the Erie Canal had recently opened a furrow for the missioner to harvest.[19]

A tall man of thirty-one, Father Farnan had been a priest for seven years. He spoke French, his sermons were down to earth, and he was hail fellow well met. Arriving in Utica in March of 1819, he had the faculties that had been suggested to the bishop by Father

Michael O'Gorman, a veteran of the Albany mission. It appears that Father Farnan organized congregations, raised money, and built churches at his discretion. At least, that is how he is remembered in western New York. He put up the first Catholic churches in Utica, Carthage, Auburn and Rochester,[20] and he started the first Sunday school in Utica. Auburn had about five Catholic families at the time, and Utica about sixteen.[21] With his altar things in a packsaddle, the servant of God roved ten or twelve counties, advertising in the newspapers for the lost sheep of the Church.[22]

The people of Auburn and its vicinity are hereby notified that the Rev. Dr. Forman (Farnan), Roman Catholic Rector of Utica, has arrived in the village and will perform Divine service in the Court House, Sunday, the 11th. inst. at half past ten o'clock, A.M., and at five P.M. Auburn, July 7, 1819.

Father Farnan was suspended by Bishop Connolly in 1823, we are told.[23] The reason that is given was his trouble with lay trustees. Now, that is puzzling. For one thing, it is not clear whether it was at St. John's of Utica, or St. James's of Carthage.[24] For another, the only trouble that we know of was a dispute over his salary at Carthage, where he threatened to sue the trustees for breach of contract. That was in October of 1823, and the missioner was in the village at the time.[25] But bishops did not suspend priests for having trouble with trustees. Lay trusteeism was chronic, involving bishops as well as priests, and priests were hard to get. A missioner might have been transferred in such a case, but he would not have lost his faculties. Yet, the best authority[26] says that Father Farnan was not only punished by Bishop Connolly with a "suspension," but that his appeal to Archbishop Maréchal led nowhere, and that the missioner was not reassigned until Bishop Connolly died. The mystery is darkened by another source,[27] which tells us that, after February of 1823, on one or more occasions, Father Farnan "interrupted" the services of his successor at St. John's of Utica.

Whatever the secret, Father Farnan stayed upstate until the Administrator of the diocese, *sede vacante,* Father John Power, sent him to Brooklyn in 1825 to take charge of St. James's. It was the first Catholic church there, and Father Farnan thus became the first permanent Catholic pastor of Brooklyn and Long Island. He served not only his own congregation, but also attended at the Brooklyn Navy Yard, at Fort Hamilton, which was then building, and at times at Flushing and Sag Harbor.

The struggle for Irish Emancipation was then raging on both sides of the ocean, and Father Farnan pitched into it. He became the president of the Friends of Ireland, while his brother, Eugene, a Brooklyn lawyer, was the chairman. What with St. Patrick's Days, July Fourths and fund raisings for the Old Country, when Catholics mingled with Protestants, Americans and Freemasons in a tide of American and Irish nationalism, life became too convivial for the pastor. He was suspended again. This time it was by Bishop Dubois in 1829, and it was for being drunk at Vespers.

After the First Provincial Council of Baltimore, which met that year, refused to hear his appeal, he founded in Brooklyn the "Independent Catholic Church." He had backing, and he went collecting as far as Philadelphia. When Catholics were warned against him, he brought a suit for libel against the priests and laymen who were behind the *Truth Teller,* a Catholic newspaper. More, he published replies in other newspapers in defiance of the sees of Rome and New York, and in assertion that he was "conscientiously opposed to Jesuits, monasteries, nunneries, the Inquisition and all other institutions incompatible with civil and religious liberty."[28]

In short, in the opinion of one historian,[29] the notoriety of this stray priest, during the eighteen years of 1829-1847, had something to do with the nativism of that time, which was marked by the burning of the Charlestown convent, the obscenities of Maria Monk, and the Massacre of St. Bartholomew's Day, so to speak, in Philadelphia. Father Farnan in time lost his following and his church, and sank into obscurity. In 1847, Bishop John Hughes of New York gave him an *exeat* to the diocese of Detroit, where he died in 1849, at peace with the Church.[30]

For the sake of verity and proportion, as well as a sweetmeat, let this chapter end with the name of Pierre-Marie Mignault. And, let him stand for all of those missioners who came to central and northern New York from Canada and Germany before the Civil War, and who cannot find a space in these pages. The Abbé Mignault[31] was the pastor of St. Joseph's of Chambly from 1817 to 1866. It still sits on the Richelieu River near Montreal and thirty miles to the north of Lake Champlain. For a half-century, the cure plodded that old "River of the Iroquois," bent on another sort of war: the pursuit of his countrymen, from Ogdensburg on the west, to Boston on the east, to Albany on the south, in order to bring them the Faith in the French tongue, without which, they fell away in numbers. He became the vicar general for the Canadians, in New England after 1828, and in New York after 1834, and he is remembered as "the virtual founder of the Church in Vermont,"[32] and "the apostle of the Canadians in northern New York."[33] In spite of an ill health that was chronic and a temperament that cost him tears, his letters[34] to the Bishops of Albany, Montreal and Quebec place him wherever the *Canadiens* settled in the North Country and along the Champlain Road. In an age of immigration and nationalism, when a mother tongue did help to preserve the Faith, he early favored the erection of a see at Ogdensburg to serve the needs of the Canadian-Americans. Father L. Sasseville of Rouses Point wrote to Bishop McCloskey in 1859:[35]

> I have seen the Vicar General, Mr. Mignault, who has been dangerously ill. Even on his death bed, he busies himself with his bishopric of Ogdensburg. This mania will pursue him into the next world.

It is a tradition that Abbé Mignault said a Mass in the home of Louis Marney of Champlain, four miles west of Rouses Point, in 1818,[36] and on October 5, 1819, he wrote to the Bishop of Quebec that he had recently baptized eighty-two children around Plattsburgh.[37] Year in, year out, the missioner tracked down the strays of his fold, at his own expense,[38] until, after a short retirement, he died in 1868, fifty-six years a priest, in the line of Melchizedek.

---

[1] The dearth of priests was aggravated by the hard traveling, the scattering of Catholics and their trilinguality. Early on, some of the laity had to journey for the sacraments to New York City, from as far away as Rochester, Rev. Frederick J. Zwierlein, "Catholic Beginnings in the Diocese of Rochester," *Catholic Historical Review,* I, No. 3 (Oct., 1915), 282-283.

[2] McCloskey to Bp. Ignace Bourget of Montreal, Albany, Sept. 26, 1852, Archives of the Archdiocese of Montreal: McCloskey to Rev. John McCaffrey, Rector of Mt. St. Mary's Seminary, Emmitsburg, Md., Albany, Jan. 31, 1854. Letterbox A25, Archives of this Archdiocese of New York (thereafter NY). This is a typed copy of the original at Mt. St. Mary's.

[3] Above, p. 55.

[4] Herbermann, *passim.* Sometimes, he had no money to bring along an assistant. In that way, he was like other frontier bishops, such as John Martin Henni of Milwaukee, of whom it was said in 1845: "What are the treasures of this sole German Bishop in America? One God, one faith, one baptism, one vestment, one chalice." Rev. Peter Leo Johnson and Rev. William Nellen (ed.), "Letters of the Reverend Adelbert Inama, O. Praem.," *Wisconsin Magazine of History,* XI, No. 4 (June, 1928), 447.

[5] Very Rev. John Power to Rev. Paul Cullen, New York, Fall of 1834, in Rev. T. Henry (ed.), "Papers Relating to the Church in America, from the Portfolios of the Irish College at Rome," *Records of the American Catholic Historical Society of Philadelphia,* VIII (1897), 470. Father Power repeated

the criticism in several letters 1833-1835, *ibid.*, 463-474. Cullen was rector of the Irish College, and had the ear of the Holy See. He later became Cardinal Archbishop of Dublin.

[6]Herbermann, p. 343.
[7]*Ibid.*, p. 344.
[8]Smith, "Ogdensburg," pp. 32-33, 185, 196. See Jeremiah O'Callaghan, Catholic Priest, *The Holy Bible Authenticated* (New York: Publ. for the Author, 1858), *passim,* wherein the priest had a go at Sectarians, Free Lovers, Socialists, Spirtualists and Bankers.
[9]Wade, "Survivance," pp. 168-169.
[10]Corrigan, "Register," III (1904), 309-310.
[11]Seward, II, 482. This page also gives a photo of Father Hourigan in old age.
[12]*Catholic Directory for 1848,* pp. 185-187.
[13]Edward White to Bp. McCloskey, Binghamton, Jan. 1, 1850, Letterbox A25, NY.
[14]William P.H. Hewitt (ed.), *History of the Diocese of Syracuse* (Syracuse: Catholic Sun Press, 1909), pp. 344-345.
[15]Seward, II, 482.
[16]Sister M.T. White, pp. 65-66. Father Hourigan died in 1892 at Binghamton, after 45 years there.
[17]Rev. John Kean Sharp, *History of the Diocese of Brooklyn, 1853-1953* (2 vol.; New York: Fordham Univ. Press, 1954), I, chap. III.
[18]In 1821, Farnan's mission was halved, and Father Patrick Kelly took the Auburn-Rochester mission. *Catholic Directory for 1822,* pp. 106, 184. Farnan then covered Utica to Auburn and the Mohawk River to the St. Lawrence.
[19]Above, p. 70.
[20]Rev. Robert F. McNamara, *The Diocese of Rochester, 1868-1968* (Rochester: Dio. of Rochester, 1968), pp. 32-34.
[21]Bishop John Timon, *Missions in Western New York and Church History of the Diocese of Buffalo* (Buffalo: Catholic Sentinel Press, 1862), p. 211; M.M. Bagg (ed.), *Memorial History of Utica, N.Y.* (Syracuse: D. Mason, 1892), p. 443.
[22]*Cayuga Republican,* quoted in Rev. Bernard Leo Heffernan, *Cross Bearers of the Finger Lakes Region* (Chicago: John Anderson, 1925), p. 32.
[23]Sharp, I, 48.
[24]Carthage is suggested by the wording of Rev. Francis P. McFarland in a letter to John Gilmary Shea, Utica, Feb. 12, 1856, in "Early Catholic Affairs in Utica, N.Y.," *United States Catholic Historical Magazine,* IV (1891-1893), 65. But there is no express identification.
[25]Rev. Thomas C. Middleton, "An Early Catholic Settlement," *Records of the American Catholic Historical Society of Philadelphia,* X (1899), 70-74.
[26]Sharp, I, chap. III.
[27]Very Rev. J.S.M. Lynch, *A Page of Church History in New York: St. John's, Utica* (Utica: Privately printed, 1893), p. 19.
[28]Sharp, I, 54.
[29]*Ibid.*, I, 62.

[30] The archives of the Archdiocese of Detroit have no papers of Father Farnan. Rev. J.V. Swastek, archivist, to me, Jan. 18, 1971.
[31] J.O. Dion, *Souvenir du Révérend Pierre Marie Migneault* (Montreal: Des Presses A Vapeur de la Minerve, 1868). The abbé always signed as "Mignault."
[32] Wade, "Survivance," p. 165.
[33] Shea, *Church,* IV, 128.
[34] There are many letters of his, all from Chambly, dating 1819 to 1864, in the archives of the archidoceses of New York, Montreal and Quebec and of the diocese of St. Jean of Quebec.
[35] L. Sasseville to McCloskey, Rouses Point, Jan. 15, 1859, Letterbox A25, NY. Ogdensburg became a see in 1872.
[36] *La Presse,* Montreal, Aug. 20, 1922.
[37] Mignault to Plessis, Chambly, Oct. 5, 1819, Letterbox "St. Joseph (Chambly) 1765-1884," Archives of the Diocese of St. Jean of Quebec.
[38] Said Bp. Fitzpatrick of Boston of him in 1847. Wade, "Survivance," p. 165.

CHAPTER VII

NUMBERS: THE CATHOLIC POPULATION

The nineteenth century saw all Christendom surge with new life. Though behind Protestantism in this regard, the Catholic Church peaked in growth. In 1847-1864, while Bishop McCloskey sat at Albany, Rome erected 4 new archbishoprics, 35 bishoprics and 10 prefectures apostolic, to reach a total of 1,007 secular jurisdictions around the world.[1] Its communicants rose, in round numbers, in the meantime, from 164 millions to 208 millions. At the end of this period, there were over 320,000 priests, 120,000 men in 8,000 communities, and 190,000 women in congregations, which were multiplying so rapidly, that their number was something, the people said, that God Himself did not know.

In the United States, at the same time, the Roman sees mounted from 26 to 47, churches, chapels and mission stations from 1,469 to 3,348, priests from 890 to 1,832, and communicants from 1,177,050 to 3,540,700.[2] The new diocese of Albany simultaneously grew, in priests from 34 to 95, in churches, chapels and mission stations from 71 to 188, and in communicants from 76,700 to 134,500.[3] All of this suggests that the members of the Catholic Church in 1847-1864 increased as follows: in the world by 27 percent, in the United States by 201 percent, and in the diocese of Albany by 75 percent.

There is no telling the exact number of Bishop McCloskey's flock. Due to the separation of church and state, this country has never had a civil census of church membership.[4] We can, however, winnow the statistics for an estimate. The Catholics of the diocese seem to have amounted to 69,200 in 1845, 138,200 in 1855 and 134,100 in 1865. Their numbers rose and fell with birth, death and the tide of migration. Gaining an average of 6,900 a year in 1845-1855, and losing an average of 400 a year in 1856-1865, they appear to have raised their share of the population of the diocese in the twenty years from 6.4

percent to 10 percent.[5]

At first, they and others hugged the lakes, canals and rivers of the young diocese, then they spread steadily upstream. In 1845, not a single church of the Faith stood in ten counties of the Catskills, the Adirondacks and the Appalachian Upland of the Southern Tier, although five of its mission stations had budded here and there in those fairly emply regions.[6] Twenty years later, at the end of the Civil War, Schoharie County, in the Catskills, with one mission station, was the only county in the diocese without a Catholic Church.[7] It was in the cities and large villages where most of the Catholics settled down, at canal junctions, river mouths and waterfalls, as at Albany, Troy, Plattsburgh, Ogdensburg, Watertown, Syracuse and Utica.[8]

The Catholics of the diocese were Whites. So far as we know, there was not a Black or Indian face among them. Of the 10,265 Negroes, who fell short of one percent of the population of the diocese, those who went to church were Methodists, Baptists, or African Methodist Episcopalians.[9] As for Indians, the only Catholics were the 338 who lived on the St. Regis Reservation, and belonged to the see of Montreal.[10]

Most of Bishop McCloskey's flock were immigrants, a fact that typified the Church throughout America at that time. Bishop Shaughnessy, who has made the most thoroughgoing study of the tie between immigration and the numbers of Catholics in the United States, puts the gain in the Catholic population of this country in 1850-1860 as 1,497,000, and breaks it down as 3 percent for converts, 9 percent for natives and 88 percent for foreigners. For the two years of 1850 and 1860, his estimates for the immigrants to this country are, respectively, 70 percent and 79 percent Catholic.[11]

The diocese reflected these ratios. As the high road to the West, it drew traffic from the two busiest ports of entry of North America, namely New York and Quebec. Passengers to New York were 896,414 in 1822-1846 and 3,211,761 in 1847-1864.[12] At Quebec and Montreal, they were 586,987 in 1816-1846 and 531,477 in 1847-1864.[13] In self-defense against a flood of aliens, and for the sake of the strangers as well, those cities prodded the immigrants inland,[14] where they converged on Albany and Troy, as at a doorway.[15] From this human flow, worn out, sick and penniless, the Catholics silted down in ethnic deltas.

Irish, French Canadians and Germans, in that order of sinking numbers, made up the bulk of the congregations of the Church in the twenty-eight counties of the diocese. Admixed, were some English, Scotch and Welsh, from the British Isles and the British North American Provinces, some French, Swiss, Dutch and other Continentals, and a trace of the more exotic peoples of the world. Though precision eludes us, we can get an idea of the size of the ethnicities, by using the data of immigration and of population by land of origin or birth, in combination with figures that have been offered by Bishop Shaughnessy. That prelate, in a study of apostasy among the Catholics of America, has made the assumption, which is as good as any, that if country A had a population that was, say, 40 percent Catholic, then country A's immigrants to the United States were 40 percent Catholic.[16] On that basis, the chief groups among the foreign-born Catholics of the diocese stood muster so:[17]

	Irish	German	Canadian
1845	(a) 49,540	(d) 2,067	(g) 13,740
1855	(b) 90,507	(e) 10,482	(h) 29,985
1865	(c) 80,186	(f) 10,980	(i) 36,685

To complete this ethnic array, the native American Catholics need to be mentioned. It is probable that there were few out-of-staters among them, and that those who were born in New York before the Civil War were, at the most, a few thousand.[18]

[1]These numbers are offered as approximations, due to the lack of scientific statistics for the entire Church then. A prefecture apostolic is the first step in the organization of a mission territory, is directly subject to the Holy See, and reports to the Congregation of Propaganda. I distinguish secular jurisdictions from religious jurisdictions, as, for example, that of the Society of Jesus. *La Civiltà Cattolica*, Serie VI, II (1865), 732: *Annuario Pontificio, 1864*, pp. 267-268, 294; *The Stateman's Yearbook for the Year 1865*, p. 324; the *Catholic Directory for 1848*, pp. 280-281; *Einsiedler Kalender für 1864 für Amerika*, p. 1. For a discussion of Catholicism in the frame of Christendom, see Kenneth Scott Latourette, *Christianity in a Revolutionary Age: A History of Christianity in the Nineteenth Century and Twentieth Centuries*. Vol. I: *The Nineteenth Century in Europe: Background and the Roman Catholic Phase* (New York: Harper & Bros., 1958), chap. V. For a focus on Catholicism with more detail, see H. Daniel-Rops, *History of the Church of Christ*, Vol. VIII: *The Church in an Age of Revolution, 1789-1870* (New York: E.P. Dutton, 1965), chaps. VII-VIII.
[2]See Appendix I.
[3]For priests, churches, etc., see the *Catholic Directory for 1848*, pp. 185-187, 234-244; the *Catholic Directory for 1865*, p. 101. For communicants, Shaughnessy, *Immigrants*, is no aid here. His numbers are only for the entire U.S. and only for the last years of decades. For my numerical series, which gives the yearly numbers of the Catholics of the diocese, see Appendix II.

⁴The so-called censuses of religion of 1890, 1906 and 1916, which reported church membership, and which were compiled by the U.S. Census Bureau, were based on the mere estimates of pastors. Shaughnessy, *Immigrants*, p. 33, n.7.
⁵See Appendixes II and IV.
⁶The counties were Chenango, Cortland, Delaware, Fulton, Hamilton, Madison, Montgomery, Otsego, Schoharie and Warren. The *Catholic Directory for 1846*, pp. 106-110.
⁷The Sharon Springs mission, in Schoharie Co., was attended from Amsterdam, Montgomery Co., in 1864. *Catholic Directory for 1865*, p. 99.
⁸"Foreign Born Population, 1855," a scatter-dot map, Thompson, *Geography*, p. 171.
⁹U.S. Bureau of the Census, *Statistics of the United States in 1860, The Eighth Census* (Wash., D.C.: Govt. Print. Off., 1866), p. 325; Rev. Timothy J. Holland, S.S.J., "The Catholic Church and the Negro in the United States Prior to the Civil War," (Unpublished Ph.D. dissertation,Fordham Univ., 1950), pp. 102, 121. In 1940, a century later, the diocese, reduced to 13 counties, had only 209 resident Catholic Negroes. *Ibid.*, p. 22. E.Franklin Frazier, *The Negro Church in America* (New York: Schocken Books, 1963), pp. 27-28. There were Negroes at St. Vincent de Paul's, New York City. *Freeman's Journal*, April 27, 1850. In the raillery that went on between Catholic and Protestant journalists, *ibid.*, Oct. 10, 1846, declared that there were no "nigger pews," meaning segregated ones, in Catholic churches.
¹⁰New York, Secty. of State, *Census of the State of New York for 1855* (Albany: Weed, Parson, 1856), pp. 500-501. This source gives the ecclesiastical jurisdiction to the see of Quebec, but it is overruled by the *Catholic Directory for 1858*, p. 180, which got its information *ex cathedra*, and lists St. Regis parish in the diocese of Montreal with Rev. F.X. Marcoux as pastor. When the Paulists gave a mission at St. Peter's, in Saratoga Springs, in 1852, they reported that there were some Catholic Indians who occasionally attended Mass there, and received the sacraments. Archives of the Paulist Fathers, "Chronicle of Missions," MS., 2 cols., I, 23.
¹¹In 1840 and 1870, his estimates are respectively 47% and 82% Catholic. Shaughnessy, *Immigrant*, p. 251.
¹²The 1822-1846 figures were for all passengers. W.J. Bromwell, *History of Immigration into the United States* (New York: Redfield, 1856), p. 86. The 1847-1864 figures were for alien immigrant arrivals only, but they were almost all of the pasengers. Friedrich Kapp, *Immigration and the Commissioners of Emigration of the State of New York* (New York: The Nation Press, 1870), pp. 232-233. The 1847-1864 landings at New York were 74% of the direct oceanic immigration to the U.S., which were 4,280,316. U.S., Bureau of the Census, *Historical Statistics of the United States, 1789-1945* (Wash., D.C.: U.S. Govt. Print. Off., 1949), p. 34.
¹³Walter F. Willcox (ed.), *International Migrations*, Vol. I: *Stastistics*, comp. Imre Ferenczi (New York: National Bureau of Economic Research, 1929), pp. 360, 362. About 66% in the thirties and early forties and over 72% thereafter went on to the U.S. Norman Macdonald, *Canada: Immigration and Colonization, 1841-1903* (Aberdeen: Aberdeen Univ. Press, 1966), pp. 52, 72-79, 86.

[14]In 1842, 54,000 arrived at Quebec, 50,000 asked for aid, and 30,000 got free passage inland. *Ibid., p. 54;* Robert G. Albion, *The Rise of New York Port (1815-1860)* (Chas. Scribner's Sons: New York, 1939), pp. 349, 351.
[15]By 1851, the New York route to the West from Montreal had lost out to the cheaper Canadian route. Edward Everett Hale, *Letters on Irish Emigration* (Boston: Phillips, Sampson & Co., 1852), p. 63. The Champlain and St. Lawrence Railroad, between the River and the Lake, was the only Canadian railroad in 1836-1850, and together with the Champlain Canal, must have bent a path from Montreal to the diocese of Albany. But the Great Western Railroad opened between Hamilton, Ont., and Chicago in 1850, and the Grand Trunk Railroad began to run west from Montreal in 1856. As a result, in 1857, the 72,251 immigrants to Quebec sent most of their number to the U.S. West via Canada and only 685 to the U.S. Northeast. There were Canadian and American steamboat lines, which ran daily on the upper St. Lawrence from the twenties on. The American Line called at Ogdensburg, Cape Vincent, Sackets Harbor and Oswego where it made connections with the railroads in the diocese in the fifties. Cowan, *Emigration,* pp. 197, 226, 283-286; Glazebrook, *Transportation,* I, 145, 160. The city of Troy, with good rail connections to Lake Champlain, from the forties on, and nearer than Albany to the southern end of the Champlain Canal, from the late twenties on, was the first to receive the immigrants from Canada. It then fanned them out by rail and canal, Hansen, *Mingling,* p. 130. Albany received almost all of the westbound immigrants from the Hudson Valley, though fewer of them after 1851, when the New York and Erie Railroad reached Dunkirk on Lake Erie. Albany also received and dispatched the immigrants from the north, who had come down to use the canals and railroads to the West. A New York State immigrant agent was stationed at Albany, and all of the immigrant forwarding companies had agents there. Kapp, *Immigration,* chap. IV, esp., pp. 67, 69.
[16]Shaughnessy, *Immigrant,* p. 108.
[17]See Appendix III.
[18]In 1825, all of the region of New England, which almost entirely colonized upstate New York before the forties, had nine Catholic Churches and 7,000 Catholics, 5,000 of whom belonged to Boston's cathedral parish, Robert H. Lord and Others, *History of the Archdiocese of Boston* (3 vols.; New York: Sheed & Ward, 1944), II, 30-31. Apropos the immigrant to New England after 1835, "the penniless newcomer had no alternative but to stay where he was." Oscar Handlin, *Boston's Immigrants* (rev. ed.; Cambridge: Belknap Press, 1959), p. 49. In view of the westward flow of the population then, it is not likely that the diocese had any native American Catholics from the rest of the U.S. We can estimate the possible number at the French Settlement on Lake Champlain, in Clinton County, in 1790. See above, p. 30. There were maybe 400 Catholic families, with 2,280 members, in the Mohawk Valley in 1798. See above, p. 43, n.1. But, if we consider the emptiness of that region right after the Revolutionary War, we must assume that they cannot have numbered more than 100 families, with 570 members, if that many, in 1790. And, that figure, I think, is generous. Therefore, in 1790, the Catholics in the region of the future diocese of Albany amounted to 740. For the period of 1790-1865, we can get the rates of natural increase, known and

conjectured, of the population of America from Shaughnessy, *Immigrant,* pp.68, 193, and from Warren S. Thompson and P.K. Whelpton, *Population Trends in the United States* (New York: McGraw-Hill, 1933), pp. 7-8. In this way, we reckon the numbers of native American Catholics in the region of the diocese of Albany as 3,536 in 1845, 4,633 in 1855 and 5,877 in 1865. But, there was that strong westward drift of Americans then, especially in New York, where the St. Lawrence River, the Erie Canal and the Delaware and Susquehanna Rivers offered easy routes to the West. In the 1830's, Father Victor Dugas, at Corbeau, in Clinton County, put aside the temptation of following many of his parishioners to Lake Huron. Taylor, p. 121. In short, we must conclude that the American-born Catholics in the diocese of Albany before the Civil War cannot have been more than a few thousands. There is very little evidence of them in the lecture to Bp. McCloskey.

CHAPTER VIII

IMMIGRATION

From the Old World to the New, death and suffering dogged the immigrant. Ireland stood out as a land that lay under the doom of Malthus, or the wrath of Jehovah, depending on who cried woe. Under a British rule, which they still remember to hate, as having robbed them, starved them, made them sneaks and assassins,[1] the Irish became the most crowded people on earth. Their lives hung on the potato. When the rot struck in 1845, 1846, 1847, 1848, for the twentieth odd time in a century, Ireland became a biblical Egypt. Horror stalked the land. Early in 1847, Father John O'Sullivan, a parish priest, walked into a room. There, on a bed, lay a dying father, a dead mother, two dead children, as, nearby, a gaunt cat was eating a dead baby.[2] Landlords, dying too in the ruination, tumbled the huts of tenants, and humanoids burrowed in the ground. Murder spread. Pestilence raged. "The land is cursed," the people cried, and fled away to the sea.[3]

Charles Edward Trevelyan, the Assistant Secretary of the Treasury, and so the lord of life and death in Ireland, was the overprincipled villain of the tragedy, says an Irish historian. Besieged by pleas for help, Trevelyan wrote: "It is hard upon the poor people that they should be deprived of knowing that they are suffering from an affliction of God's providence.[4] Benjamin Jowett, the scholar, said:[5]

> I have always felt a certain horror of political economists since I heard one of them say that he feared the famine of 1848 in Ireland would not kill more than one million people, and that would scarcely be enough to do much good.

No one knows, but some think, a million died in five years, a million left their land.[6] Most of them were Catholic.[7]

But the Irish stampede was unique. Usually, the immigrant-to-be, whether Irish, or German, or someone else, was a peasant or villager, who, in spite of his troubles, had to hear the Lorelei song of the passenger agent before he left his native soil. That drummer, bent on commissions, duped the clodhoppers along the Rhine and the Shannon with tall tales of North America, its jobs and wages, its free land, free tools, free support.[8] The desperate Paddy could start to work on arrival for a fat dollar a day.[9] The gullible Hans could buy a farm that was cleared and equipped for a song.[10] In New York City, in 1846, one Owny Hogan and others testified before a Committee of Assistant Alderman that they had been cozened into emigrating by ship brokers, that they had searched for work here in vain, and that they had ended up in the poorhouse.[11] Agents were known, on occasion, to guarantee a ten-day trip, when the average sailing time to America was six weeks.[12] Sometimes, the steamboaters on the Rhine promised their passengers a cash bonus when they reached Amsterdam and a free trip across the ocean.[13] An American in Mainz, by the name of Washington Finlay, directed a network of agents in southern Germany and the Rhineland. In 1849, he shipped 12,743 Germans to the port of New York alone.[14] Agents aside, even a family letter could skew the picture of the States. "Everyday here is as Christmas day at home."[15]

Immigration was an ordeal. It scarred the body; it ravaged the mind; it cut the purse. The moment a man left his native village, he was an alien, swept by a tide, rarely knowing his destination.[16] Disorientation would vex him till he died, and his children after him. Uprooted, in transit, he was vulnerable. This writer recalls, living on a farm as a boy, the time a neighbor was burnt out, house, chicken coop and all, and brought his fowls over to roost with ours. In a week, the strange birds were pecked bald. So it was with the immigrant.[17]

His journey began with tears. On a spring day in 1851, in the southwest of Ireland, a visitor was watching as some villagers said goodbye to their homes and their *soggarth aroon,* that is, their dear priest.[18]

> The people gathered about (the priest) in the most affectionate manner. He had a word of advice to Pat, a caution to Nelly, a suggestion to Mick; and he made a promise to Dan to take care of the "old woman" until the five pounds came in the spring to his "Reverence" to send her over to America. Then ensued a scene of tears and lamentations, such as might have softened a much harder heart than mine or that of the priest. He stood for a while surrounded by the old and the young, the strong and the

infirm on bended knees, and he turned his moistened eyes towards heaven, and asked the blessing of the Almighty upon the wanderers during their long and weary journey.

The mass migration of the middle of the nineteenth century caught the Atlantic world by surprise. Ships and ports were not ready to see armies of immigrants across the ocean in safety. Neither were laws, nor ethics, nor medicine.[19] The immigrants themselves were unprepared. In 1873, an investigator for the Treasury Department of the United States reported:[20]

> the large majority of this people are of the lowest order of humanity. They are filthy in their habits, coarse in manner, and often low in their instincts. There are frequently petty thievings, discords, and treachery practiced among themselves, and their ignorance is in many instances appalling, and the women are ofttimes worse than the men....A great amount of discomfort among these emigrants arises from their own ignorance and lifelong habits. Many of them have lived in hovels to which the steerage of the steamship, in comparison,is a palace.

In the eyes of those who watched him pass, the immigrant was a problem or a pariah.

Till the sixties, he usually sailed to America on a vessel that was both a windship and a tramp freighter.[21] Its time of departure was as unpredictable as that of a non-scheduled flight today. As a result, the ports of Europe brimmed with human traffic jams, and vultures swooped where the bodies lay. In spite of the efforts of officials and philanthropists, many an immigrant fell prey to a species of human predator, who was called a "runner" in America and a "crimp" in Britain. The modern ticket scalper is a pale imitation. The runner worked for a boarding-house keeper or for a passenger broker. In cahoots with each other, they varied their wiles on the immigrant from overcharging to downright theft. In short, the immigrant in a port city was a bumpkin in Babylon, a butt of fraud, debauchery and pauperization.

Any old-fashioned theologian who wants to paint a picture of hell can use the steerage life of that time.[22] The so-called passenger vessel was built for cargo, not men. Eastbound, it carried timber, or fish, or pickled pork. Westbound, it freighted immigrants. A broker chartered a ship to America, then retailed the space to passengers. He profited by packing them in. There were laws, but enforcement was lax, and, anyway, the immigrant himself demanded the cheapest of berthing. Take a landlubber to begin with, who knows nothing of ship life, or seasickness, or hygiene, or the food he has to bring for the voyage, or even the language of the crew. Think of him as cattle. Squeeze 500 head of him, male and female, into a leaky, sea-going tub that ought to hold no more than 400, or 450, according to the vague and contrary laws, and launch them on an ocean voyage that usually lasts six weeks, or, sometimes, unforeseeably, four-and-a-half months. Will you not have a "floating coffin?"

In 1847, an Irish gentleman by the name of Stephen De Vere, en route to Quebec, sampled the steerage for two months:[23]

> Before the emigrant has been a week at sea he is an altered man. How can it be otherwise? Hundreds of poor people, men, women and children of all ages, from the drivelling idiot of ninety to the babe just born, huddled together without light, without air, wallowing in filth and breathing a fetid atmosphere, sick in body, dispirited in heart, the fever patients lying between the sound, in sleeping places so narrow as almost to deny them the power of indulging by a change of position, the natural restlessness of their disease; by their ravings disturbing those around, and predisposing them, through the effects of the imagination, to imbibe the contagion; living without food or medicine, except as administered by the hand of casual charity, dying without the voice of spiritual consolation, and buried in the deep without the rites of the Church.
>
> The food is generally ill selected and seldom sufficently cooked, in consequence of the insufficiency and bad construction for the cooking places. The supply of water, hardly enough for cooking and drinking, does not allow washing. In many ships the filthy beds, teeming with all abominations, are never required to be brought on deck and aired; the narrow space between the sleeping berths and the piles of boxes is never washed or scraped, but breathes up a damp and fetid stench.....
>
> No moral restraint is attempted, the voice of prayer is never heard...Once or twice a week ardent spirits were sold indiscriminately to the passengers, producing scenes of unchecked blackguardism beyond description...
>
> The case of this ship was not one of peculiar misconduct; on the contrary, I have the strongest reason to know, from information I have received from very many emigrants well known to me, who came over this year in different vessels, that this ship was better regulated and more comfortable than many that

reached Canada.

Disease and death among the emigrants, nay, the propagation of infection throughout Canada, are not the worst consequences of this atrocious system of neglect and ill usage. A result far worse is to be found in the utter demoralization of the passengers, both male and female, by the filth and debasement and disease of two or three months so passed. The emigrant, enfeebled in body and degraded in mind, even though he should have the physical power, has not the heart, has not the will to exert himself. He has lost his self-respect, his elasticity of spirit; he no longer stands erect; he throws himself listlessly upon the daily dole of Government, and in order to earn it carelessly lies for weeks on the contaminated straw of a fever lazaretto.

The *Thomas Gelston*[24] which sailed from Londonderry to Quebec in 1834, was such a vessel, what with short supplies, cholera and crowding. For lack of space, the passengers in steerage ate in their berths. One berth contained a man, his wife, his sister and five children. In another, there slept six young women. Five men crowded into the berth above them, and eight men into another berth to one side. Nine weeks that lasted.[25]

In 1860, Congress had to pass a law for the protection of females at sea from seduction and violation by ships' crews and officers, let alone the other men in steerage. But four years later, Thurlow Weed, the politician and journalist, in laying the cornerstone of the Emigrant Hospital on Ward's Island, in the port of New York, spoke of the white slavery that continued to lurk for the girls from Europe.[26]

Diseases bloomed in steerage as flowers in a hothouse. The fiercest of them were typhus, or ship fever, smallpox and Asiatic cholera. In May of 1845, the *Hottinguer* was a Liverpooler bound for New York. She carried a crew of 26, a half-dozen in the cabins, and 397 in steerage. Eight days out, the pox killed two children, aged five and seven. Dr. Richard Fraser chanced to be a passenger.[27]

> The bodies were thrown overboard the instant life had ceased; their beds, bedclothes, and linen were also thrown into the sea, and their berths purified with burnt tar.

In 1832, cholera walked the waters. On one vessel, a Scotchman named Sholto counted fifty-three corpses, his mother's and sister's included, cast into the Atlantic. "One got used to it — it was nothing but splash, splash, all day long."[28]

But, in 1847, death outdid himself. Month after month, the Irish thronged to the ships, ragged, starved and dying, some with nothing but a ticket for passage. Then, as the multitude of sail, overcrowded, underprovisioned, beat its way across the ocean, typhus did its deadly work. A few in Quebec saw calamity coming, but begged for preparation in vain. It would be tedious to detail the death and suffering, the piteous survival, the desertion and heroism, the trail of tombstones, real and fancied, from Liverpool and Sligo to Lake Ontario and the diocese of Albany. It lasted from early May to late October, and ended only when winter iced the St. Lawrence in.

Thirty miles below Quebec, the river laps a spot of land that is named Grosse Isle. It was Quarantine in 1847. It was the "Isle of Death." A cross stands there now, Celtic, granite, and an inscription reads:

Sacred to the memory of thousands of Irish immigrants who to preserve the faith suffered hunger and exile in 1847-8, and stricken with fever ended here their sorrowful pilgrimage.

Over 88,000 Irish Catholics set out for North America that year. Thirty-one thousand of them died along the way.[29]

But there are rays of light in this dark picture. One of them was a multiple deed of charity to warm the heart and one of the most extraordinary sermons ever to be preached in a church of God. After the year of death, there were six hundred Irish orphans in the hands of the authorities of the Church in Quebec.[30] The *habitants* soon took four hundred of them into their families, but two hundred remained in the orphanage. Father Charles-François Baillargeon, the curé of the city of Quebec and the archbishop-to-be, brought one of them, a boy of two, into his own home. There, the child lived happily and noisily for a few years, till the roles of priest and parent became too much for one man. One day, a curé from a mission station came to the house on a visit. He was charmed by the child, and at the urging of his host, took him home to show to his people. Imagine the thoughts of the congregation on the next Sunday, when their cure stepped from the sacristy with a little boy in his arms, and when they heard him say:

look, my dear friends, at this beautiful child, who has been sent by God to our care. There are 200 as beautiful children as this poor forlorn infant....Their fathers and mothers now lie in the great grave at Grosse Isle....The pious mothers....left them to the good God, and the good God now gives them to you. Mothers, you will not refuse the gift of the good God.... Go

quickly to Quebec; there you will find these orphan
children....Take them and carry them to your homes, and they
will bring a blessing on you and your families.

"The next day," said the traveler who wrote this down in 1866, and who must have had it from the living principals,[31]

there was to be seen a long procession of waggons moving towards Quebec; and on the evening of that day there was not one of the 200 Irish orphans that had not been brought to a Canadian home, there to be nurtured with tenderness and love, as the gift of the *Bon Dieu.*

The Germans also suffered. True, the ports of Hamburg and Bremen and their registered ships were better than their British counterparts at mid-century.[32] A scene at Quebec in the summer of 1847 sticks in the mind. To one side, the Irish were being dumped on the shore under the cliff. "I have one day seen thirty-seven people lying on the beach, crawling on the mud, and dying like fish out of water," wrote a priest.[33] To the other side, there were shiploads of Germans, sailing by on their way up the river, unaware of the tragedy, apparently, and singing.[34]

But the German record, early and late, was marked by death. When the *Leibnitz,* out of Hamburg, arrived in the Bay of New York in 1868, to report that cholera had killed 108 of its 544 passengers, two officials of the port went aboard to investigate. "We spoke to some little boys and girls, who, when asked where were their parents, pointed to the ocean with sobs and tears, and cried, 'Down there!'"[35] Yet, the worst of the Atlantic migration was over.[36]

In Europe, the immigrant had been a slow-lived peasant, following family custom, and moving with village tradition.[37] Now, still alive, in New York City, he was plunged into a hurly-burly of sharp wits and free enterprise. Friedrich Kapp, a Commissioner of Emigration and an ex-immigrant himself, looked on.[38]

There seemed to be a secret league, a tacit conspiracy, on the part of all concerned in dealing with emigrants, to fleece and pluck them without mercy, and pass them from hand to hand as long as anything could be made out of them.

The frauds on aliens mounted when they began to pour into the port in the thirties. Some Europeans were unwanted, as paupers, jailbirds and lunatics, who were dumped here by landlords and overseers. Of 187 persons who entered the almshouse of Clinton County in 1833, 152 were aliens who had been sent through Canada.[39] A newspaper wrote: "We have seen herds of them on the way."[40] The people had a name for the ships that brought them: "the Workhouse Line."[41] When they begged in the streets, and filled the public institutions, the taxpayer raised a cry.

In the absence of a federal law on the admittance of aliens, the state of New York enacted in 1824 that anyone who landed an alien in New York City[42] had to post a bond with the mayor to cover the cost of the alien's care, if he were likely to become a charge on the public. Afterwards, a city ordiance gave the mayor the right to commute the bond by accepting in its stead a payment of one to ten dollars. This was insurance, in effect, which the alien paid for in his fare, and the insurer was the bondsman or the city, depending on whether the alien was bonded or commuted. Of course, the money that flowed from this became a boodle for politicians, and the bondsman, bayed by claimants, now and then skedaddled.

The bondsman used every trick to fob off on the city his obligation to the immigrant. Sometimes, he doctored the record. One immigrant could not get relief from a bondsman, because he was fifty years old, and his age in the passenger list had been falsified as twenty. To reduce the payments that the bondsman had to make to the city for those aliens who were in the institutions of the city and under his bond, the bondsman opened his own shelter for immigrants, or made a contract with someone who did. Those places sprang up in the forties as toadstools in the rain.[43] They cut their costs to the bone, and they reeked with scandal. At Eighth Avenue and Eighty-Ninth Street, one "Emigrant Hospital" contained 110 men, women and children in a two-story, family house that measured thirty feet by forty.[44] Tapscott's Poor-House and Hospital in Williamsburg, in Brooklyn, was another. In 1846, it was so bad that the neighbors had to send in food, and to remove the women and children. An official report of it pictures a scene from the demi-world of Charles Dickens: rotten food, verminous filth, ragged clothing and a careless commingling of the sexes. At one meal, the inmates were fed the flesh of a sick sow that had been butchered before it could die of its disease. Another time, nine of the inmates bought bread on the outside, and ate it, without the leave of the overseers. Before you could say Star Chamber, they were in jail on Blackwell's Island, in the East River, without a trial, for whatever the reason. (The bondsman, in such a case, was wont to argue that his obligation to support the alien was at an end.) At that time, Tapscott's had about thirty inmates, men, women and orphan breastlings. All were Irish, apparently, and, in the eyes of the matron and the house doctor, the adults were lazy, dirty and undisciplined. When bad came to worse, some of the shelters got rid of inmates by giving them the fares to non-existent jobs in other states.[45]

Quarantine was the first brush that the immigrant had with America. In the port of New York, it was the Marine Hospital of the state, on Staten Island, overlooking the bay. There, offshore, the Health Officer boarded the vessels for a duty that was distasteful to both sides. The officer could smell an immigrant ship on a breezeless day at a distance of gunshot,[46] and the immigrant had learned from scuttlebutt to dread the name of Quarantine. At best, the inspection by a doctor who was overworked was hasty. One mother of a sick daughter was able to sneak the girl through by impersonating her with a quick change of dress.[47] There, the contagious were plucked out, and the rest were sent across the bay. Not only were the families broken up and the baggage lost, but there was a good chance that death lay in wait. In 1851, fourteen of every hundred who entered Quarantine left in a coffin.[48] The place became so dreadful that a mob of neighbors in 1858 burnt it to the ground, and the sick inmates had to fight for their lives.[49]

Before 1855, the immigrants were put ashore on Manhattan, anywhere, day or night, rain or shine, to find their own way. It was common for them to sleep in the open for days and nights at a time. Those who did not die in a doorway, or were not found by relatives, wandered the streets, pitied and loathed, until they came to the sill of a public institution, said an Almshouse Commissioner, "a sickening picture of human destitution and suffering."[50]

The port had the usual pitfalls. In one case, two German girls were beguiled into a brothel.[51] Another case involved a man named O'Connor, his wife and three children. All landed with typhus, and were sent to Quarantine. While there, their money ran out. The man, who recovered first, left his family in the hospital, and set out for St. Louis to get help from his father. When he returned, he was told that his wife had died, and that the bondsman had taken the legal option of shipping the children back to Liverpool instead of paying the greater cost of their care in New York. At last report, one child had died at sea, and the other two were lost.[52]

Evengeline of Acadia was reborn a thousand times, in those years, among the immigrants, under many names, to search, to suffer, to die. In July of 1851, she reappeared in Malone, in Franklin County.[53]

INFORMATION WANTED: Of Michael Kennedy, who sent 15 pounds to his wife Rose Kennedy, to bring her and two children and brother-in-law, named, I think, Connors, and from the Province of Connaught, with instructions that they had their choice to come to New Orleans, Quebec, or New York.

He wrote from Fairmount (Onondaga Co.). The wife and family are at present in Section 4, Ellensburg, Clinton County, New York, where they are sick on the Railroad. Address Rev. Bernard McCabe, Malone, N.Y.

Worst of all for the immigrant was the side web of extortion, spun by a conspiracy of runners, brokers and boarding-house keepers, which stretched from Europe to the Great Lakes. Those middlemen between the traveler and the transit lines, as most of them were, had the same lust for the immigrant, as spiders for a fly. In New York and Albany, many were foreigners themselves, who, for its greater effect, preyed on their own countrymen. Using blarney or force to grab the baggage, they lured the immigrant to a boarding-house that fleeced him, then to a broker, who stripped the rest. It was common for the greenhorn to pay the broker five dollars for a one-dollar ticket for the trip from New York to Buffalo. If the victim balked, his baggage was held. One Scotsman was bled of $145 for fares that cost the agent $8.61. Such was the vampirism that paralyzed aliens in the ports.[54]

The legislature of the state of New York, in 1847, made an investigation. Among the witnesses were some of the ringleaders in that banditry. "The notorious James Roach," a broker in Albany, called the immigrants "cattle," and kept a gang of plug-uglies to tame them. George W. Daley, "the notorious One-eyed Daley," rigged his scales to overweigh luggage by forty percent, and had accomplices in the Customs House at New York. It was political pull and the ignorance of the immigrant that gave them an impunity.[55]

As a result of the inquiry, the legislature began a series of laws in 1847, which created a Broad of Emigration Commissioners, and laid the basis for a system of social welfare for every immigrant to the port of New York. Immigrant aid societies had been around for a half-century, but their means were small.[56] The system did not become effective until the immigrant had suffered for eight more years. Then, in 1855, the Commissioners won their struggle for an Emigrant Landing Depot, as the only legal landing place, over which they had sole control. It was fitted out in an old fort and music hall at the Battery, called Castle Garden. There, for the first time, the Commissioners were able to receive and forward the immigrants without interference from runners.

The system comprised, in the main, the installations at Castle Garden, at the foot of Manhattan Island, the State Marine Hospital, or Quarantine, on Staten Island, the Refuge and Hospital for paupers and the non-contagious sick on Ward's Island, in the East River, the Labor Exchange, on Canal Street, and the agencies at Albany and Utica. In addition, any public or private institution in the state might bill the Commissioners for the care of an immigrant who was "chargeable" to them. That meant that the Commissioners, having levied upon the immigrant a head money, or a commutation,[57] of one dollar after 1847, and of two dollars after 1853, were obliged for his support, if he fell into need, anywhere in the state, at anytime within five years after his arrival. Although the Commissioners divided amongst themselves on whether they were insurers, or guardians of the poor, as is so today, they did whatever they could to set the immigrant on his feet. In fact, they did for him, more or less, what social welfare does for those in need today.

For example, in 1860, the Commissioners received 105,162 alien passengers and $209,534 in commutations; they found jobs for 6,640 men and women; they turned over to the immigrants $14,788 in remittances from friends and relatives; and they assisted a total of 20,715 aliens throughout the state, who were chargeable to them. They lent $1,756 to 173 families, on a pledge of baggage, to travel inland, and at the end of the year, had been repaid $1,658 by 168 families. At Ward's Island, they admitted 3,700 persons, of whom 1,664 were Irish and 1,400 were German, and they buried 59 of the Irish and 73 of the Germans. For the care of chargeable aliens throughout the state, the Commissioners disbursed the following sums, to name a few: $475 to St. John's (Catholic) Orphan Asylum in Utica, $404 to the Troy (Catholic) Orphan Asylum, $1,035 to the Troy (Catholic) City Hospital, and $16,207 to sixteen of the counties in the Albany diocese for non-denominational costs. They wrote 1,867 letters for the newcomers, received 713 replies with enclosures of $7,654, which they gave to the immigrants, and they spent $878 on shipping immigrants back to Europe and $644 on forwarding 301 of them to the interior of the United States. In the same year and in the same ways, the agent of the Commissioners at Albany helped 915 foreigners. Once, he received $230 in settlement of two paternity suits, which he had brought on behalf of some immigrant children.[58]

All of this was worth doing, said Commissioner Kapp, because the value of the immigrant was $1,125 in potential labor and $150 in property, and that was the loss to America in case of harm to him.[59] But there were those who saw immigration as somewhere between Heaven and Hell. Either it spread the Kingdom,[60] or it cost the loss of souls.[61] With David, they might have sung: "They that go down to the sea in ships, and do business in great waters, they see the works of the Lord, and His wonders in the deep."

[1]All of the Irish and Irish-American historians whom I have read agree on this. "Their vices are imposed upon them — Their virtues are their own," said a mid-19th-century Englishman. Quoted in George W. Potter, *To the Golden Door* (Boston Little, Brown, 1960), p. 58.
[2]Cecil Woodham-Smith, *The Great Hunger* (New York: Harper & Row, 1962), p. 182.
[3]Sowing disease as they went. Thirty Catholic priests died of the fever that they caught from the Irish to whom they ministered in Great Britain in March-December, 1847. W.A. Carrothers, *Emigration from the British Isles* (New York: Augustus M. Kelley, 1966, originally 1929), p. 200.
[4]Woodham-Smith, *Great Hunger*, p. 177.
[5]*Ibid.* p. 375.
[6]The population shrank from eight-and-a half million to six-and-a-half million in 1846-1851. T.W. Moody and F.X. Martin (eds.), *The Course of Irish History* (New York: Weybright and Talley, 1967), p. 274.
[7]Woodham-Smith, *Great Hunger*, p. 412. The reasons for immigration from Europe to the U.S. then were, in general, economic, political and religious, in that order of motivation. Maldwyn Allen Jones, *American Immigration* (Chicago: Univ. Chicago Press, 1960), chap. IV.
[8]Cowan, *Emigration*, p. 150.
[9]Edwin C. Guillet, *The Great Migration* (2d ed.; Toronto: Toronto Univ. Press, 1963, originally 1937), p. 45.
[10]Herman Wätjen, *Aus der Frühzeit des Nord-Atlantikverkehrs* (Leipzig: Felix Meiner, 1932), p. 177.
[11]Kapp, *Immigration*, p. 51.
[12]Edith Abbott, *Immigration: Select Documents and Case Records* (Chicago: Univ. Chicago Press, 1924), pp. 128-130.
[13]Mack Walker, *Germany and the Emigration, 1816-1885* (Cambridge: Harvard Univ. Press, 1964), p. 8.
[14]Wätjen, *Nord-Atlantikverkehrs*, pp. 123-125.
[15]Quoted in Adams, *Irish Emigration*, p. 180.
[16]Guillet, *Great Migration*, p. 204.
[17]Oscar Handlin, *The Uprooted* (New York: Grosset & Dunlap, n.d., originally 1951), *passim*, esp. p. 6 and chaps. II and IX. The surplus of men over women and young men at that, among the immigrants, was one source of trial for people who were used to marrying early. Donald R. Taft, *Human Migration* (New York: Ronald Press, 1936), pp. 205-208. See also Kapp, *Immigration*, pp. 42-44.
[18]Quoted in Guillet, *Great Migration*, p. 44. For a sketch of the scene from the *Illustrated London News*, n.d., see *ibid.*, opp. p. 36.
[19]For the details of the ocean voyage, I follow scattered pages in Abbott,

Adams, Cowan, Hale, Kapp and Watjen.
[20] Quoted in Abbott, *Immigration*, p. 51-53.
[21] In 1856, 97% of the immigrants to the port of New York came under sail. In 1869, 89% came by steam. Kapp, *Immigration*, p. 38.
[22] I follow the scattered pages in Abbott, Guillet, Hale, Kapp, and the U.S. Senate, *Report of the Select Committee of the Senate of the United States on the Sickness and Mortality on Board Emigrant Ships, August 2, 1854* (Wash., D.C.: Beverly Tucker, Senate Printer, 1854).
[23] Quoted in Carrothers, *Emigration*, pp. 194-195.
[24] It brought Bp. John England from Ireland to his see of Charleston in 1820. Shea, *Church*, III, 309. No doubt, he travelled cabin class.
[25] Adams, *Irish Emigration*, p. 20.
[26] Maguire, *Irish in America*, pp. 181, 339-340, gives an extract from the act.
[27] U.S. 29th Congress, 1st Session, *House Executive Documents*, Vol. 6, No. 182, "Surgeons on Packet Boats."
[28] Guillet, *Great Migration*, p. 90.
[29] That was 35%. Totals for the Irish were 109,000 emigrants and 38,000 deaths among them. Woodham-Smith, *Great Hunger*, chap. 11. Catholics among them were 81%. Shaughnessy, *Immigrant*, p. 112. The worst ships made for Quebec, steering clear of the stricter U.S. passenger and landing laws. For more detail on Grosse Isle, see Maguire, *Irish in America*, chap. VIII.
[30] New York City had its share. "Any Catholic Lady or Gentleman wishing to adopt a fine healthy male child, four months old, can have one by applying at 327 Eight Street, any day during the week." *Freeman's Journal*, July 12, 1851.
[31] Maguire, *Irish in America*, pp. 139-142.
[32] Starting in the late thirties, Hamburg and Bremen improved their accomodations on land and sea, in order to win the German emigrant trade from the Atlantic ports. Wätjen *Nord-Atlantikverkehrs*, Book Two, chaps. I-II, esp. pp. 113-114.
[33] Maguire, *Irish in America*, p. 136, quotes this.
[34] Woodham-Smith, *Great Hunger*, p. 225.
[35] Kapp, *Immigration*, pp. 189-195, contains this quote. Plague and saturnalia blot the German record. Wätjen, *Nord-Atlantikverkehrs, passim,* esp. p. 162.
[36] The period of 1840-1860, the "golden age of sail," which coincided with Bp. McCloskey's residence at Albany, passed away with the increase of steamships, responsible shipping lines and governmental regulation. Guillet, *Great Migration*, chap. XXII, "The Passing of the Sailing-Ship." By the way, that "golden age" took a toll of lives in shipwrecks. Seventeen vessels with 700 persons were lost in a single season in the Gulf of St. Lawrence. Kapp, *Immigration*, chap. II.
[37] Handlin, *Uprooted*, chap. I, "Peasant Origins."
[38] For the immigrants' voyage from New York port inland, see Kapp, *Immigration*, chaps. III-VII, and appendices II-V; Abbott, *Immigration: Case Records*, pp. 97-181; and the New York, Commissioners of Emigration, *Reports,* annually 1847-1864. For the inland trip via Canada, see Guillet, *Great Migration*, chaps. XVI-XVII.

[39] Abbott, *Immigration: Case Records,* p. 112, quoting a newspaper's report of the findings of an investigator for the city of Boston, in 1835.
[40] *Ibid.,* quoting *Niles' Weekly Register,* Oct. 3, 1835.
[41] Edith Abbott, *Historical Aspects of the Immigration Problem: Selected Documents* (Chicago: Univ. Chicago Press, 1926), pp. 572-574. The North Country received many such paupers.
[42] This did not cover the landings, known and unknown, licit and illicit, at Perth Amboy in New Jersey (near Lower New York Bay), at Sag Harbor on Long Island, and at Ogdensburg on the St. Lawrence. U.S. Scty. of State, "Report of Passenger Arrivals," annually 1821-1838, *U.S. Govt. Documents Serial Set,* Vols. 69, 83, 103, 118, 140, 154, 175, 187, 198, 209, 221, 235, 257, 275, 291, 304, 331, 340; Abbott, *Immigration: Case Records* (1924), pp. 122-127. For the smuggling of aliens at Perth Amboy, see Albion, *New York Port,* pp. 349-350.
[43] And became targets of controversy, as, nowadays, nursing homes and homes for the aged.
[44] "Report of the Committee appointed by the Young Friends of Ireland to investigate the condition of the Emigrant Hospital kept by Hezekiah Williams in Bloomingdale," in the *Freeman's Journal,* June 20, 1846. The report was countersigned by aldermen and doctors.
[45] Kapp, *Immigration,* chap. III; Abbott, *Immigration: Case Records* (1924), pp. 134-139.
[46] Some thought them worse than slavers. Cowan, *Emigration,* pp. 150, 156.
[47] Guillet, *Great Migration,* p. 180.
[48] Including four staff doctors. New York, Commissioners of Emigration, *Report for 1851,* pp. 45, 48.
[49] New York, Commissioners of Emigration, *Report for 1858,* pp. 21-25, 71-72. There is more detail in Charles W. Leng and William T. Davis, *Staten Island and Its People* (5 vols.; New York: Lewis Historical Pub. Co., 1930-1933), I, pp. 262-267. The same thing happened to an immigrant reception center on Long Island in 1847. Guillet, *Great Migration,* p. 183.
[50] Quoted in Abbott, *Immigration: Case Records* (1924), p. 28.
[51] New York, Commissioners of Emigration, *Report for 1861,* pp. 66-67. For the systematic seduction of Irish girls, see *Freeman's Journal,* Nov. 7, 1846.
[52] Kapp, *Immigration,* p. 58.
[53] *Freeman's Journal,* July 12, 1851. Every issue of this Irish Catholic newspaper, which went into every Catholic community, contained a half-dozen or more of such ads. Father McCabe was the pastor of St. Joseph's, Malone, and the mission stations around.
[54] Maguire, *Irish in America,* chap. X; Kapp, *Immigration,* chap. IV. "The transportation of emigrants has become a kind of slave trade among white people." Baron A. van der Straten-Ponthoz, *Recherches sur la situation des émigrants aux Etats-Unis de l'Amérique du Nord* (Bruxelles, 1846), quoted in Abbott, *Immigration: Case Records* (1924), pp. 26-27.
[55] Roach had made $2,000 in three months in that year, and Daley $1,500 for the same period. Compare that to the salary of the chief physician at Quarantine in 1852, which was $1,600 a year. New York, Commissioners of Emigration, *Report for 1852,* p. 21. New York City, in 1847, had about 100 runners and boarding-houses keepers in the employ of just the three largest

companies of immigrant forwarders. Albany had about 20 runners for the three companies. The New York City runners received a wage of about $70 a month each, not counting what they creamed on their own from the immigrants. The equivalent Albany wage was $55. The most notorious of the big three companies was H.D. Smethurst & Co., which had offices in New York, Albany and elsewhere. It was Smethurst who had bilked the Scotsman, aforementioned. Kapp, *Immigration,* chap. IV.

[56] Almost every ethnic group in the city had one. The Irish and German societies were the most active, and worked hand in hand with the Commissioners. In fact, the presidents of those two societies, by law, were *ex officio* commissioners.

[57] Commutation was a way of getting around the U.S. Constitution's bar against a state's interference with foreign commerce. The New York State law of May 5, 1847, required a bond to be posted for every immigrant to the port of New York in order to cover the cost of his care by the public authority, if he fell into need. In lieu of the bond, the law permitted a payment of money, called a "commutation," which was voluntary and therefore constitutional. *Ibid.,* chaps. V, XI.

[58] New York, Commissioners of Emigration, *Report for 1860, passim.*

[59] Kapp, *Immigration,* chap. VIII.

[60] From the Pilgrim Fathers of the seventeenth century to Catholic bishops in the nineteenth century, many believed in the providential mission of the immigrant. See Bishop John Lancaster Spalding, *The Religious Mission of the Irish People and Catholic Colonization* (New York: The Catholic Pub. Soc. Co., 1880).

[61] Shaughnessy, *Immigrant,* chap. XIV, "Alleged Catholic Losses."

CHAPTER IX

A LAND OF MILK AND HONEY

The waterways of New York bred the congregations[1] of the diocese. Clustering about the episcopal see, and about the capital city, of Albany, at the meeting of the Hudson and the Mohawk Rivers, the churches, chapels and mission stations strung out from there, north and south on the Hudson, and westward on the Mohawk. They dotted the many rivers that ran down the slopes of the Adirondacks, east to Lake Champlain, and north to the St. Lawrence. They grew up along the creeks that fed Oneida Lake, and along the Black and Oswegoa rivers, which flowed into Lake Ontario and pointed to the West beyond. On the upper Delaware and upper Susquehanna, they appeared, in the region of the Southern Tier. Some of them, in the Catskills and in the Adirondacks, in particular, lived a short life, due to the migration of lumbering, or to a separation from the main routes of trade.[2]

America boomed in 1847-1864. The wealth of the nation tripled, and its area widened by twenty-three percent.[3] New York was the Empire State in riches as in name, owing to a combination of markets, raw materials, fuels, waterpower, capital, law of incorporation, and, especially, transportation.[4] "Transportation is king," said a merchant in Philadelphia of New York[5] In the opinion of a Yorker historian, the state of New York, with Pennsylvania, blazed the American way, a style of life that is dynamic, urban, pluralistic and democratic.[6] The diocese of Albany, on the crossroads of the state, so to speak, and with the biggest bloc of counties in the state, shared those advantages in a number of ways.[7]

If we bear in mind that Troy and Albany, the hub of the diocese, ranked thirteenth and seventeenth, respectively, among the cities of America in the dollar value of manufactures in 1860,[8] we may itemize the superlatives of the economy of the diocese without stretching its image. The city of Albany led the country in the manufacture of sawed lumber, alcohol, malted and distilled liquors, road vehicles, farm drainage tiles, and stoves. As Americans multiplied by 71 percent in 1845-1865,[9] and buildings arose to keep in step, Albany turned out more stoves for cooking-heating than any place else in the land. Rathbone's Stove Works was known on the Egyptian Nile. In a peak year, 500 men there made 40,000 stoves. Ransom's, in the same city, turned out another 30,000.

The biggest American brewery was in Albany. John Taylor's Sons covered two acres along the Hudson, some of its buildings rearing up six and seven stories. Elevators hoisted grain from riverboats to the top of the brewery at the rate of 1,000 bushels an hour. Incidentally, the office building housed a 10,000-volume library, and its tower was 130 feet high with a clock that was six feet across and was lit up at night. The city also made much farm machinery, furniture, cigars, clothing, cottons, woolens, edged tools, flour and meal, hats, hosiery and steam engines.[10] Albany was the top market for lumber in America, till Chicago took its place in the fifties, and it was in Albany, in 1865, that the country poured its first Bessemer steel. During the Civil War, Albany made arms.[11]

Troy, six miles north, on the other side of the Hudson, was more industrial. It was big in the manufacture of iron products for the railroads, from cars to spikes, in the making of shirts and collars, road vehicles, stoves,[12] sawed lumber, surveying instruments and paper. Other important manufactures were boots and shoes, brushes, clothing, flour and meal, leather goods, safes and sheepskins. Troy's iron factories were among the largest and most modern in the land. The Albany Iron Works, in Troy, using a process that had been discovered in Germany in 1852, made perhaps the only American puddled, or semi-steel, with a tensile strength of 108,000 pounds to the square inch. The Troy Iron and Nail Factory, Henry Burden and Sons, proprietors, with its patented spike-making machines, almost singlehandedly fixed down America's railroad tracks. Burden's patented horse and mule shoe machine (at the end of the War, they had five in operation and five more on order) stamped out 3,600 shoes per hour in 38 different sizes, shapes and weights, and it was said that Burden's horse shoes trod the highways of the world. Their plant on Wynant's Kill was powered by the country's biggest waterwheel, 60 feet across, and in 1862, they built, between the Hudson and the Hudson River Railroad, the most modern steam-powered forge and rolling mill in America. The Burden works

A LAND OF MILK AND HONEY

employed as many as 1,500 men at a time in the sixties. Another factory in Troy, famous since turnpike days, was Eaton, Gilbert & Company. In 1850, it turned out 100 stagecoaches, 50 omnibuses, 30 railroad passenger cars and 150 freight cars.[13] In 1860, Troy sewed enough shirts and collars to equal the value of its iron products, and it led the state in paper-making in 1850.[14]

Just upriver, at West Troy (now Watervliet), Meneely's Bell Foundry cast 600 bells a year, six-ton behemoths included, and shipped some of them around the world.[15] To the west, the Schenectady Locomotive Works, seventeen miles from Albany, and flanked by the Erie Canal and the New York Central Railroad, rolled out a monthly quota of five or six locomotives of dreadnought size.[16] Cohoes, where the Mohawk cascades to the Hudson, knitted an immensity of hosiery and underwear.[17] That was the home of the Harmony Cotton Manufacturing Company, the largest of its kind in the state.[18] At Hoosick Falls, east of the Hudson, Walter A. Woods led America in the manufacture of mowers and reapers. Holding some thirty patents, he supplied one-half the European market for such machinery after 1857.[19] Ilion, on the Erie Canal, eighty-three miles west of Albany, was the site of E. Remington and Son's Armory, one of the biggest gun factories in the United States. A chief contractor with the Union Army, and an employer of 600-700 men at Ilion and 200 at Utica, at the end of the War, Remington's capacity of output per year was 50,000 rifles and 150,000 revolvers.[20]

At a time when flour milling was the leading American industry in value of product, Hart and Munson's Mill Stone Manufactory in Utica, on the upper Mohawk, was famous for its patented inventions of a complete line of machinery for that trade.[21] Oswego, in the northwestern corner of the diocese, where the Oswego River runs into Lake Ontario, quickened in the fifties to challenge Rochester's primacy in the milling of wheat. By 1859, Oswego was grinding out 9,000 barrels of flour a day and 1,000,000 a year.[22] To the southeast, at Syracuse, the springs at Onondaga Lake welled up 7,000,000 bushels of salt in 1859, or 59 percent of the national total. Syracuse led too in the manufacture of canalboats.[23] Years before, Amsterdam, on the Erie Canal, to the east, had already begun to win attention for the carpets it was spinning out.[24] Lead was mined at Ticonderoga, the American Graphite Company there digging out 500 tons in 1860. At the same lakeside, Westport and Port Henry were known for the ships they built.[25] The Adirondacks, overlooking the North Country, was among the ten big iron ore regions of

America, when Bishop McCloskey dwelt at Albany. After Pennsylvania coal came to the Hudson valley in the thirties, and Lake Superior iron ore arrived in the fifties, the Hudson, upper and lower, continued as one of eight American river valleys that were important for their iron manufactures.[26]

Because manpower was then costly, the manufacturers in the region of the diocese, as elsewhere in the country, had an urge for invention. Patents were issued to residents of Albany, Troy, Oswego, Waddington, Fort Edward, Hoosick Falls, Ballston Spa, Whitehall, Utica and Greenwich, for methods of making paper, paper collars, leather, steam engines, stoves, knitted wear, farm machinery, pianos, millstones, railroad wheels, horse shoes, endless chains and sewing machines. As New York, with the help of Rensselaer County, led the nation in the production of farm machinery, it was fitting of the United States Agricultural Society to hold a grand national field trial of mowers and reapers in the state at Syracuse in July of 1857.[27]

It was during the Civil War that tax and currency laws and governmental contracts spurred the concentration and consolidation of industry. On the war's eve, most manufacturing was still scattered in small proprietary units. It was especially so for sawmilling, which went with the clearing of land, and for some of its related industries, as the making of potash, paper and tanned leather. Till 1860, New York and Pennsylvania were the leaders in lumbering,[28] and in New York, the wood and paper production centered in the Albany diocese.[29] Although every stream in the diocese had its sawmill, the heart of the industry was the upper Hudson, between Whitehall and Albany. There were the great sawmills of Glens Falls, Sandy Hill (now Hudson Falls) and Fort Edwards. Glens Falls alone, in 1851, devoured 26,000,000 feet of logs, and swelled its appetite by 260 percent in the next year. There also were the smaller mill villages of Mechanicville, Palmer Falls (now Corinth) and Schuylerville. At the head of Lake Champlain lay the village of Whitehall, which funneled the lumber of the lake's watershed down the Champlain Canal to Troy and Albany. Ticonderoga on the lake and Watertown on the Black River spewed the many products of the forest, and the noise of logdriving rang on the headwaters of the Delaware and the Susquehanna in the Southern Tier and on the rivers that rushed to the St. Lawrence through the North Country. In those days, too, the hemlock forests of the Catskills sent forth over one-third of all of the American-made sole leather, and Zadoc Pratt of Prattsville, in Greene County, ran perhaps the world's biggest tannery. (Pratt is

A LAND OF MILK AND HONEY

still remembered for interring his horses under stone monuments, fittingly epitaphed.)[30] Nearby, Shandaken was a smaller center of tanning, and is named here with other villages and cities for the reason that they all had Catholic congregations at one time or another. It was, in fact, while Bishop McCloskey oversaw the diocese, that New York's woodland industries topped out in importance.

In textiles, the upper Mohawk and the upper Hudson were humming, as the New Englanders had made them. Troy, Albany and Cohoes have already been mentioned. Other places of brisk manufacture were Utica and Whitestown on the Mohawk River, and Hudson, Greenwich and Ballston Spa on the Hudson River.[31] Of the 64 principal cotton mills in the state in 1860, 53 were in the diocese.[32] In iron working, northern New York was strewn with small forges that made and repaired farm equipment for the local trade. St. Lawrence and Jefferson Counties had furnaces and rolling mills. Carthage on the Black River, Clintonville on the Ausable, and Saugerties on the Hudson were particular centers.[33] Johnstown and Gloversville, in Fulton County, north of the central Mohawk, made leather goods; Schaghticoke on the Hoosic had the state's only linen mill; and the city of Hudson on the Hudson River was still sending whalers out to sea in the forties.[34] The diocese of Albany ranked above that of Buffalo and below that of New York in industry, in general. In 1860, for example, the diocese of Albany made 26 percent of the dollar value of the manufactures of the state. Buffalo diocese's share was 14 percent, and New York's was 60 percent.[35]

In 1847-1864, the farmer of New York was undergoing a quick and painful change.[36] Railroads were spreading; canals were enlarging; and the New West, beyond the Ohio, was gushing cheap wool, beef, wheat and pork. The farmer in the diocese of Albany, as throughout the Northeast, had to change his ways to compete for the growing urban market. The idyllic world of Washington Irving was going commercial. For farm folk, self-reliance had been almost religion, hard work and thrift near commandments. Now those old certitudes were giving way to risk, guile and fickle prices, to railroads, banks and commission merchants. Now cash was cutting the familial bond. Daughter left home for a factory town, and son set his face for Michigan. As homespun turned to "boughten," mother idled, and hankered after fashions. In spite of the New West, cleared land continued dear. Abandoned farms lay about in New York; tenancy and share-renting spread; mortgages mounted; and harvest hands scorned the going wage.

Still, the farmer did adapt, and during the Civil War, he reached the apex of his economic stature in New York. Although upstate remained mostly crude and lightly settled, its edge of arable advanced. The farmer had needed no urging to turn his off-season hand to sugaring, teaming, lumbering, canalling or railroading, or to sell supplies to those who did. In New York, he continued to turn out large amounts of the old staples of wool, beef, wheat and pork. But now, on the advice of agriculturists, as slowly or as quickly as he was able to overcome his bucolic inertia, he varied his crops, bred up his livestock, spread fertilizer, bought machinery, and, all in all, intensified his cultivation, while the new-fangled telegraph put him in touch with the daily market.

Self-sufficiency made way for special crops. The closer the farmer to train or market, the more he turned to perishables. Whole milk, butter, cheese, fresh fruits and vegetables sped to the city, and cheese went on to Europe. The diocese of Albany, then spanning most of the Hudson and all of the Mohawk, was the dairy capital of the United States.[37] It was near Rome, in Oneida County, in the spring of 1851, that America saw the birth of commercial dairying. It was in the factory system for making blue-ribbon cheese. In no time at all, it centered in Herkimer County, and made it famous.[38] Besides dairy products, the diocese was a major source of all of the common American cereals, except rice and Indian corn. It grew Irish potatoes, fruits, vegetables, wool, beef, pork, flax and flaxseed (for linseed oil), hay, beeswax, honey and maple sugar, in bonanzas. In particular, the diocese was almost the only American source for hops and the fuller's teasel.[39] Viewed at large, the diocese of Albany, in 1850, had almost 45 percent of the dollar value of all of the farm property in the state of New York.[40] The landscape of the diocese can be envisioned from the fact that 62 percent of its area was farmland in 1860, and almost a third of that was still wilderness.[41]

The infant diocese throve on a web of travel routes in all directions. Their spine was the Hudson-Mohawk Corridor, the "gateway to the interior." It was the easiest and cheapest pass through the Appalachians, from the populated Atlantic shores to that lap of Mother Nature, the American Middle West. In the wake of a transportation revolution, and at the outbreak of the Civil War, the diocese had 43 percent of the railroad tracks of New York, 47 percent of its navigable waters, and it was capillaried as well with roads and turnpikes. The revolution was at core a permanent plunge in the cost and time of transit. In 1830, the wagon freight rate averaged 20 cents per

A LAND OF MILK AND HONEY 109

ton-mile. Its equivalent on the railroad was 4 cents in 1851 and 2 cents in 1860. Canal rates were cheaper yet. As for speed, the steamboat and steam locomotive in 1860 sped five or six times faster than the wagon or canalboat. Passenger travel changed in the same way.[42]

When Bishop McCloskey came to Albany, most of the turnpikes had gone to grass. In their heyday, the twenties and thirties, more than 270 of them crisscrossed the state with 4,000 miles of hard-packed highway. Some of the big ones laced the diocese from its cities on the Hudson River to the west. But the canals and railroads did them in, and only 10 of them were kept up in 1868. In their stead, a fad arose for plank roads. The first one in the United States was built in 1845-1846 over the 14 miles between Syracuse and Oneida Lake. Called "the farmers' railroads," and costing only $1,800 a mile, they caught on in the diocese due to its abundance of cheap timber. In February of 1850, the state had 182 plank-road companies with $3,700,000 of capital and 2,019 miles of road. By 1857, 352 of such companies had sprung to life in the state, but the canals, the railroads and, finally, the panic of 1857, put an end to them too, and in 1868, only 17 were left.[43] In addition, there were country roads, bridges and fords, which at best were obstacle courses, and at worst *culs-de-sac*. A letter from Watertown in April of 1864 said: "It is cold, rainy, unpleasant weather this week, and the roads — well it is impossible to give a description of them. Mud! Mud! Mud!!!"[44]

No sooner had the New York State Canal System opened for business than the traffic forced it to enlarge. The state spent millions in 1835-1862 on continual improvement. The Oswego Canal alone, with only 7 percent of the diocese waterways, absorbed $2,511,992 in 1852-1862 for that reason. That was more than four times its original cost in 1825-1828. There were other expenses on all of the canals as well. For example, the legislature voted $390,000 in 1853 to build bridges at Troy, Utica and elsewhere. In 1854, the annual spring cleaning of the canals, called "bottoming out," cost $100,000. A culvert caved in at Schenectady in 1858, taking $6,000 to repair. In the fall of 1858, when a cold snap froze in 430 boats on the Eastern Division of the Erie Canal, in the diocese, the state had to pay $20,000 to haul them out to the Hudson. Muskrats in 1852 gnawed a 600-foot breach in the Champlain Canal, halting traffic for six days, while crews worked around the clock to plug the hole. By 1882, the cost, over the years, of collections, superintendence and "ordinary repairs" on the canals, with 47 percent of their mileage in the diocese, added up to $48,399,287. As a result, under Bishop

McCloskey's gaze, as it were, the annual tonnage that moved on the State Canal System almost doubled during his residence. The diocese reached out, via its 560 miles of navigable lakes, canals and rivers, to the entrepots of North America, and its cities on the Hudson were oceanic ports of call.[45]

Railroads were the liveliest of the industries just before the Civil War, and upstate New York hived with their activity. In 1858, the diocese had 24 railroads with 1,077 miles of track, showing an average growth of 73 miles a year, at an average cost of $50,704 a mile.[46] Of the 6 all-rail routes that pierced the wall of the Appalachians in 1850, the first 3 to do so cut across the diocese. The New York Central followed the Hudson-Mohawk Corridor; the New York and Erie threaded the Southern Tier; and the Northern, also called the Ogdensburg and Lake Champlain, opened up the North Country.[47] When Bishop McCloskey arrived at his procathedral in 1847, he found himself in a hub of railroads, mostly short, which spoked in all directions.[48] He was 11 hours away, railroad running time, from his westernmost missions around Syracuse, but two years later, the same trip took 7 hours.[49] In the fall of 1850, the bishop could board "the cars" at Albany to visit more and more of his congregations, year by year, in the North Country.[50] But it was not till 1854 that the rail gap closed between him and the Catholics in the Southern Tier.[51] By the way, travel had its dangers then as now. In July of 1859, the bishop escaped injury in a carriage wreck on the way to Port Kent. But he was not so lucky in the following January. En route to a provincial council in New York City, his train collided with another one, near Tarrytown, and his right foot was broken.[52]

The railroads stirred the diocese. Nearly two million passengers rode the Mohawk and Hudson over the 17-mile heart of the diocese between Albany and Schenectady in 1843-1850.[53] In 1851-1856, the freight tonnage on the New York Central between Albany and Buffalo leapt by 765 percent.[54] The Watertown State Fair, in the summer of 1856, drew $11,000 in passenger fares to the Watertown and Rome Railroad.[55] In 1849, one record-making locomotive on the Utica and Schenectady (a link in the later New York Central) pulled 22 cars, that is, 14 first-class passenger, two emigrant, five baggage and one mail.[56]

On top of all of that, the "magnetic telegraph" came to central New York in December of 1846. It first appeared between Utica and Schenectady.[57] In April of 1850, Bishop McCloskey received a

A LAND OF MILK AND HONEY

message over the wire of the New-York, Albany & Bufffalo Telegraph, inviting him to officiate at a wedding in New York City in four days, and saying that his reply was prepaid.[58] Two years later, every corner of the diocese was wired to Boston, Philadelphia, Montreal and New York City, and at the end of the decade, the diocese was linked, in addition, to St. Louis, New Orleans, the District of Columbia and the British Isles.[59] One effect of that whirring, clanking bustle, of the tempo and profits of the Civil War, was that Saratoga Springs came alive with its spa and its racetrack, like a shade of ancient Nineveh.

---

[1]"Congregation" means, here, a group of neighboring co-worshipping Catholics, with or without church property of any kind, or resident priest, who were recognized and listed as such by the bishop in the *Catholic Directory*. Turn to pages xiii-xiv for two maps on which I have plotted the sites of the congregations of the diocese of Albany in 1847 and 1864. Sixty-seven congregations disappeared from the *Catholic Directory* between those two years. Many of them were in the mountains. I compiled this information from the *Catholic Directory,* for 1848-1865.
[2]On the effects of a separation from the main routes of trade, see Appendix IV and Frost, *Susquehanna,* pp. 82-84, 96. On the importance of waterways as lines of settlement, see Noble E. Whitford, *History of the Canal System of the State of New York* (2 vols.; Albany: Brandow Printing Co., 1906), I, 889-908. By 1825, years before the railroads, the state's "basic patterns of farms and villages had been set." Thompson, *Geography,* p. 140. In 1942, the majority of American sees, 79 to be exact, were on waterways. Rev. William Schaefers, "Growth of Episcopal Sees in America," *The Ecclesiastical Review,* CVII (Nov., 1942), 367-371.
[3]U.S., *Historical Statistics,* pp. 9, 25.
[4]Flick, *History of New York,* VI, chap. X, "New York Becomes the Empire State."
[5]Quoted in Whitford, *Canal System,* I, 833.
[6]David M. Ellis and Others, *A History of New York State* (rev. ed.; Ithaca: Cornell Univ. Press, 1967), p. 3.
[7]To gauge the economics of the 28 counties that coincided with the diocese we must remember that, though they had 59% of the area of the state, they also contained all of the Adirondacks and three-fourths of the Catskills, which in those days were a wilderness.
[8]Rochester and Buffalo, in the diocese of Buffalo, were fifteenth and sixteenth, respectively. J. Leander Bishop, *A History of American Manufacturers from 1608 to 1860* (3d ed., 3 vols.; Phila.: Edward Young & Co., 1868), III, *passim,* Vol. III is, in its entirety, a summary of the "statistics of the Principal Manufacturing Cities and Towns in the United States, Compiled from Census Returns for the Year Ending June 1, 1860, with Descriptions of Remarkable Manufactories." According to another source, New York City led the nation in manufacturing altogether. It also had 40% of the state's manufactures and 20% of its factories. Victor S. Clark, *History of*

Manufactures in the United States (3 vols.; New York: McGraw-Hill Book Co., 1929), I, 465.

[9] U.S., *Historical Statistics,* p. 26.

[10] Bishop, *American Manufactures,* III, 240-248.

[11] Clark, Manufactures in the U.S., I, 467, II, 17, 19.

[12] In 1866, an Albany priest found a Troy stove in a Franciscan hospice in Jerusalem. The priest was Father Edgar P. Wadhams, the first Bishop of Ogdensburg-to-be. Rev. C.A. Walworth, *Reminiscences of Edgar P. Wadhams, First Bishop of Ogdensburg* (2d ed.; New York: Benziger Bros., 1893), p. 150.

[13] Richard Henry Dana, the author, saw one of their passenger cars on a Cuban railroad in 1859. Albion, *New York Port,* p. 177. In the 1860's, Troy had 10,000 Irish who worked in the mills and below stairs, and were treated with indifference or harshness by the Presbyterian mill owners. Rev. A.J. Thebaud, S.J., *Forty Years in the United States* (New York: U.S. Cath. Hist. Soc., 1904), pp. 110-120.

[14] Bishop, *American Manufactures,* II, 468, II, 249-253; Flick, *History of New York,* VI, 207-208, 219.

[15] In May of 1850, Meneely's shipped out a bell of 480 lbs. to the Sandwich Islands (Hawaii) one of 784 lbs. to Ningpoo, China, and one of 1,200 lbs. to Cuba. *Freeman's Journal,* May 25, 1850.

[16] Bishop, *American Manufactures,* II, 254-257.

[17] Clark, *Manufactures in the U.S.* I, 559.

[18] Flick, *History of New York,* VI, 196.

[19] In 1865, Woods employed 450 men. Bishop, *American Manufactures,* II, 602.

[20] *Ibid.,* III, 260-261.

[21] *Ibid.,* II, 602, III, 260-262.

[22] Flick, *History of New York,* VI, 232-233.

[23] Ellis, *History of New York,* (1967), pp. 268-269.

[24] Flick, *History of New York,* VI, 203.

[25] *Ibid.,* VI, 213, 220.

[26] Clark, *Manufactures in the U.S.* I, 348, 497-499.

[27] Bishop, *American Manufactures,* II, 481-513.

[28] Clark, *Manufactures in the U.S.,* I, 467, 478, II, 39.

[29] William F. Fox, *A History of the Lumber Industry in the State of New York* (Wash., D.C.: Govt. Print. Off., 1902), *passim,* Flick, *History of New York,* VI, 215-220.

[30] Edward Hungerford, *Men of Erie* (New York: Random House, 1946), p. 91.

[31] Clark, *Manufactures in the U.S.,* I, 535-552.

[32] Bishop, *American Manufactures,* III, 541.

[33] *Ibid,* III, 275; Clark, *Manufactures in the U.S.,* I, 386, 477, 512; Flick, *History of New York,* VI, 206.

[34] *Ibid.,* VI, 202, 217-218; Ellis, *History of New York* (1967), pp. 259-261.

[35] U.S. Bureau of The Census, *Eigth Census: 1860, Manufactures* (Wash., D.C.: Govt. Print. Off., 1864), p. 411.

[36] Percy Wells Bidwell and John I. Falconer, *History of Agriculture in the Northern United States, 1620-1860* (New York: Peter Smith, 1941, original-

A LAND OF MILK AND HONEY

ly 1925), chaps. XIX, XXXIX; Hedrick, *Agriculture in New York*, chaps. XI-XX.

[37] New York led the states in dairying, and in 1864, the diocesan share of the state's dairy business was 60% of the milch cows, 89% of the cheese factories, and of products, 61% of butter, 81% of cheese and 69% of whole milk. *N.Y., Census, 1865*, pp. ciii, 394-409, 415.

[38] The town of Fairfield, on the Erie Canal, was dead center. Bidwell, *Agriculture in Northern U.S.*, chap. XXXV.

[39] The teasel was a plant burr, used to raise the nap on cloth. Onondaga Co. was almost the sole American source. As for American hops, almost one-third came from Otesgo Co. *N.Y., Census, 1865*, pp. 394-409.

[40] U.S. Bureau of the Census, *The Seventh Census of the United States: 1850* (Wash., D.C.: Robert Armstrong, Public Printer, 1853), pp. 121-125. Farm property here means land, equipment and livestock.

[41] It was probably more than 62% to judge by the censal methods of measuring land and counting farms. U.S., Bureau of the Census, *Agriculture of the United States in 1860: The Eighth Census* (Wash., D.C.: Govt. Print. Off., 1864), p. 100.

[42] George Rogers Taylor, *The Transportation Revolution, 1815-1860* (New York: Holt, Rinehart and Winston, 1951), pp. 137-139. The diocesan railroad mileage is my calculation based on John H. French, *Gazetteer of the State of New York* (n.p.: Author, 1860), pp. 66-79. The diocesan navigable waters are my calculation based on Whitford, *Canal System*, I, map facing p. viii, II, folded map in pocket under rear cover, and pp. 1030-1036, 1466-1467.

[43] The turnpikes along the canals and railroads had been abandoned by the forties. Flick, *History of New York*, V, chap. VIII, "The Turnpike Era." The "construction of plank roads was carried farthest in central New York State." Taylor, *Transportation Revolution*, p. 31.

[44] E.B. Wynn to Rev. M.E. Clarke, Watertown, April 14, 1864, Letterbox A25, NY.

[45] Whitford, *Canal System*, I, 955-1025, II, 1031, 1062, 1068

[46] In 1850-1860, trackage in the U.S. more than trebled, and capital investment in rails almost quadrupled. John F. Stover, *American Railroads* (Chicago: Univ. Chicago Press, 1961), pp. 29, 38. New York led the states. Henry V. Poor, *Manual of the Railroads of the United States for 1868-1869* (New York: H.V. & H.W. Poor, 1868), pp. 20-21. The diocesan mileage and growth, given above, was for 1847-1858. French, *Gazetteer*, pp. 66-79. See also Hungerford, *Erie*, p. 86, and Edward Hungerford, *The Story of the Rome, Watertown and Ogdensburg Railroad* (New York: Robt. M. McBride & Co., 1922), pp. 35, 43. Average cost was for the entire state, in 1850-1860, although the Albany, Vermont and Canada RR., built in 1853, cost $61,232 a mile. *U.S., Census, 1860, Statistics*, p. 326.

[47] The New York Central was not so called till 1853. U.S., Bureau of the Census, Supt. (Joseph C.G. Kennedy), *Preliminary Report on the Eighth Census, 1860* (Wash., D.C.: Govt. Print. Off., 1862), pp. 103-104. See also Balthasar Henry Meyer (ed.), *History of Transportation in the United States before 1860* (New York: Peter Smith, 1948, originally 1917), Plate 4 after p. 654, map of "Railroads in the United States in Operation in 1850."

[48] French, *Gazetteer*, pp. 66-79.
[49] Frank Walker Stevens, *The Beginnings of the New York Central Railroad: A History* (New York: G.P. Putnam's Sons, 1926), pp. 321-327.
[50] He could take the N.Y. Central to Rome, and there transfer to the Rome and Watertown, which was building northwards, and which reached Watertown in Sept., 1851, and Cape Vincent in April, 1852. Hungerford, *Rome, RR.*, pp. 43, 50. True, the Northern was the first railroad in the North Country. It broke ground at both Rouses Point and Ogdensburg in March, 1848, and completed its 117-mile traverse between Lake Champlain and the St. Lawrence in Nov., 1850. *Ibid.*, p. 15. But to reach its railhead at Rouses Point, the bishop would have had to take a lake steamboat, which was icebound from Nov. to April. After the two big North Country railroads opened, branch roads appeared in 1853, 1857, and 1861, tapping in other villages with Catholic congregations as Potsdam, Malone and Sackets Harbor. Carthage, with an old and active congregation, did not get tracks till 1872. *Ibid.*, pp. 36, 73, 75, 153.
[51] In 1847, there was a twig of track in Broome Co., belonging to the New York and Erie. It was building west from Deposit, in the diocese, and reached Binghamton in Dec., 1848. Hungerford, *Erie*, pp. 48, 86. But the bishop had no direct access to it from Albany. He would have had to take a Hudson River steamboat to its Piermont terminal, opposite Irvington-on-Hudson. In 1854, the Syracuse and Binghamton made connection between the N.Y. Central and the Erie. French *Gazetteer*, p. 73.
[52] Shea, *Church*, IV, 480; Richard H. Clarke, *Lives of the Deceased Bishops of the Catholic Church in the United States* (3 vols.; New York: Author, 1888), III, 422.
[53] Alvin F. Harlow, *The Road of the Century: The Story of the New York Central* (New York: Creative Age Press, 1947), p. 24.
[54] *Ibid.*, p. 84.
[55] Hungerford, *Rome RR.*, p. 57.
[56] Harlow, *Road of the Century*, p. 29.
[57] *Ibid.*, p. 32.
[58] Thomas E. Davis to McCloskey, New York, April 19, 1850, Letterbox A24, NY. The masthead of the telegram shows that the offices of the company were in Albany and that its wires reached 21 places in New York State between New York City and Buffalo, and made connections with Vermont, Pennsylvania, Ohio, Michigan, Indiana, Illinois, Wisconsin, Kentucky, Tennessee, the Iowa Territory and Canada. The diocese of Albany had nine terminals, between Syracuse and Albany.
[59] U.S., Bureau of the Census, *The Seventh Census (1850) Report of the Supt. of the Census for Dec. 1, 1852, (and for) Dec. 1, 1851* (Wash., D.C.: Robt. Armstrong, 1853), pp. 112-113; John Homer French, *Gazetteer of the State of New York* (10th ed.; Syracuse: R.P. Smith, 1861), p. 81.

CHAPTER X

LAY TRUSTEEISM IN TROY

Now, let us turn to people. Let us listen to the voices in old letters from the missions of the diocese of Albany, across the gulf of time, the voices of Catholics and Protestants, of laity and clergy, and of the bishop who shepherded that field of the Church. But, in doing so, let us remember that we will be hearing only the words that survive. While most of those men and women drudged on in the shadows of life, there were some who wrote to their bishop in appeal, or complaint, or quarrel mostly, due to the nature of his office, or sometimes in insult, or devotioh, or simply with news of local affairs. The bishop, on his part, making no copies, sent replies that are now largely scattered or lost. In 1847-1864, a total of 263 missioners labored in the diocese at some time or other, and 138,000 Catholics dwelt there in 1855.[1] But the 1,300 or 1,400 letters in the ecclesiastical archives of Canada, Ireland, France, Austria, Italy and the United States that relate to the life of the Catholic people and priests of the diocese of Albany come from the hands of no more than a few hundred writers, most of whom were troubled.

"The fatal time is come when we must elect trustees," growled a priest in 1848. It was Father Philip Mark O'Reilly, the pastor of St. Peter's, in Troy, writing to the bishop.[2] County Cavan-born, Bologna-schooled, Father O'Reilly became a Dominican in Spain, traveled through the Continent and the British Isles, as chaplain to the Catholic Duke of Norfolk, came to New York in 1829 as a "missionary apostolic," served in Utica, built churches at Saugerties and Cold Spring, and was to toil on the missions of New York and New Jersey for five and twenty years. He was a large man, active, outgoing and a talker. Collecting money from one and all in Cold Spring, opposite West Point, in the thirties, he set Protestant against Protestant for "abetting the idolatry of the Mass." Years later, after his death in 1854, Cardinal McCloskey used to reminisce about Father O'Reilly, how he had been a military buff, able to spin from memory the entire story of Napier's *Peninsula Wars*.[3]

The missioner was mercurial. When the bishop once ordered him to take up a collection for the Pope, he replied: "I know nothing of the Pope but through you who are my master. With respect to him, your commands shall be obeyed."[4] Later, when he sent the money, and described the stiff-neckedness of certain men and their families, who had either shunned the church on the day the baskets passed, or walked out right after the Gospel, he wrote: "I question the wisdom of the Council of Baltimore that could by any measure produce such results."[5] But thirty-three dollars in those days could keep a seminarian for a quarter-of-a-year, and the priest assured his bishop that he would have handed the money over in person, half-blind or not, if the cholera had not laid him low. But, that packhorse of the Lord had a burr under his saddle, and he tried his master's patience. Bishop Fitzpatrick of Boston thanked Bishop McCloskey, a year later, for a kind and frank letter about the missioner, recognizing that his diocese could not receive him, because he was too old to hope for reform.[6] "Mad Phil O'Reilly," they called him for his humors.[7]

Now, in 1848, Father O'Reilly was damning lay trustees and all their works. "This matter, at all times a dangerous one, is doubly so now, when the Irish in America like their fellows in Ireland are an insane and bloody mob of Jacobins."[8]

A half-century of lay trusteeism lay behind that spleen. As a form of assistance by the laity in the care of the goods of the Church, so long as it clung to the canon law, it was accepted by the clergy, who were burdened by the care of souls. But, as "trusteemania," when lay trustees used their civil rights of incorporation to usurp the canonic rights of the clergy, as, for example, to appoint and dismiss a pastor, then lay trusteeism became a seed of schism. It was the ghost of lay investiture "come out on's grave." It was the collision between the canon law and the civil law.[9] According to one authority, all of the difficulties of the Catholic Church in America in the early nineteenth century were brewed by lay trustees, egged on by troublemaking priests, and it was that that lurked behind the removal, in the thirties, of Bishop Conwell of Philadelphia and Bishop Dubois of New York from the administration of their sees.[10]

Lay trusteeism was planted in New York in 1784 and 1813 by the legislature of the state. In response to the weight of Protestantism around them in 1813, the lawmakers passed "An Act for the Incorporation of Religious Societies." It authorized the men of a congregation to elect trustees, three to nine in number, who were thus empowered to take the title to, and to manage, all of the property of the congregation, as money, pewrents, graveyard, meeting house, and so on. The only thing the minister could do about the temporalities was to call for the election, and to hope, perhaps, to be chosen as one of the trustees. His salary was to be fixed by the same voters. As an expression of the spirit of the Protestant many, who saw authority flow from the people up, the act throttled the Church in New York for fifty years, a Church in which authority flows from the bishops down.[11]

But the bishops in the state of New York learned to live with the act. They would not accept a congregation, unless it used its option, under the act, of deeding its property to the ordinary and not to the lay trustees. That, however, raised a new problem. As an owner under the civil law, although a trustee under the canon law, the ordinary had now to see to it that the property, at his death, went to his successor. That was done by a bequest to a fellow bishop and to a second one, on contingency, who then, after the death of the devisor, made over the property to his successor. But, bishops were but men to the civil law. They could die intestate, or leave a faulty will. A sacred altar could be entailed against its purpose, or escheat to the state, or fall into the hands of a good-for-nothing brother-in-law. (Bishop McCloskey's sister's husband was a sot and a wastrel.)[12] Be that as it may, in 1852, the bishops in New York, namely, Bishop John Hughes of the see of New York, Bishop John Timon of the see of Buffalo, and Bishop John McCloskey of the see of Albany, held in fee-simple, that is to say, in as full ownership as the civil law did recognize, almost all of the religious and charitable properties of the Catholic churches in their jurisdictions.

Three years later, a Pharoah arose who knew not Joseph. The spirit of Know Nothingism moved the legislature to have another go at the Church. It enacted that all conveyances of real estate for religious use had to be a corporation of lay trustees as organized under the Act of 1813. But it was only in the cities of Buffalo and Rochester, in the diocese of Buffalo, that the "Putnam Act"[13] of 1855 found any live coals of lay rebellion. Finally, in 1863, the legislature, feeling friendly to the Catholics during the Civil War, repealed the "Putnam Act," and provided, in the "O'Connor Act,"[14] that any Roman Catholic church or congregation might incorporate, if its bishops, vicar general and pastor chose two laymen, and the five presented themselves to the state as a board of trustees. Thereafter, the successors of the three clergymen, by right of office, were to be trustees of the congregation. On the other hand, the two lay trustees, now in the minority, were to serve for one year, and to be replaced in the same way as first appointed.

To return to St. Peter's, in Troy, when Bishop Hughes turned over to Bishop McCloskey the diocese of Albany in 1847, having appealed to Catholic consciences where he could, and having threatened to withdraw priests where he had to, lay trusteeism was caged, for the most part, although "Mad Phil" O'Reilly was feeling the claw of the beast. He was wringing his hands over the new church. The old one had burnt down, and the new one was rising from the ashes, a dilatory Phoenix. Winter lay ahead, the church was unroofed, the money was running out. The pastor felt helpless. He saw ruin coming. A new board of trustees was needed, the pastor was convinced, who would be willing to mortgage the property of the congregation in order to speed the building. He, the pastor, had to sit on that board to prevent an "interminable confusion," to watch the dollars, and to account for every one of them to the bishop and the people. The bishop had no choice, urged the missioner, but to send him a letter, which would enable him, the pastor, that is, to override the opposition to an election of a new board of trustees. "Without the assistance and protection of the Bishop's as yet almighty name, I nor any other simple priest can hope to do but little."[15] Although Father O'Reilly must have known that the bishop held the title to the property of the corporation of St. Peter's of Troy,[16] he beseeched him to brandish his shepherd's crook in order to save the new church.

A few weeks later, the pastor wrote again.[17] There was a new board of nine trustees, but he was not among them. "A butcher of infamous character" had run the election. Because the honest people had not turned out, in dislike for trustees, an edge of five votes had defeated a ticket of religious men, who had been hard to find, and had elected a bunch, whom the people were calling "the Troy Gang." Excepting the three trustees who were as crooked as the rest but had the sense to bow to public opinion, Father O'Reilly painted the others as "almost always drunk and one of them yesterday disabled for life by a dangerous wound." They had stopped the work on the church, immediately, to the scandal of all, and had sent word to the pastor that they would start it again, if the bishop let them mortgage the property of the congregation. More, they had turned down the bishop's letter.

We do not know for sure what the bishop wrote. But a guess is that he advised the pastor and trustees to raise more money by pledge, to pay as they went, and to avoid a big mortgage like sin. After all, as coadjutor to Bishop Hughes, he had seen five of eight churches in New York City pass under the auctioneer's hammer.[18] The bishop must have called their attention to the fifth decree of the First Provincial Council of Baltimore of 1829: "No church shall be erected or consecrated in future unless it is assigned by a written document to the Bishop..."[19] Probably, Bishop McCloskey asked for the deed to the new church, and that was what the trustees rejected.

Three weeks later, in early fall, Father O'Reilly sent a third urgent plea.[20] To roof the church before winter was his obsession. "Waiving every technicallity (sic)," the bishop ought to allow the trustees to mortgage the land of St. Peter's as they wished. That meant, to judge by the logic of the situation, that the bishop ought not to demand the deed to the new church for the time being, or all would be lost. For, wrote the pastor, the trustees

> refused to be seen to receive your letter which I read to the Congregation, declaring in their primary meeting, which was a secret one, that they would not admit the authority of the Bishop. This sentiment has been expressed by some of the principle scoundrels amongst them since their formation into a body. They won't have the Bishop interfere. The same feeling was expressed by their predecessors in the time of Bishop Hughes.

In all of those goings on, it is not clear whether Bishop McCloskey put any more stock in the self-avowed prudence of "Mad Phil" than he did in the Troy Gang.

It came to pass, whatever the reason, that Father O'Reilly was soon sent to another mission, as Moses to Pisgah Peak, the Troy Gang quiesced, and Bishop McCloskey dedicated the beautiful Gothic church of St. Peter's in the week before Christmas of 1849.[21] But the people of St. Peter's lived to see the face of bankruptcy, no blame to lay trusteeism, and the fall from grace of another and unwise pastor.[22]

[1] Appendix II.
[2] O'Reilly to McCloskey, Troy, Aug. 22, 1848, AA.
[3] Corrigan, "Register," II, Part I (1901), 45; photocopies of several newspaper clippings from the Dominican Archives of St. Joseph's Province,

Wash., D.C., courtesy of Rev. James R. Coffey, O.P., archivist; Rev. Victor F. O'Daniel, O.P., *Dominican Province of St. Joseph* (New York: National Headquarters of the Holy Name Society, 1942), pp. 157-158. Father O'Daniel resented Father Frederick J. Zwierlein's use of the term "wandering religious" for another such Dominican in the state of New York then, and insisted that the proper term was "missionary apostolic," which meant that the Dominican missionary did not belong to the Dominican province in which he was serving.

[4]O'Reilly to McCloskey, West Troy, July 7, 1849, Letterbox A25, NY.
[5]O'Reilly to McCloskey, West Troy, July 16, 1849, Letterbox A25, NY. He was questioning the wisdom of the Council for ordering the collection.
[6]Fitzpatrick to McCloskey, Boston, May 31, 1850, Letterbox A22, NY.
[7]Corrigan, "Register," II, Part I (1901), 45.
[8]O'Reilly to McCloskey, Troy, Aug. 22, 1848, AA.
[9]Rev. Patrick J. Dignan, *A History of the Legal Incorporation of Catholic Church Property in the United States (1784-1932)* (New York: P.J. Kenedy & Sons, 1935), chaps. II-IV; Rev. Robert F. McNamara, "Trusteeism in the Atlantic States, 1785-1863," *Catholic Historical Review*, XXX, No. 2 (July, 1944), 135-154; McNamara, *Dio. of Rochester*, pp. 69-77; Bp. John Hughes, "A Pastoral on the Administration of the Sacraments, Secret Societies and Church Property," (1842), Kehoe, *Works*, I, 314-327; Guilday, *Councils of Baltimore, passim;* Rev. Dr. Joseph Salzbacher, *Meine Reise Nach Nord-Amerika im Jahre 1842* (Wien: Wimmer, Schmidt & Leo, 1845), pp. 335-340.
[10]Dignan, *Church Property*, pp. 74, 124, 163.
[11]*Ibid*, chaps. II-IV. For the text of the Act of 1813, see Appendix V.
[12]E. Mullen to McCloskey, New York, Sept. 11, 1850, Letterbox A24, NY. Mullen was the bishop's brother-in-law. He was replying to a letter from the bishop, in which the bishop had taken him to task for drunkenness and had said that he, the bishop, had been avoiding the Mullen home for that reason. In 1890, the heirs of Father W. B. Hannett, the late pastor of the Church of the Immaculate Conception, Hamilton, Madison Co., were threatening to sue the congregation for $9,000. Wm. P.H. Hewitt (ed.), *History of the Diocese of Syracuse* (Syracuse Cath. Sun Press, 1909), p. 327.
[13]*Laws of the State of New York, Pased at the Seventy-Eighth (1855) Session of the Legislature* (Albany: Van Benthuysen, 1855), Chapter 230, pp. 338-340.
[14]*Laws of the State of New York, Passed at the Eighty-Sixth (1863) Session of the Legislature* (Albany: Weed, Parson, 1863), Chapter 45, pp. 65-67.
[15]O'Reilly to McCloskey, Troy, Aug. 22, 1848, A.A. See also the *Catholic Directory for 1849*, p. 173.
[16]Ledger labeled "Real Estate Owned by R.C.D. (Roman Catholic Diocese)," unpaginated, last page of entries, AA. For St. Peter's, in Troy, the entries show that, in 1843, a Francis W. Mann made a conveyance of real estate to the trustees of St. Peter's; in 1844, the trustees deeded it to Bp. John Hughes; and in 1844 (sic), Bp. Hughes deeded it to Bp. John McCloskey. This was for the land, not the church building.
[17]O'Reilly to McCloskey, Troy, Sept. 8, 1848, AA.
[18]Dignan, *Church Property*, p. 163.

[19] *Ibid.,* p. 145.
[20] O'Reilly to McCloskey, Troy, Sept. 29, 1848, AA.
[21] *Freeman's Journal,* Dec. 29, 1849; O'Reilly to McCloskey, West Troy (now Watervliet), July 7, 1849, Letterbox A25, NY.
[22] It was Father Michael A. McDonnell, whom we have already met in Keeseville. McDonnell to McCloskey, Glens Falls, Jan. 5, 1856, AA.

CHAPTER XI

THE PROFANATION OF THE
TEMPLE OF OSWEGO

Compared to the Troy Gang, the congregation of St. Paul's of Oswego really raised the roof. In the forties, the village had been booming for twenty years, what with traffic on the Oswego Canal and Lake Ontario, the salt trade from Syracuse, the flour mills, and the real estating of such as Gerrit Smith. After the panic of 1837 and its after-lull, the flush times roared back in 1845 to stay for a few years. It was a "golden age." Irishmen and *Canadiens* swarmed, of course, with a clump of Germans for good measure. St.Paul's had gone up in 1838, the first "mass house" in the county, and in 1844 had had to enlarge itself.[1] With a heavy debt, a bulging church, a fiery brew of Teuton, Celt and *Québecois*, the same board of lay trustees for ten years, a history of chasing their priests out of town, and Father John Kenny, a block of Irish granite, St. Paul's erupted in 1846. There was name calling from the pulpit, a lawsuit in the courts, and bloody fighting in the church after a Sunday Mass around a corpse in a coffin at the foot of the altar.

That was the year before the see of Albany appeared. Bishop McCloskey was yet the coadjutor of New York, and handled the imbroglio in Oswego for his ordinary, Bishop Hughes. Soon after New Year's Day, the trustees of St. Paul's wrote to beg the bishop for a new pastor. Father Kenny, they said, had been calling them names from the altar, and accusing them of wanting to "plunder the Church." And, they said, it was simply because they, who had been re-elected as trustees for ten years, were zealous in their duties, and did not see eye to eye with the pastor on the best way of renting the pews, in order to pay for the recent renovation.[2] It was all the spark that the powder keg at St. Paul's needed.

Memory was still green among Catholic and Protestant of establishment and patronage, that is, the support of religion by government and magnate. But America expected her people not only to run their churches, but to pay for them too. After a church of any denomination had been built with gifts or loans of land, money, labor and materials, the money having been ordinarily collected by a "subscription," or pledge, the congregation had to meet the upkeep, either by a general assessment,[3] or by a rent or sale of the pews. Sometimes, during a period of rising prices, an auction was tried, but it made for hard feelings.

In renting, there were differences of method. One price might be the policy for all the pews in a church, or the rents might vary with location, as do the season tickets at the Metropolitan Opera today. A front pew cost more for its status and its nearness to pulpit and winter stove. Whatever the case, the pew holder had a piece of property (in New York, it was real estate) for a term or life.[4] The owner and his family made it a home away from home, with cushions and foot warmers, and woe to him who trespassed. When reformers, in that "ferment of the forties," called for free churches,[5] that is, the abolition of pew rights, along with emancipation, bloomers and tub baths, the issue of pew holding became almost as hot as open housing in our own mad, mad world.

In canon law, the pews belong to the parish church, and the right to permit a layman to reserve a pew, or the right to cancel such a reservation, lies with the ordinary and with the pastor, as his agent.[6] But the civil law in the several states is something else, and pew rights in this country of ours have been an extra-complication of legalities. When Catholics in the nineteenth century quarreled with their bishops and pastors over such a matter, or sued them in the civil courts, they did not always come off second-best,[7] and sometimes the noise of the wrangle reached the ears of Rome.[8]

The typical Catholic church of that time, in its poverty, was small and bare. It had one altar, a sacristy that doubled as a confessional, an organ, if it could afford one, a heating stove, and a gallery on three sides and as many pews as possible in order to stretch the capacity and the income.[9] St. Joseph's (German) of Rochester, which was built in 1836, had an external area of 1,530 square feet (it was thirty by fifty), an internal space of 1,359 square feet, and 361 linear feet of pews, or room for about 240 persons.[10] Such crowding was dangerous. In March of 1859, St. Mary's of Oswego was packed with Irishmen, Germans and French Canadians for a mission by the Redemptorist Fathers, when the floor caved in, killing four and hurting many.[11]

To return to St. Paul's of Oswego, a month after the trustees asked the bishop for a new pastor, 301 men of the congregation rallied to their *soggarth aroon*. Irishmen all, but for thirty-eight *Canadiens*, five Germans and one lone Italian, they mailed a petition to Bishop McCloskey.[12] A concatenation of scraps of paper, stuck together with a dark red sealing wax, it measures six feet in length. One can imagine a grotesque fist, wrapped around an alien quill, scrawling its name laboriously

> in Vindication of the Caractor of A zealous pious & exemplariary Clergyman. Clergymen have been heartofore assailed in the discharge of their duty in this Congregation (this dear Bishop) is an old Custom amongst a few nominal Catholicks that wants to get Rid of A good Clergyman who will not depart from his duty to please them. But we are happy to inform you (Dear Bishop) that the number of Such men are few and amongst them are the old trustees who we heartily wish to get Rid off & to come under the administration of the Dioces...

On the same day, the trustees, now the former ones, due to a recent election, over the signatures of their partisans, 110 of them and likewise Irish in the main, after repeating their own merit and their request for the removal of Father Kenny, spread before the coadjutor a scene of profanation.[13] The pastor, they wrote, had been reviling some of them from the pulpit on Sundays for over a month, but they had borne it with patience in the hope that the bitterness would pass away. But, it was in vain. Father Kenny had given notice of an election for a new board of trustees, to be held on the Sunday of February 1, 1846, after Mass. He had named three candidates of his own, and had instructed the people to name three more. Excitement followed. When the day arrived, and Mass was over, the meeting began in the church.

Father Kenny, wrote the old trustees, called for a vote on his candidates. At the same time, he told those "in favour of the church" to come over to his side. One man replied: "Sir, we are all in favour of the church." When the pastor ordered his partisans to put the man out, a fight began.

> It was in a few moments a scene of confusion and bloodshed in the Temple of the most High ... At the time of all this contention and strife there was laid at the foot of the alter the Remains of one of its most worthy members. No more regard was paid to the dead body than if it was the remains of a Jew or

a Heathen.

In the margin of this letter, and as clear as if written yesterday, are two affidavits in support of the old trustees. One is by the man who spoke up at the meeting, and the other by one who swore before a justice of the peace that he had been "assaulted and beaten with blows under the direction & orders of the Revd. Mr. Kenny."

On the very day on which the above-mentioned two letters were written, and before he could have read them, Bishop McCloskey, in New York City, wrote to Father Kenny, taking him to task for his part in the dispute. The missioner replied in a tone as if to say: "Et tu, Brute! "[14] The truth was, he wrote, he had fallen heir to the rivalry between the trustees and Father John Rogers, who had been the pastor in 1836-1844, until the trustees had run him off. Now, they were up to new shenanigans. They wanted to push the French and others to the rear of the church, and to monopolize the front with their friends and their "fine dressed Ladies." To do so, the trustees, who were among the oldest and richest in the congregation, fixed the rent on the front pews at ten dollars a quarter and on the rear pews at eight dollars. There were 136 pews on the ground floor.

Then, wrote Father Kenny, the trustees went further. They decided to assign the pews on the basis of the amount of money that the members had given to the church from the time of the laying of the cornerstone. The result was that everybody tried to swell his account. Confusion reigned for a month of Sundays. Old people were insulted. Young men and servant girls threatened to leave the church. At last, the congregation would have nothing to do with the pew assignments. They demanded that the trustees resign, and that the church come under "the regulation of the Dioces," that is, the control of the pastor. But the trustees would not give an inch. They threatened the pastor and everybody with the law, if one pew was rented or occupied without their say so. Wrote Father Kenny: "This is the second time they threatened me with the law. Oh! they are great lawyers." It was then that the pastor called for an election of trustees, and gained control of the board when five of his supporters won seats together with four of the opposition. And, he did so, he pointed out to the coadjutor, "in order to carry out the views of the people — to transfer the deed of the church to Bishop Hughes."

As for his use of "intemperate language" against the old trustees, it was not true. He had put up with their highhandedness. He had implored and entreated them to auction the pews to restore the peace, in vain. But, Father Kenny wrote to Bishop McCloskey, when the old trustees went around to tell the people that "if Bishop Hughes or yourself once got possession of their church you would sell it, make away with it," and when they "charged my Bishop with dishonesty, selfishness & sinister views, I thought it was time to let them know their place." He told the people, at the election, apparently, that Tom Lyons, who was a pedlar, and David Cuddy, who was a bootmaker, and Peter Lappin, who was a "kitchen boy or servant," all might be good at their trades, but that "they knew very little of Catholic Bishops, or the respect due to them."

Now, finally, the pastor of St. Paul's of Oswego was satisfied. He had beaten the old trustees. he had rented almost all of the pews by himself; peace was restored; and the future was bright. In closing, he wrote:

> I will pledge my word that the Priest who will come after me to Oswego will have peace if the fault is not his own. ... I most humbly conjure you, Dear Bishop, not to condemn me before investigating the matter ...

But, the trouble at St. Paul's continued. On March 4, that is, a month later, six of the new board of nine trustees, namely, Michael Lynox, Patrick Kelly, Edward Huker, Cornelius Dunn, Michael O'Brien and William Keho, wrote to their "dear & beloved bishop," in defense of their "much esteemed & beloved pastor."[15] Those who were attacking Father Kenny, had attacked Father Rogers in 1836-1844, and Father Francis O'Donoghue in 1834-1835,[16] and were the very same persons who had "çaused the Rev. Mr. Macknamara to die of a Broken hart by the accuseing him of money in the treasury that he never Received."[17]

On March 9 of that year, 1846, the old trustees made good their threat of having the law on Father Kenny or anybody else in his camp who dared to meddle with the property of the church. A trial took place on that date. What the outcome was will be seen below, although the identity of the parties is beyond our ken. But it did happen, according to a D.M. Nagle, who wrote a few days later to the bishop against Father Kenny.[18] He was probably the same one who put the following ad in the *Freeman's Journal* on May 22, 1847:

> Laborers wanted. 5000 healthy and able bodied laborers are wanted immediately to work on the New York and Erie RR, Good wages and constant employment given. Tickets to pass over the railroad free of expense will be furnished till the first day of July next, by applying at the corner of Duane and West Streets to D.M. Nagle, Agent of Contractors.

Nagle had been a trustee of St. Paul's when Father Francis O'Donoghue was the pastor in 1834-1835, and had been assailed by that priest, "who was bitter in his denunciations of those who sacrificed their time and means to elevate the character of the Catholics of Oswego." So Nagle wrote. Now, on March 9, he came to Oswego, where he met friends who invited him along to the trial, at which he discovered that he was involved in the trouble, he wrote, inasmuch as Father Kenny hnad been denouncing him from the pulpit as "Priest-Hunter Nagle," who had slurred the pastor to the bishop as a drunkard. Nagle denied this hotly, and asked the bishop to stop the priest from slandering him.

> I have no desire to interfere with his difficulties — difficulties I dread will increase and multiply as long as he remains Pastor of the Catholic Church of Oswego. I hope you will pardon all this trouble in trespassing upon your valuable time. But having reared a large family in respectability and in the religion of my forefathers will I trust plead my apology ...

In early April, the coadjutor received a supplication from four hundred and eighty men with signatures appended. They were 381 Irishmen, 93 *Canadiens,* five Germans, and that one lone Italian (by the name of Gaetano Volta).[19] Representing themselves as "the greater part" of St. Paul's, which they must have been, if you count their families, they begged the bishop, with a sound of tears, not to take away their "much Beloved and pious pastor," and to grant their wish "to come under the Administration of the Diocess."

Ten months later, the cathedral spoke. Bishop McCloskey had visited Oswego, in the meantime, at the behest of his ordinary, Bishop Hughes, to see the situation for himself. Then, back in New York City, writing to a man in Oswego, whose name does not appear on the copy of the letter in the archives, but who was evidently an old trustee and was behind the litigation, the coadjutor sent this reprimand:[20]

> Bishop Hughes acknowledges the receipt of your letter dated 21st inst. & requests me to give you the following reply. In the first place, you seem to think that he has not investigated the unhappy state of things in Oswego.
> In this you labour under a serious mistake. He has carefully read all the letters which have been written, & listened to a faithful report of all the statements which have been made on *both* sides. He himself wrote a letter to Rev. Mr. Kenny directing & advising him — he wrote also a letter to the *congrega-*

tion, which has read by Rev. Mr. Kenny from the altar, & the tenor of which you can hardly have forgotten.

All this failing to produce the e%ect desired, he sent me to Oswego, giving me all necessary instructions how to act as in his name & for himself. I confined myself as closely as I could to his instructions. The arrangements we then entered into, if they had been adhered to, would have fully restored harmony & peace.

But you would not abandon the suit; you appealed to the Bishop he *decided* — you were not satisfied with his decision — & you *appealed again to the Vice Chancellor* (a judicial officer of the state). You set aside the authority of the church, & placed *above* it the authority of the law.

You rejected the advice of your Bishop, you slighted his admonitions, you put at defiance his commands, you set yourself up together with others in open rebellion against the ruler of your church, & now you ask whether the Bishop has any charge against you, or whether you have ever done anything contrary to his wishes. You have been strangely deluded, my dear Sir, if you were not aware that for several months past you have been almost continually opposing his wishes. A more aggravated case than that of Oswego you can hardly point to. Trustees in many places have been set aside even more unceremoniously than you were, their feelings much hurt & offended, yet they never went so far as to forget that they were *Catholics,* or call in the interference of a civil tribunal to protect them, & to impose heavy costs & fines upon their fellow Catholics, & even their lawfully appointed Pastor.

All this you have done, & it is this which has provoked the hard language of which you complain. If Rev. Mr. Kenny has spoken as you represent, Bp. Hughes is very far from authorizing or approving such sort of severity. But as long as you persist in your present very unwise & imprudent course, consulting your *lawyer* first, & your Bishop afterwards, & seeming to desire to drive away your clergyman by vexatious suits, & legal fines, no effectual remedy can be applied to the evils of which you so bitterly complain.

Your prejudices and resentment against Mr. Kenny lead you astray. You think he wishes to injure you in your property & character, whereas he only wants to lead you back to your rightful obedience as a Catholic. If he is imprudent in his attempts at doing so, it is to be deplored, but you yourself by taking the authority into your own hands, defeat the very purposes you have in view.

The course which you & your associates have pursued, & which you seem determined to persevere in, is wholly at variance with the discipline of the *Catholic* church, & with your duties as professing to be members of that church — & believe me, my dear Sir, unless you listen to the teachings of your holy faith & submit in obedience to the laws of your church, you will only be daily invoking upon your heads fresh calamities.

Bp. Hughes asks you to *pause* before you implicate yourself in a new suit. The law may prove you to be an honest man & a peaceable citizen. That I have no doubt you are. But the law cannot & does not interfere with your character as a *Catholic* or with the duties which you owe your church. It may procure for you satisfaction in money, but be assured it will only plunge you into new difficulties.

The day will come when you will bitterly regret having preferred the counsel of your lawyer to that of your Bishop, & he now admonishes in all earnestness & all charity to retrace your steps, to make your full submission, to offer reparation as far as in you lies for the scandal already given by your iniquitous suit, & to avert from your head the censures which must otherwise inevitably fall upon it.

It was by Bp. H's own request, no deference was made in the late proceedings before the Vice Chancellor; the Church will not set itself up against the law; but it will within its own pale, enforce its discipline, & they who will within its own pale, enforce its discipline, & they who will not abide by it, must if they continue obstinate be severed from her communion, & from the participation of those sacraments which she can only dispense to her faithful & dutiful children.

When Bishop Hughes is apprised of your willingness to refer your present differences *solely* to his decision, to withdraw the *threatenings* of the law, & to consent yourself to abide by it, he will then decide & act — reserving to himself the privilege of still acting with reference to the case in which his *decision* was given, & his authority & injunctions afterwards set at defiance, as in his conscience & his sense of duty he shall best. I have endeavored in the above as accurately as possible to convey to you Bp. Hughes reply to y[our] letter. The sentiments are *his* &

mine are in accordance with them. Very truly yours in Xt./ [signed] John McCloskey Coadj. of NY.

With this threat of excommunication, the shepherd of the flock stilled the wind and water at Oswego for a while, but Father Kenny, alas, was to fall on evil days.[21]

[1]Snyder, *Oswego,* Introduction and chaps. 6-9.
[2]Trustees of St. Paul's of Oswego to McCloskey, Oswego, Jan. 4, 1846, Letterbox, A23, NY.
[3]A Baptist church in Kentucky, in 1820, assessed its white, male members $21 for the year. William Warren Sweet, *Religion on the American Frontier: The Baptists, 1783-1830* (New York: Henry Holt, 1931), p. 515.
[4]Carl Zollman, *American Civil Church Law* (New York: Columbia Univ. Press, 1917), chap. XV.
[5]"The pew No. 18 in the south aisle of St. Patrick's Cathedral [New York] (lined and cushioned)" was advertised for sale in the *Freeman's Journal,* May 11, 1850. On Oct. 24, 1846, the editor of *ibid.* observed that all but two of the Methodist churches in New York City had free seats, and called it "an example worthy of imitation." In 1844, the Church of the Holy Cross (Episcopal), in Troy, was built as one of hte first free churches in that denomination. A.J. Weise, *History of the City of Troy* (Troy: Wm. H. Young, 1876), p. 193. Father Jeremiah O'Callaghan lumped the pew right with usury, burking and Gallicanism. Bp. John England of Charleston saw it as a hindrance in conversion and a burden to the poor. Lucey, "Diocese of Burlington," p. 148.
[6]Rev. Charles Augustine [Bachofen], *The Canonical and Civil Status of Catholic Parishes in the United States* (St. Louis: B. Herder, 1926), pp. 219, 294-295, 320.
[7]Zollman, *Civil Church Law,* chap. XV.
[8]In 1860, the congregation of St. Patrick's of Watertown split in two, for and against their pastor, Father Patrick McNulty, and their trustees, for introducing a pew auction instead of their old system of pew renting at a fixed price. Dr. John Binsse, of continental French stock, one of the founders of that church, who had paid a rent of $5 a quarter, watched his pew go in the auction to an Irish greenhorn, who recklessly bid $31 a quarter. Mrs. Binsse refused to vacate. Although Father McNulty said that the split was between the rich, high-class continental French and the poor, low-class immigrant Irish, there were a few Irishmen of standing, who lost their old pews, and who therefore asked the bishop for permission to make their confessions to the French Canadian priest at Cape Vincent. Dr. Binsse, likewise, kept his family away from St. Patrick's for fear of unpleasantness. Feelings ran so high, wrote one Irishman to the bishop, that clubs and knives were brought into the church, the pastor was accused of drunkenness and adultery, and Dr. Binsse, whose brother was L.B. Binsse, the Pontifical Consul in New York City, sent a complaint to Propaganda about the pastor and, apparently, about Bishop McCloskey. Father McNulty was transferred out that very year, and later fell into money straits, although he remained in service in the diocese. There are 13 letters in the archives of the Archdiocese of New York

and the Diocese of Albany, dated 1859-1860, which detail the facts. See also Kenneally, *Documents in Propaganda, Volume II,* Item Nos. 1589, 1696, 1698, and 1718.

[9] Salzbacher, *Reise,* pp. 332-341. St. Patrick's, New York, was an exception. In 1817, it made $37,000 in one sale of pews to private families. Rev. John Grassi, S.J., "The Catholic Religion in the United States in 1818," *Woodstock Letters,* XI, No. 3 (1882), pp. 237-240.

[10] Zwierlein, "Diocese of Rochester," p. 287.

[11] Snyder, *Oswego,* p. 147.

[12] Members of the congregation of St .Paul's of Oswego to McCloskey, Oswego, Feb. 5, 1846, Letterbox A23, NY.

[13] The old trustees and members of the congregation of St. Paul's of Oswego, to McCloskey, Oswego, February 5, 1846, Letterbox A23, NY.

[14] Kenny to McCloskey, Oswego, Feb. 9, 1846, Letterbox A23, NY.

[15] The New Trustees to McCloskey, Oswego, March 4, 1846, Letterbox A23, NY.

[16] Dates are from the *Catholic Directory for 1835* and *1836,* sections of the diocese on New York.

[17] No doubt, this was Father Michael McNamara, who, as pastor of St. Patrick's, Rochester, had trustee trouble there, beginning in 1829, and was accused by the trustees there of pocketing some of the collection for St. Patrick's. He was removed by Bishop Dubois in 1832 for some reason, and could have been in Oswego in 1833. McNamara, *Diocese of Rochester,* p. 71.

[18] David M. Nagle to McCloskey, Syracuse, March 14, 1846, Letterbox A23, NY. He had been traveling around the western part of the North Country, on business apparently, when he came to Oswego.

[19] Members of the congregation of St. Paul's of Oswego to McCloskey, Oswego, April 4, 1846, Letterbox A23, NY. I sorted them by the looks of their names into ethnic groups.

[20] McCloskey to ?, New York City, Jan. 30, 1847, Letterbox A38, NY. Italics are the bishop's. Paragraphing is mine. I give the entire document, on account of its importance.

[21] He was suspended for drunkenness in 1850, was transferred to Cooperstown and died in 1852 at the rectory of St. Peter's, Troy. Kenny to McCloskey, Oswego, Aug. 2, 3, 1850, Letterbox A24, NY. *Catholic Directory for 1851,* p. 61; *Catholic Directory for 1852,* p. 62. *Freeman's Journal,* March 27, 1852.

CHAPTER XII

THE INTERDICT IN CARTHAGE

An interdict is a scourge. To the children of Holy Mother Church, such a loss of the sacraments is like being cast into outer darkness. "Turn not thy face from me, O Lord, lest I sink into the abyss!" But the Church saves this weapon to the last, for schism, as repentance, may come of it. History records its use against the kingdom of France in 1200, for example when Philip II divorced his Danish queen; against the realm of England in 1208, when King John vetoed the election of Stephen Langton to the see of Canterbury; and in 1909 against the city of Adria in northern Italy, when the populace mobbed their bishop to stop him from moving his home out of town.[1]

In the United States, during the first half of the nineteenth century, when the flint of the frontier struck against the rock of Rome, and the sparks flew, the interdict was laid on at a number of places. Buffalo, Rochester, New York, Norfolk, New Orleans, Charleston, Detroit, Philadelphia and even the village of Norwalk in Ohio, all saw congregations of Catholics forfeit the comforts of their faith for the sake of home rule. In Buffalo, the Church of St. Louis lay under an interdict for seventeen months in 1843-1844 and eleven months in 1854-1855.[2]

So it befell St. James's of Carthage, on the Black River, in Jefferson County, in 1861-1862. For almost two years in that church, the people, meeting, heard no Mass, sinning, received no pardon, and dying, went to their graves unblessed.[3] God's grace flowed elsewhere. Such was the censure, such the chastisement that Bishop McCloskey visited upon his people, for rioting in their church, for raising fists against their priest, and for usurping the rights of their bishop. Years later, at the end of the century, two priest-historians would debate the guilt and innocence of the Catholics of Carthage, but that is not a question for men to settle.[4]

The village of Carthage, off the beaten path, was struggling along in 1855, as if against the will of nature. After a half-century, it had only 785 inhabitants to greet the Reverend Michael Edward Clarke when he came to St. James's as pastor.[5] But Father Clarke was no stranger. At the age of three, he had come from Ireland with his parents and six brothers and sisters to a small farm near Carthage, where the children had grown up, and where the parents had died, years later, in their old age. Michael Edward had worked in the village as a shoemaker till the age of twenty-three, when he had left to become a priest.

Having made his humanities in three years at the new University of Notre-Dame-du-Lac in Indiana, he had moved in 1845 to the new College of Regiopolis in Kingston, Ontario, for theology (maybe because it was closer to home). There, while teaching the undergraduates for his keep, he had won a name for himself as a good student and a proper young man. And there, he had written to Bishop McCloskey in 1847 to ask to become his subject, and had enlisted Father Francis P. McFarland of nearby Watertown to bespeak the bishop for him.[6]

Ordained by Bishop McCloskey on August 15, 1850,[7] Father Clarke had been posted to St. John's of Utica as the assistant. He had served there from October of 1850 to March of 1855.— In 1854, he had taken a leave of absence of eight months for his health, during which he had traveled to Europe with the Nicholas Devereux family as their guest.[9] He had then returned to St. John's for another five months. Now, in July of 1855, he pitched into his duties as the pastor of St. James's of Carthage.[10]

Thirty-six years old, Father Clarke was then. A daguerreotype of 1870 shows him in the public garb of a priest, standing over the middle height, it seems, with a burly frame, a full head of dark hair and a commanding face, looking younger than his fifty-one years.[11] Take away the Roman collar, add military insignia, and he might have been one of Mathew Brady's Union generals. All of the evidence, pro and con, says that he was a hard worker, aggressive and dedicated. How could he not have been, and stuck it out for seven years in that Siberia of the state, where winter half-buried the houses in snow, and spring drowned the roads in mud. What slogging must have been his, as he made the rounds of Carthage, Antwerp, Redwood, Sterlingville, Harrisburgh, Lewisburgh, Montague, Rossie, Gouverneur, Copenhagen, Fullerville and Pinckney, a circuit that reached into three counties, and stretched across for fifty miles.[12]

Yet, he was content. Before a half-year had passed, he wrote to Father James Rooney, a veteran of the North Country, and now, in his old age, the chancellor of the diocese. In a plain, legible hand, the younger man said:[13]

You wrote an inspired letter filled with divine truth we must all admit that squander our time, so precious to God, to ourselves and to our neighbors. I see my faults now more plainly than ever, and I hope through God's help and your prayers, I will make amends for all. Do not delay in sending me another cone of honey ...Please excuse my bare note I am called away. Your most afft. child in Domino ...

More than content, Father Clarke was a happy, active missioner. Another letter, a half-year later, to the bishop this time, showed the priest in touch with his people and with the landlords of the locale on behalf of his people.[14]

I acknowledge with many thanks your kind and affectionate letter of the 9th June, which gave me time to collect the Seminary fund, and in your absence I sent 94 dollars to F[ather] Rooney for you, which he informed me that it arrived safely. Since then I collected the amount assessed for Cathedraticum 30 dollars which I sent through the kindness of Mr. Stewart of this village to Mr. Brenard of Watertown, who will inclose a check for the above amount to you.

Everything goes on prosperously here. I have a number of Deeds for you, and among these I have the deed of Belfort Church, which you are aware was a source of a great deal of trouble to you. A few kind words from me to Mr. Stewart prevailed and I have the deed as you wished to have it drawn. [See note 15]

I visited Rossie as you wished me to do, and I got the deed of all the land we want and one hundred dollars from Mr. Parish towards the Church. [See note 16] I intend to visit Rossie in about ten days, and to procure fromt he congregation enough to inclose their Church. I will be able to accomplish all this without incurring a debt.

I intend to commence soon to build at Sterlingville, and also at Lewisburgh. I am waiting for the titles of the land which Mr. Sterling promised me, and also a subscription towards each. [See note 17] There are two other stations that I am trying to procure lots for Churches, and a prayer from you and your approbation, will I hope enable me to succeed.

Since I came here I paid for indebtedness on Churches, buying lots & Burial Grounds, repairing and fixing the above which amounted to three thousand dollars, and I intend still to expend about three hundred dollars in repairing and painting Antwerp Church, still not being one dollar in debt.

You are aware of the generosity of both Catholic & Protestant all helping me to carry on the good work, which was so backward in this part of his vin[e]yard. I received seventy Adults into the Church since I came here & I have as many more awaiting the happy day in which they can say, we are of that one fold, having one Divine Shepard watching over us, who will never permit us to go astray.

You may my beloved Father think yourself happy, which I hope you are, but I can assure you that I feel myself truly happy in discharging my duties faithfully, and the fruit so abundant that I cannot but behold it. I do not know what trouble is, it never approaches me. I tell my people to seek only to please God, and they will be enabled to practise what their religion requires of them.

May I have a share in your prayers, and believe me to be always your most ob[edien]t child in Xto ...

There was the life of a frontier priest: getting deeds, gathering money, buying lots, building churches, laying out cemeteries, fixing, painting, coaxing, baptizing, praying, and, glory to God, avoiding debt. "I do not know what trouble is," exulted the missioner, as if in the prelude to a Greek tragedy. But elation became exaggeration. John Gilmary Shea, was then collecting the data for his 1856 edition of Henry DeCourcy's *The Catholic Church in the United States*. In it, there is a paragraph on the Black River valley, which echoes the Acadia of Evangeline. Drawing on Father Clarke, the historian glanced at the Catholic pioneers of Carthage,[18] who,

with their descendants, still occupy the spot, directed by a clergyman brought up in their midst [Father Clarke]. Having had the advantage of living together under the shadow of the Church, they are as faithful to their religion as though they lived in the most favored Catholic country. By their industry most are now easy farmers, owning the greater part of two townships, and numbering about ten thousand. Their schools, made up exclusively of Catholics, are well attended and well conducted.

But the priest and the historian erred. For one thing, 10,000 was far too great a number for the Catholics of Father Clarke's mission. His largest congregation, St. James's of Carthage, had 300 members and a usual attendance of 400.[19] If each of the other seven mission stations had had as many, where could he have found more than 3,-200 Catholics? Secondly, Shea's mention of the Catholic pioneers of Carthage, most of whom had been Frenchmen from Europe, and their descendants, calls up the vision of a French-speaking countryside. True, there were many French to the immediate north. But, as a matter of fact, in Father Clarke's own cure, especially in and about Carthage, the Irish had the large majority.[20] Thirdly, all was not farming. There was mining and manufacturing at Antwerp, at Rossie and at Sterlingville, and Carthage had two axe factories and a nail factory, two iron furnaces, a rolling mill, a big tannery, and sawmills and gristmills.[21] Fourthly, Carthage had no parochial school till 1885,[22] and the public schools could not have been "exclusively" Catholic with the many Protestants about.[23] And, fifthly, that the Catholics there were "as faithful to their religion as though they lived in the most favored Catholic country" was a vaunt that remains to be seen.

Sometimes, in human affairs, an alarm bell in the night will forebode a Civil War. In a lesser way, soon after Father Clarke's ordination, and long before he became the pastor of St. James's, a letter went from Carthage. John Clarke, one of the priest's four brothers, was writing to the bishop.[24]

> Having seen the notice that my brother Michael Clarke has been ordained to the holy Priesthood, while now engaged in an unjust lawsuit against me and Mr. Le Ray de Cha[u]mont, I thought best to make you acquainted with the circumstances, so that you can judge weather he has acted worthy of the high honor bestowed upon [him]....

The Chosen Peoples of history have been of Adam's seed.[25] As Jacob was a deceiver, so this letter displays one hard trait.

Litigiousness came with the Irish to America, along with other scabs of body and mind from a history of subjugation. In the Old Country, during the first half of the nineteenth century, acts of murder, arson and kangaroo justice became a part of daily life. In America, the Irish drank and brawled and sued. They say so themselves.[26] Besides, the bond of priests with people in Ireland was due to a common enemy, the British government, and was an accident of history. America was different. If Father Clarke had the truculence of his race, we do not know it. But, the record shows that he and the Carthaginians were continually at law with one another.

The summer of 1857 marked the second anniversary of Father Clarke at St. James's. Before it was past, the five years of feuding had begun. It was on the wind in July. Richard Gallagher was a trustee and a businessman. It was he who had once advertised for a choirmaster,[27] and who had shared with two other trustees the burden of lodging their missioners.[28] Now, in July, in a letter to the bishop, he boomed the church and the village.[29]

I have long wished to call your attention to this Carthage mission being one of the largest & oldest in the Albany Dioces, and I dare say the most in want of at least one more priest. It is not possible for one priest to do the labour required neither do we expect it, but we of Carthage do want a priest to ourselves and until we have such we will be on the back ground.

We are numerous and able enough to do all that would be in reason required of us for the support of a priest and I think and in fact know that the ballance of the mission is able & willing to support another.

I feel a deep interest at this time to have our holy Religion take a new start here. The time is come that we can do something. We are receiving the benefits of our Publick works as you will see in articles I mark in one of the county papers. Our Catholic population is increasing in this village by the erection of large tanneries & other improvements.

We have now a subscription of about $1200 for a parochial House with near $800 paid in & on interest. The balance could be collected & more with it if the House would only Start. And all I can see in the way is a want of time on the part of our priest to attend to it, as he is engaged in seeing to the erection of several small chappels on the mission.

We want a Catholic School. We who are raising Families want it now if ever, that is as soon as it can be brought about, which I think might be in another year. Our Sunday School also wants the vigilant eye of a pastor, as the people, or a portion of them want constant urging to do their duty to their children.

It is the intention to have mass here now twice in the month but we sometimes have [it] but once on account of Duty on the outborders of the mission, which arrangement will never permitt the Carthage Church to go ahead. Will Your Grace give us a trial. I'll be bound we can and will do our duty here. Our House once complete and we can have a verry good house here for about $1800.

I am looking with strong hope to the building of the Hudson

River & Lake Ontario Rail Road. Then will be the time to build a good Church on our realy magnifficent lot, *the best in the State.* In the meantime a good Catholic *School.*

This is not all visionary. I have never lost sight of those things. It has only been a question of time with me. As Your Grace will see from the enclosed epistle from that saintly man, Father McFarland, over 4 years since. I also send you a country paper to show the benefits which we are beginning to derive from our Black River Canal & River Improvement.

I fear I am trespassing on your time and will close by appealing to you in the name of God, to do what you can for us, which I have faith to believe you will ... With great respect I remain your faithful servant in Christ ...

Was that the voice of religion or business, of the Faith or Rotary, of St. James's or the Black River Canal? A priest of their own, a priest's house of their own, a school of their own, Mass twice a month for themselves, and a bigger and better church, those were the heart's desires of some of the Catholics of Carthage on that second anniversary of Father Clarke. They were proud of their church. They were ambitious for it. And, let caution take note, they were losing patience with a pastor, who was away much of the time to put up chapels elsewhere. It was not to be the first falling out between that congregation and their priest.[30] Nor would they have a pastor to themselves in the nineteenth century.[31] The doom of geography lay upon Carthage.[32]

At Sunday Mass, on August 30, 1857, in St. James's, the quarreling began. Its story lies in two bodies of contrary evidence, to wit, the Cardinal McCloskey Papers and the article on St. James's of Carthage, by Father Thomas C. Middleton, which appeared in print in 1899, and which has already been cited here. The one has the letters from participants. The other is drawn from interviews with the same, and their descendants, in Carthage, in 1896. In the one, the accounts are fresh. In the other, senility had to reach back forty years. Yet, the article has detail that the letters lack.

Mrs. Richard Gallagher attended that Mass and five days later, wrote a complaint to the bishop.[33] Hoping that he would not frown upon her, as a woman, for addressing him so, she was determined to defend herself and husband against accusations that were unjust. A few weeks ago, wrote Mrs. Gallagher, a woman of the congregation died. Her bereaved son told Mr. Gallagher that Father Clarke wanted three dollars for celebrating the requiem and two dollars for a Mr. Haberer for singing it. Mr. Gallagher advised him to give the offering to the priest but not to Haberer, who had sung unasked. At the next funeral, a week ago, wrote Mrs. Gallagher, Father Clarke refused to say Mass. He gave the reason that a prominent member of the congregation had "stepped between him and the Altar," that is, had interfered with him in his religious role by telling the young man not to give an offering.

Since gossip named Mr. Gallagher as the prominent member, he wrote to Father Clarke for an explanation. It came last Sunday, wrote Mrs. Gallagher, at Mass. The pastor attacked her husband from the altar in a "tirade," without naming him, "most probably for fear of legal consequences." He accused him of "falsehood" and "hypocricy [sic]." He insinuated that "the people's money would be unsafe in his hands." After Mass, the pastor summoned the Altar and Rosary Society. He appointed a new president and secretary, thus ousting Mrs. Gallagher from office. He said that those affairs had prospered in Catholic hands, but had declined in the control of others. He charged that money to the Society had not been recorded, wrote Mrs. Gallagher, "intimating that I as treasurer had practiced dishonesty." Father Maurice Roche, the pastor in 1852-1854, had said a Mass for the Society once a month, but Father Clarke had said not a one. All he did was to ask about the Society's funds, once in a while.

> Now the whole end and aim of this persecution seems to be a desire, a secret determination to crowd my husband and myself out of the Church, to bring disgrace and ruin upon our inoffending family, and all to gratify some secret malice or purpose ...

A convert from the "school of Protestant prejudice," Mrs. Gallagher vowed that no amount of ill treatment from Father Clarke would ever destroy her faith in the one "Holy Church of God." Her husband had not spared time or money in promoting St. James's. It was he who had gathered the children for catechism in the church on Sundays when there was no Mass. "But now that is vetoed." Last Sunday, the pastor had forbade that activity, saying that once the key had been left in the door, and the children had made a playhouse of the church. Mrs. Gallagher denied it. Some old and pious people were always there with the children after catechism, saying the Rosary with them, and saying their own prayers.

> It is our most heartfelt desire to have everything pertaining to Catholicity advance and prosper, to see the Priest and people united and happy, a state of things which I fear is not in a

very rapid progress at present.

When Mrs. Gallagher said that Father Clarke had insinuated that the money of the congregation was not safe with her husband, she was talking about the fund for the future rectory. That brings us to the edge of the knife. As we already know, the Catholics of Carthage were proud of their congregation as one of the oldest and largest in the diocese, and were unhappy in the thought that it was the most in need of another priest. To such as the Gallaghers, the plan for a rectory augured a priest for St. James's alone, and so, in turn, more Masses, a Catholic school, and prosperity for the congregation and village. To Father Clarke and Bishop McCloskey, the priest's house would also be a sign of faith, that is, the willingness of the people to support their religion.

In 1855, St. James's had no such house. The two pastors of 1849-1854, Fathers Michael C. Power and Maurice Roche, the first of their line to live in Carthage, had bought their own residences there. But, when Father Clarke came as pastor, which is to say, when he came home, he went to live on his brother William's farm. It was in the *Irish Settlement,* five miles from the village. It is probable that he had grown up on that farm, or near it, and evidently had a stake in it. Whatever the reason, he made his headquarters there for seven years.[34]

Right off, the new pastor and his several congregations busied themselves to get a rectory. Father Clarke named a committee, the trustees, apparently, to take up a subscription for it. In July of 1857, the pledges totaled $1,200, of which $800 had been paid in, and was on deposit in a bank and drawing interest.[35] Then came the wrangling. Father Clarke wanted the house next to the church, but the Carthaginians wanted it elsewhere.[36]

At that time, St. James's had been standing alone, for thirty-seven years, near the road, at the foot of a gentle hill. All of the rest of the slope, three acres of it, was a sacred soil, dotted with family stones.[37] It was dear to the people. Once, in the thirties, the village had surveyed a road across it, but a trustee had scotched the intrusion. He was Edward Galvin, one of the incorporators of St. James's. On the eve of the cutting, in the dark of night, he had taken a long and dangerous wagon ride on the rutted road to Antwerp, in order to buy a yet unburied corpse there, so the story goes, and had carted it home and buried it in the path of the coming road. The law that prohibited road diggers from disturbing graves had saved that burial ground.[38] Now, in 1857, the congregation saw another such threat in the pastor's plan for the rectory with a barn and other outbuildings. For Father Clarke, on the contrary, a dwelling that was next to the church would save his time, "so precious to God, to ourselves and to our neighbors."

More light on the priest's house comes from another letter by Richard Gallagher to the bishop.[39]

I have as I informed you continued to swell our subscription list at the urgent solicitation of the Priest, until we have together an amount equal to our most sanguine expectations & more. I am accused of dishonesty, in fact & [in] intent.

Now all I can say is that I am perfectly willing to submit all to our building committee and have always done to everyone interested in our welfare until we were threatened from the Alter that our money would go to Antwerp or some other place to build or buy a priest's House.

Nor have I refused to exhibit the accounts at any time, but did refuse to let them out of my hands, after I was publickly and shamefully attacked from the Alter of God. I have done so for my own protection. I could do nothing less.

I trust I have a good reputation to sustain. At any rate I defy a liveing man to say that I ever took a dollar wrongfully from him & why should I cheat the House of God. I will submit it to any Priest who has ever known me, but this is all to destroy me, to put me out of the way in church matters & also in my business, it appears to be intended for both.

So far as I can learn, this man Haber[er] used to work for me, is now on his own account. [See note 40)] He & a man by the name of Kenna are the principal & in fact the only men who would sustain the priest in the course he is takeing at present.

Our people were all in favour of buying the House that Father Roche built from the beginning & the verry best men in our Church will hold up both hands for it & say with one voice if it is bought now, it will be paid for unto the last farthing within ninety days. Those are facts, no guess work about it. It can be had for a very low figure, say $1150 or $1100. Several hundred less than cost.

The committee met this evening at Mr. Stuerts [Stewart] office for the purpose of consultation. [See note 41] We met thare because the fact is, the priest has made a confident of him. We consulted with him in regard to the matter. He is altogether in favour of buying Father Roche's House as all of the committee, the two Mr. Walshes, James & Patrick, Mr. Farrell N[e]ary & myself. Mr. Ken[n]a is not really in favour of it.

Your Grace may think my conduct a strange contrast between the present & the past but I was strongly urged to press his coming here. [Father Clarke as pastor] at the time by himself, which I have his letters to show & will do if necessary in his own words for at least six months & what is my thanks, you will determine.

I think that Mr. Clark[e] does not want a House here at present. I think he finds it far pleasanter where he is 5 miles in the country. We see him but seldom.

So, it appears that all of the trustees but one wanted to buy the house that Father Roche had built near the church,[42] because it was a bargain, and, it turns out, that Gallagher had had a hand in Father Clarke's coming to St. James's. But the Gallagher letters reveal a darker side to the problem of the priest's house than its location. According to them, the pastor had used words from the altar, which gave them to believe that he was accusing them of mishandling the funds for the rectory and the Altar and Rosary Society, or, to put it bluntly, of stealing them. Furthermore, the pastor, out of patience with the Carthaginians over the plan for the house, was threatening to use the money, which they claimed as theirs, to build a house for himself at the mission station of Antwerp or Montague. That was why the satellite congregations, with Montague in the van, rallied to Father Clarke's side when the two factions formed, and the affair became a sort of Shakespearean feud between the Montagues and the Carthaginians.[43] But, as the Gallagher letters show, there were other brambles in that mission patch. There were the priest's fees, the use of the church, the catechism for the children, the control of the several funds and records, and, above all, a driving priest with an active lay apostolate.

All the while that the wind was rising in Carthage, Father Clarke journeyed to and fro on behalf of his other mission stations, riding the stagecoaches, sleeping in hotels, not only to bring the sacraments, but to handle mundane matters. On one occasion, he bought land for the church in Redwood. At another time, he traveled as far as Ogdensburg in order to buy stoves for the congregation at Rossie. As if his vexations at home were not enough, the trip to Ogdensburg, into the territory of his neighbor, Father James

Mackey, aroused the lion in that missioner to complain to the bishop that Father Clarke was poaching.[44]

Such a friction was common on the frontier, where settlements rose and fell, and Catholics with them, where the immigrant, in his religious needs, could not know, or did not care about ecclesial districting, and where the circuit-riding priest did not always stickle at a man-made line to bless a marriage or baptize a child. But when the bishop wrote to Father Clarke on a variety of matters, the complaint included, the missioner explained that he had stopped at Morristown, in St. Lawrence County, merely to wait for a stagecoach. And, he added: "So a good clergyman who loves his flock cannot leave his own mission according to Rev. Mr. Mackey's principle, in search of that which is nessary for their comfort."[45]

It was in this reply to the bishop, who had apparently also asked Father Clarke whether he could help out another neighbor, Father Patrick McNulty of Watertown, with a loan of cash, that Father Clarke first showed his feelings about the shape of things in Carthage.

I am sorry to say that I fear we cannot help Rev. Mr. McNulty being that Mr. Gallaghar has not given us any return as yet, nor much sign of it, he is very stiff and impertinent, he is not afraid to say in public that if you do not answer his letter, that he will write to the Archbp. [Hughes], he does not believe in eclesiastical aristocracy.

I have not provoked him, nor neither have said anything to him, but I prayed for his conversion. I hope that you will show him that he has no right to dictate to your Priest concerning the stipend of his masses, nor his Choir, nor to keep the Book containing the names of those who paid their money, and also the money since the last of May (for the priest's house). I am sorry that I have been so easy with him but I thought all for the best, and done all for the best. Every thing thank Providence goes on well and prosperously in this mission. Forgive me if I said anything wrong in this hasty note. And believe me always your most obt. child in Domino ...

As things stood at St. James's now, in the fall of 1857, both sides were appealing to the bishop, Father Clarke against an impertinent laity, and the Gallaghers against a priest, whom they viewed as despotic. Now, too, the heart of the quarrel lay bare. Mr. Gallagher did not "believe in ecclesiastical aristocracy."

Gallagher journeyed to Albany to ask the bishop to settle the dispute over the rectory in favor of the trustees, but the bishop refused to do so, and, on top of that, rebuked him for complaining about Father Clarke, when Gallagher was one of those who had asked for him as pastor in the first place. As the trustee wrote to the bishop a few days later, he was writhing under the lash of the pulpit innuendoes.[46]

> I know of but one way to get redress & that is to appeal to our Bishop. If this fails the Law of the land will protect private character. This is the last extremity. Your truly in Christ ...

In December, Gallagher was still clutching the money and the subscription book for the priest's house, and the insurance policy for the church as well, saying that he had the bishop's approval of his course of action. Father Clarke, in the meantime, was trying to muffle the strife, in the hope that the bishop would soon step in to check the trustees. He wrote to the bishop:[47]

> I consider it necessary for you to interfere for the good of religion and the future peace of this congregation. Should you deem it not necessary for either, I will resign immediately and you may send one more capable to take my place.

In January of 1858, the pastor informed the bishop that the trouble had spread to the pew rents, and was now a scandal in a court of law.[48]

> I have delayed longer than I should on account of duty to answer your kind letters, and at present I regret much to have to inform you how Mr. Gallagher continues not only to be obstinate, in not surrendering the money and accounts still in his hands belonging to this church, but he has tried to form a league in the church to annoy me by not paying Pew Rent. Finding this be about the time Revd. Father Thebaud was here [See note 49], I asked his advice what would be the best course to pursue. He advised the following plan, to request that all would remain in their pews until their names and the number of each Pew and Pew Rent would be taken.
> Accordingly I did so, and I further announced to them that all those who did not answer for their Pews on that occasion, they would be rented to the first applicant. All remained and cheerfully answered to their names, and paid their Pew Rent, but Mr. Gallagher who walked out contemptuously and did not pay his Pew Rent.
> Accordingly the Committee and Collectors consulted me how to act in this matter, and we jointly concluded to rent his Pew

THE INTERDICT IN CARTHAGE

to another person who paid for it, and on the following Sunday, this man & family came and occupied his Pew. On the same Sunday, Mr. Gallagher & family came to church, and forced his way into this man's Pew, regardless of any rule or regulation, and his family occupied it for that Sunday.

In a few days after he [Gallagher] sued this man for his Pew, and yet did not pay his Pew Rent, before a Justice of [the] Peace who is a Protestant Preacher in this village, whom he knew to be an enemy of the Catholic Church and the jury being of the same material with the addition of one bad Catholic, who decided in favour of Mr. Gallagher putting thirteen dollars cost on this poor man.

Whilst in public court he [Gallagher) encouraged and insisted upon his Lawyer to ask all the scandalous questions he could think of, and among the questions were these, are not the Catholic Laity tools in the hands of Bishops and Priests, intending to draw odium and disgrace upon the Bishops and Priestly functions and the discipline of the Catholic Church in a crowded Court Room for the space of nearly two days and the greater part of the night.

He has no provocation from me for his rebellious course, in as much as I have not mentioned his name from the Altar on any occasion nor will not until I receive your advice as my Bishop how to act in this matter.

Now I have given you a precise statement of Mr. Gallagher's conduct and it is for you to determine how to settle this now, for he seems by the present appearance of things, and the bold stand he takes, he is only beginning his troublesome course in this congregation.

I think this man will continue coming to the Church to raise a public disturbance, so on these grounds, I think it best for me not to attend the Church until I hear from you....

Another source tells us what happened in the court. Gallagher sued a Joseph Savage, for trespass, probably, over pew number thirty-four, which he and his family had occupied. During the hearing, or trial, before a Justice of the Peace, one Marcus Bickford, on January 4th and 5th, Father Clarke, as a witness for the defendant, was interrogated by the magistrate. The court awarded $5.31 in damages to Gallagher, while the costs to Savage came to thirteen dollars, which must have been the better part of a week's pay for him. Illustrative of the nature of that litigation and of the strife at St.

James's was the yelp of the Know Nothingism of that time in a statement by Gallagher's lawyer: "Roman Catholics here are slaves to the bishop and clergy."[50]

It appears that Father Clarke's temperament had a bit to do with the discord. At least, that was the complaint of some of his contemporaries and the tradition of their descendants. Father Middleton, the historian, met a few of the old families when he visited Carthage in 1896. There were the Walshes, the Galvins, the Nearys, the Giblins, the Bossuots, and in all likelihood, a Clarke or two as well. Though he spoke to some of the old partisans of Father Clarke, most of his informants were related to the trustees of the trouble. Peter Walsh was one of them. He had been confirmed in 1822 or 1823 in St. James's by Bishop Connolly, and was a brother of James and Patrick Walsh, who had been trustees and ringleaders of the anti-Clarkes. Another informant in 1896 was Edward Galvin, whose mother had been a Walsh. He was descended from the trustees and incorporators of St. James's, spear and spindle.[51]

While those of 1896 remembered Fathers Roche and Power[52] with affection, as Middleton recorded it, the best that they would say of Father Clarke was that he had been active. They recalled him as a hard bargainer, vindictive, self-assertive, proud, even strange. He had resented slurs about his low start as a cobbler. It was recollected in 1896 that he had told the people of St. James's more than once that "he'd put his foot on their neck," or that "as Christians and men they were no match for Montague."[53] Sometimes, when he had been out riding alone, "he heard voices, saw faces."[54] (Middleton did not ask his informants how they had learned that.) On one occasion, the bishop had sent his vicar general, Father John J. Conroy, to Carthage to make a peace, but the pastor was supposed to have told him to "go home and mind his own business."[55]

It was this irascibility in Father Clarke that moved one of its victims to appeal to the bishop for justification. Farrell Neary, a trustee and a farmer, wrote:[56]

> I am an old man and for the first time in my life I was on as a witness in a suit between two persons in this congr[eg]ation where our pastor took a very active part. I testified on the trial to the Rules which pews were rented and regulated but to my surprise after the trial I learned that it is reported among the people of this Mission that I swore on the Trial that the Laity had control of temporal & Spiritual matters.
> I am a Resident of this Town for the last 35 years and now to

> be charged with advocating a principle which would control the Clergy of my Church in their Spiritual Duties it is painful to me indeed and more so when I am calumniated by a person [Father Clarke] who Should give his counsel and advice and not Stir up and Encourage Litigation and Strife amongst his congr[eg]ation.
>
> I have raised a family of 11 children all now grown up to the age of men & women and now to have their father charged with advocating a heretical Doctrine and to be branded as a perjurer is worse than death and to Sustain my reputation at Least in the Estamition of the Bishop of my dear religion I Enclose the proceedings on the trial which I refer to....

Here was an echo of the "lay investiture" controversy. Here was a layman, in America, in the nineteenth century, denying that he wished to invade the spiritualities, but being as vague as usual about the line that separates them from the temporalities.

Of course, the letters that have been quoted herein were not disquisitions, and do not tell us exactly where the pastor and his flocks stood on the points of their relations with each other. But the spring of 1858 unfolded one ill effect of the trouble at St. James's and a note of indifference in Father Clarke to it. He wrote to the bishop at the end of May:[57]

> I have prepared the children of Redwood & Rossie for confirmation having to help me the Fathers from Montreal. [See note 58] I trust there will be a great many in both places for confirmation ... There are but few if any at Carthage for confirmation but if you see fit you may visit it....

Two weeks later, Richard Gallagher gave in enough to send the bishop a copy of the subscriptions for the rectory and the insurance policy for the church, saying, at the same time: "I do insist that I should be protected from those charges if false."[59]

In 1898, when Father Middleton wrote his article on St. James's, the man who had built the second church on that site, in 1864, was still alive in Carthage. Arnold Galleciez was his name. To make a guess on the basis of his good French prose, he belonged to the French gentry who had pioneered the village, and who had been cultured enough to support a public library of five hundred books from 1818 to 1845.[60] The letter that Galleciez wrote to the bishop in the first week of 1859 showed Father Clarke and his antagonists as moving on two collision courses.[61]

> Lord Bishop of Albany/ I address you on the subject of my

congregation at Cathage. Permit me to give you a little information about the position in which we find ourselves, and at the same time, to give you some news about the conduct of the Reverend Mr. Clarke.

I tell you that we are quite disheartened by the situation at present. I tell you also that it is a scandal for our religion to see a man behave as he does. To begin with, he has put out the principle men of our church. He has put them out by abusing them publicly, by blaming them for deeds, which all the people know are false.

For me, more than a month has passed since I last attended the church at Carthage. The reason is that when I did go I heard nothing but blickering and wrangling. His sermons heaped blame on the congregation, abused them, threatened them, even made them hear that they were worse than thieves. I was shocked to hear the pastor preach such things, and I stopped attending the services.

The disputes began in this way. When Father Clarke came to Carthage, he flattered the people by promising them this and that. He would build a parsonage. First he named his officers to collect money. They accumulated, I think, $1100 in the space of a year or a year-and-a-half.

The leading men of our congregation felt that we had enough to start with, and that when the people saw what we could do they would give more. We laid this idea before the pastor, but he hemmed and he hawed. He said that we ought to buy a ready-built house.

He sent his committeemen to see if such a house were for sale. They reported that there was one for sale, but he was no longer satisfied. After that, someone proposed that they buy Reverend Mr. Roche's house, but this did not please him, because of a grudge against him [Roche].

After all were [illegible] we let him have his own way. He continued until he had money in his pocket, wherefrom we do not know. Now he speaks of it [the parsonage] no longer. I tell you, my Lord, that he looks for nothing but to create trouble and disorder wherever he can.

At this point, Galleciez told how Father Clarke had thrust himself into the affairs of the writer's family, in particular into the division of the family farm among the children after the death of their parents, and how the writer had to tell the pastor that it was none of his business. Then Galleciez continued.

The other day I found myself at the home of a man named Guyot. There came in a poor man who worked for him to ask him for 12 dollars to have his infant baptized. He said that he had to go as far as Constableville [over 30 miles] to have the child baptized. "It has been three times that I have brought him to Father Clarke. He never has the time to baptize him."
Another poor man who has a big family of 7 or 8 children was telling me on Thursday of last week I brought my infant to be baptized, but Father Clarke said to me, Have you any money. I answered him, no, but I will pay you shortly. The Pastor answered him, keep your child until you have money to pay me.
There is Christianity. The name of this man is Maloney. My Lord, if the time permitted, I could cite more, but I think that you will be satisfied that Father Clarke does not suit us at all, and that our religion is not prospering in Carthage as it ought to prosper.
Please believe me, my Lord, that we are not infidels, indeed not. All of the people in our congregation are ready to do all for the good of our church, and pay as much as possible. All that we need is a good priest. A devoted priest who will preach the Gospel rather than divide the people one against the other. He looks upon his congregation as if we were [illegible], brutalizing, abusing and threatening.
All that he knows how to do is to flatter himself. In that he is not lacking. He tells how this one and that one liked him, the great wonders he has performed, that is the most of his sermon on Sunday.
Now, my Lord, you see our condition. You see how our religion prospers in Carthage. Our salvation is in your hands. It is up to you to see if Father Clarke is good for us. Your devoted servant....

This letter suggests at least two explanations for the unhappiness at St. James's over and above original sin. It is possible that Father Clarke, as an Irishman of the early nineteenth century, had grown up with the idea that Catholics ought to be childlike under the hand of a pastor, and here he had a congregation who could think and do for themselves, thank you. Furthermore, amidst the poverty on the frontier, it was difficult to draw a line between simony and how much a missioner had the right to ask for his support.

In the letters between St. James's and the cathedral, there now followed a silence of about a year-and-a-half, from January of 1859 to May of 1860. We may suppose that the next one to write a letter was as much, or more, a man of affairs than the educated Frenchman. His name was George O'Leary. "Squire" O'Leary they called him, until he died in Carthage in 1895 at the age of eighty-one. An immigrant in 1833, and a shoemaker at the start, he grew in wealth and respect. He served at various times as a postmaster, a justice of the peace, a deputy sheriff and a police justice. At St. James's, he never missed a Mass, and he saw to it that his five children were all baptized in a proper way. He wrote this lament to the bishop in May of 1860:[62]

I am aware of the responsibility that I take upon myself when I address the Bishop of this Dioces, but why should I hesitate, although for writing to you I should be held up to ridicule and branded as an infidel by the Reverend Mr. Clark, but matters have at present gone and caried to such an extent that I consider it a sin before God if I did not at least inform your Lordship of the total disregard of all Religious precepts.

Why should I hesitate when I see in this Congregation all respect for the doctrines and precepts of that Church of which I claim to be an unworthy member trampled under foot and disregarded.

I write to you not to find fault with the pastor or people. There is a great responsibility somewhere which this pastor or people has to answer for. There is at present over half of this Congregation which do not attend Divine worship and those charging the pastor with being guilty of acts and Language which I think is not fit to mention and near all the congregation do not partake of the Sacraments. About 200 children who has no religious training whatever.

The greatest portion talk ap[l]enty charging the pastor with turning the confessional into a place of Speculation in proposing to Peeter Kelly that he should Sell his land and that in a few days after that his Brother [Father Clarke's] called on Kelly to Sell it to him. Kelly says that he [Father Clarke] made him promise on his knees to sell it and that if he did not Sell it he was living in a State of Mortal Sin and that he has turned females of tender age away from the confessional because they went to the fathers to Watertown to confession. Refusing to attend to the Sick and dying. One of those cases is a Woman

about 3 miles from here. He was cal[l]ed on did not go the woman died. She was a practical Catholic. These are only a few isolated Cases.
There is nothing here only dissention and strife in this congregation. There are about 250 Children. No first Communion not for years. No confirmation.
There is Great Excitement at present. Mr. Clark has commenced suits against the following persons, that is, they are sued to Redwood he has transferred what he calls his accounts to be Sued in the name of a man that resides in Redwood 26 miles from here.
Enclosed I send you one of his Claims which he has sued for[.] the following are the names that are Sued William Reily, Lawrence Cunningham, Farel Neary, John Gormanly, James Moran, Philip Sullivan, Patrick Reily who resides in Harrisburgh and a number of others. Reilys suit is to come off on next Tuesday in Lewis Co.
I tell you Bishop that if you were to know the Deplorable State of Religion in this Section you would at least investigate the matter....

Such was the state of affairs at St. James's of Carthage in the spring of 1860, according to an opponent of Father Clarke. The people were staying away from the church and the sacraments; the children, the sick and the dying were neglected, and the priest was a moneychanger in the temple. Worst of all, the pastor was hounding his people through the civil court. The reason was, to take a guess at it, that either they had not paid the pew rents that they had contracted for, or that they had not paid the contributions that they had subscribed for. Having read these letters of rancor against Father Clarke, one may begin to wonder whether American Catholic historians have been correct in drawing a sharp line of separation between the Know Nothings, outside the Church, and the Catholic laity, inside the Church.

Father Clarke and his people spent the rest of 1860 in suing each other, and in raising the tension in Carthage. According to the land agent, Patrick Somerville Stewart, the pastor was ill treated by those who should have respected him, in a civil action toward the end of that year.[63] It may have happened in one of the suits that the priest himself began against his own people, or in the one that Richard Gallagher brought against him for libel apparently, and later lost.[64]

We come now to the immediate cause of the interdict on St.

James's. There was a bloody free-for-all in the church at the Sunday Mass on December 30, 1860. Though the accounts vary, they all agree that it was the issue of the priest's house, which had been smoldering for five years, and which now burst into flame. According to Father Middleton, the historian of St. James's, Father Clarke yielded to the demands of the people, and called for a vote by the congregation on that Sunday, in order to settle the question of the house once and for all.[65] But that is not probable, and the reason for the vote escapes us. Under the Act for the Incorporation of Religious Societies of 1813,[66] only the trustees might make such a decision. What Father Clarke had the right to do, and what the logic of that impasse suggests that he did do, was to call for the election of a new board of trustees. In fact, a letter of the time says that that happened.[67] But it was from a man who had the facts second-hand, and there is no word elsewhere about an election or a new board. Furthermore, Middleton showed no awareness of the possibility that the vote was an election.[68] As a matter of fact, he dismissed lay trusteeism as no cause of the trouble at Carthage.[69]

Emotions ran high throughout the mission, as the Sunday drew near. The priest's house aside, a second issue was the right of the other congregations to vote at St James's. They did not have the right under the Act of 1813, if it were an election. But they claimed it on the ground of their contributions to the fund for the rectory. The Carthaginians denied that claim with the argument that the question was local. Whether a vote or an election, whether the non-Carthaginians had the right to participate or not, it was standing room only on that Sunday at St. James's. Present were the Catholics of Carthage, who were anti-Clarke, the Catholics of Montague and the other stations, who were pro-Clarke, and the Protestants, who were agog.[70] Richard Gallagher was there. So were Patrick Walsh and his sister, Ann, an old spinster, who was called "Aunt Nancy." The two men were trustees; the Walshes were children of one of the founders of the church; and all three were to be in the thick of things that day against the pastor.[71] What a meeting it was going to be!

St. James's was a small, white building, thirty feet by forty, with a bell tower and an adjoining vestry. Under the vaulted ceiling, the pews seated four hundred. The sancturary had only the altar and a pulpit, and somewhere on the walls were two pictures of St. James, the Apostle.[72]

After communion, as told by the various accounts we must patch together, some of the people from the other mission stations signed their names in support of Father Clarke's idea for the priest's house. Then the pastor harangued the throng. He demanded a vote for the non-Carthaginians. He attacked his opponents. He called them rebels and schismatics. They retorted. The words flew back and forth. Fighting began. Someone tore the legs off a table to use them as clubs. Pews were broken. Heads were bloodied. Those from the other mission stations were thrown out. It was pandemonium. When Aunt Nancy screamed "put him out," meaning the priest, some of her cohorts leaped the communion rail, and went for him.

In one version, told thirty-six years later, they grabbed him, hustled him to the vestry, shucked the vestments off him, and cried: "Go — leave Carthage and never come back."[73] Another version denies that a hand was laid on the priest. He simply ran into the vestry, locked the door, changed clothes, and left the church, before his pursuers broke in.[74] Patrick Somerville Stewart heard the uproar and hurrahs when he was hundreds of feet away.[75] In the riot, one incident stands out. It was a sign of the times, of the anticlericalism of that era, of what some called "red republicanism." Two days later, an eyewitness wrote that Patrick Walsh, Richard Gallagher and their mob carried off books and papers from the vestry. "Then they walked up on the alter with their hats on and shouted three cheers for Garabaldi."[76]

Having fled the church, or been run out of it, before he could end the Mass, according to Father Middleton,[77] Father Clarke lost no time in asking the land agent for a testimony to lay before the bishop. Stewart, who was also a lawyer and a Methodist, wrote:[78]

I have known you for many years, but more paticularly since you have had charge of this Parish. I have and still do consider you as a very laborious, indefatigable priest. I have never heard anything against you except in this place. I know the Catholics at Redwood and Sterlingville & some at Copenhagen, and those who I have heard speak of you has been in your praise. The difficulties that have existed here I know but very little about, except what all know, but the merits the right or wrong, I have not inquired into or investigated.

You have been ill treated as a Priest by those who should have respected you, not only in a recent lawsuit, but yesterday after Mass a very uproarious time was had outside the Church. I heard loud hurrahs when I was several hundred feet from the Church. The idea I have of the duties of Catholics towards the Church and their priests has been violated by men who know or should know better.

1st Jan[uar]y. I heard that the persons who I refer to did last Sunday shut up the Church by nails & locks, and they had a meeting in the Church yesterday. I heard that these men had applied to the Military to aid them if you and your friends interfered. I say I heard so — and I think it is so.
Great disrespect has fallen on the Catholic Religion in this place, and I say for one taking into account all I have seen & heard, that the authority of the Roman Catholic Church and her Priests have been set at nought & indeed trampled under foot....

At the same time, a member of St. James's who had attended the last Mass sent a letter to the bishop in defense of the pastor.[79]

A sense of duty induces me to embrace the present oppertunity of conveying to you an expression of my indignation at the Ruffinly Conduct of a Lawless faction of nominal Catholics. This Rascally mob led by Patrick Walsh and the Renegade Galagher has committed acts of violence in the Catholic Church on last Sunday which has outraged the feelings of all the respectable inhabitants of this place.
You are aware that for some time past the prospect of building a house for the Priest on St. James Church lot in Carthage was in contemplation but oweing to the opisition of Galagher and his faction the work has been retarded but thanks be to the praiseworthy exertions of our worthy Pastor, the Rev. Mr. Clark who is determined that the building of a parochial house shall not be abandoned.
I know that for the earnestness in which he has devoted himself in the faithful Discharge of his duty he seeks no human praise but Looks up to him for his reward who will render unto every one according to his work.
However it may be interesting to you as it is highly gratifying to me to be able to state that since he came to this Mission he has diligently exerted himself with his money and his services in promoting the harmony and advancing the interest of all the Catholics who happened to come under his care.
But principles such as I have just stated and a character that proves the sincerity of them was not sufficient to secure him from the abuse of some of his own Rebellious flock . On last Sunday, a number of Catholics from all parts of the Mission, who felt interested in the Erection of a priest's house met at Carthage and cheerfully subscribed for that purpose but in-

stead of receiving thanks from the Rebel faction of Carthage Congregation, they received the most unsufferable abuse. They were taken from their seats and draged like fellons into the street. Next they abused the priest, Broke in the door to the vestry, took the Books and papers they found there and carried them off. Then they walked up on the alter with their hats on and shouted three cheers for Garabaldi.

All these indignities our worthy pastor and the virtuous members of the congregation patiently endured, recollecting that our saviour suffered far more without makeing any resistance.

Now, Rev. sir, I feel a sort of anticipated consolation in reflecting that the religion which gave us comfort in our early days and enabled us to endure the stroke of affliction and endeared us to each other and when we see our friends sinking into the earth fills us with the expectation that we rise again that we but sleep for a while to wake for ever.

But what kind of communion can we hold, what enterchange expect, what confidence place in that renegade Gallagher who is labouring under an incureable disease [pride?] and fond of his own blotches when the belief of Eternal justice is gone from the soul of man, horror and execration take up their abode. I have the honour to be Reverend Sir with profound respect your Faithful humble Servant/ [signed] Thomas Brady.

The brawl in St. James's also conjured up a spirit of malevolence, whose owner hinted at being a Catholic, but who sounded more like a brother of Orangemen and the son of Ulster Presbyterians. His vituperation against the pastor and the bishop set a record for anticlerical longwindedness. But, because it pulls almost all of the stops of Know Nothingism, let it lie here in its entirety.[80]

Sir/ I write to you for the purpose of informing you what my own sentiments are and to inform you what are the sentiments of three quarters of the Roman Catholics of the Carthage mission on the subject of your endorsement of the damnable villiannies committed by Michael E. Clarke among those to whom he was sent in the capacity of a Catholic priest.

It is scarcely necessary to inform you of the many crimes and iniquities that this clerical imposter has committed during the time that he had officiated as priest in this mission; for I am well aware that you have been informed of all these things repeatedly, and that is by the most reliable and trustworthy

Catholics in father Clarke's mission, that you are well aware of the injustice practiced against the members of the catholic church, and of the scandal given to all catholics thereby, and that this villianny and scandal is still farther aggravated by the fact that father Clarks conduct receives your official sanction and endorsement, in your utter refusal to remove him from this mission.

The causes stated above are the only inducements I had in addressing these lines to you. For I am not foolish enough to suppose that anything that can be said or written to you will have the effect of causing father Clarks removal from this place but merely for the purpose of informing you that Clark during his ministry here, has been a disgrace to that religion which it is our interest to respect and honour, and which has honoured you by elevating you to the high and holy office of one of its Bishops, in return for which, in connection with father Clark, you are a disgrace to the high office you hold — to the religion you profess — and the country that gave you birth.

For it is a notorious fact well known to both Catholics and Protestants that you have been informed, that father Clark has attempted in numerous instances to pervert the sacrament of confession to objects of his own personal interests such as speculating in bonds and mort[ag]es upon real estate, for purposes of personal revenge, for manufacturing witnesses to give in testimony in his favour in the numerous lawsuits in which he is steadily engaged in the business of horse-trading, the confessional box also furnishes him with all the information he wants with regard to the good points and comparative value of his parishioners horses.

Among the rest of his astounding feats as a Catholic Priest, [he] has been the Plaintiff in not [less] than thirty lawsuits during the last eight months, and he also [has] been the Defendant in as many as two or three suits in each of which he has committed perjury as many times, and as often as he thought it was necessary for his own interests to do so.

He has sold out the Catholic vote of his mission as often as he could find a purchase for it; and made his boast that before he came to this place he recieved one thousand dollars from O.B. Mattison of corruption money for his influence among the Catholic voters of Oneida County.

But of what use is it to multiply facts of this nature, and of which the above is but a mere outline, and the truth of which you are as well aware as is father Clark himself for Clark has never dared to challenge an investigation of those charges that are in every mans mouth in this part of the state.

You have been informed of those both when you were in Carthage and in Watertown, but you pretended that you did not believe them because they were not proved by witnesses under oath and yet you refused to give the individuals who made those statements time to produce the witnesses which they offered to do thus showing your anxiety to support father Clark in all his villianies whatever they may be.

He has collected large sums of money throug[h] his mission for the avowed purpose of building a priests house in the village of Carthage, yet no hous[e] has been built and he refuses to refund back the money to those from whom he has swindled for the said purpose of building, thereby enriching himself and his brother at the expense of those catholics who were decieved by his fair promises and serpent-like subtlety, for when he first came to this mission nearly all the catholics of this place considered him little less than an angel.

The last specimen of his piety that I have heard of occurred one week ago last Sunday in the villiage of Carthage where he assembled all the offscourings of Catholicity that he could find in Lewis, Jefferson and St. Lawrence Counties to take possession of the church in Carthage and elect trustees of a suitable degree of villiany who would be his pliant tools in any emergency that might arise, the result was what might have been expected, a fight took place in the church, during which pews were broken, a table was torn to pieces that the legs of it might be used as offensive weapons, the priest made his escape into the vestry, the door of which was smashed in, and the priest was obliged to make his escape bare-headed through the streets of Carthage [it was December 30] followed by the contemptible rabble that he had brought there for the purpose of taking possession of the church.

It is but proper to state that the uproar and noise attracted the attention of all the inhabitants of Carthage who were witnesses to the disgraceful proceedings from the windows, and roofs of their houses and from all of the streets leading to the church. With regard to this transaction I presume that you have had another version before this time for I have been told that Clark started for Albany the next day after its occurrence.

In conclusion I will now say that you are wholly responsible for all the scandal and disgrace that has fallen upon the church in this place for you are well aware, and this fact is as well known by protestants as by catholics. Your conduct in supporting the Priest in the manner has driven many from the church forever men ... who have spent their youth and middle age as catholics are now going down to the grave, with nothing but hatred in their bosoms for the faith in which their ancestors from time immemorial lived and died and for your comfort. I will tell you that all the writings and publications of the whole Protestant world combined would never be able to do this even father Clark himself could not do it; but when they seen the bishop supporting the Priest in his criminal designes they then bid farewell to the catholic church.

There are many who still remain in the church firmly as they ever did who declare firmly and emphatically that if Bishop McCloskey ever reaches heaven they do not want to go there. The truth of the matter is your reputation in this place is worse than that of any states Prison convict in the United States for it is the general remark in this place that a man who will support a murderer, a thief, and perjurer as you have done is none too good to commit the same crimes himself.

In conclusion I have only to say that I consider you to be a damnable and sacriligious villian who willingly sacrifices the whole catholic church rather than desert the Priests interests in anything he may undertake.

There is one conclusion that everyone has arrived in this place with regard to you; that is the money has been plundered from the poor catholics of this place by this clerical despot your agent, has been divided with you, that your decisions on this subject have been dictated by bribery and corruption instead of being the offspring of that disinterested regard that a Bishop should feel for the church of which he is a member./ [signed] Patrick F!ynn.

Vote selling, horse dealing, revenge, extortion, subornation and embezzlement were the business of the Church; old men were dying with hate in their hearts for the Faith; and the priest and the bishop were dividing the spoils. Can this have been anything else but the bile of an apostate?

Father Clarke went to Albany the day after the profanation of the temple. As soon as the bishop heard the news, he laid an interdict[81] on the Church of St. James and an excommunication on Patrick Walsh.[82] During the censure of the church, the pastor went on serving his other mission stations, but moved his ministry at Carthage from St. James's to the home of one Dennis Geraghty on Tannery Island in the Black River. There, on one Sunday a month, he said Mass, heard confessions and gave instruction to about one hundred. The rest of the time, he ministered at his brother William's farm in the *Irish Settlement,* where he lived. It was there that the bishop saw him soon after the sacrilege. At the farm, some of the anti-Clarkes asked this ordinary for another priest. "Father Clarke would not attend them," they said, or if he did, he "always came late,"[83] and a priest from another mission cost ten or fifteen dollars per visit, which was too high. But the bishop would not replace the priest whom they had driven from the sancturary. Nor would he do so when "Squire" O'Leary led a group to Albany.

Seven months later, in July of 1861, as secession raged in the United States, and royalism, nationalism and republicanism, in Italy, plotted against the heart of the Church, the man named Patrick Walsh, an immigrant from Ireland, a new American, and a lay trustee, in the village of Carthage, in a far corner of the state of New York, humbled himself before his bishop.[84]

After leaving your Lordship on last Monday I saw Mr. John Collins and made arrangements with him to call a meeting in the Church on next Sunday which is today and he was to send word round in his part of the town and I was to give them notice in the Irish Settlement. I did so and it was well understood that there was to be a meeting this morning at ten o'clock.

I went there at that hour and there was but few there and the Church was closed. I called on Mr. Haberer and requested him to open the Church and he refused saying he did not recognize my authority to have the Church opened. I told him he herd the Bishops direction and wish and if he did not open the Church he must expect to assume the responsibility. He said he would be no worse than he was. I went to the Church prepared with the writen resignation of myself and my Brother James of all offices in the Church which I herewith enclose to Your Lordship. My Lord you see the position in which I have placed myself for I blame no one and I hope you will see fit to remove the Censure pronounced against me and I solemnly promis never to interfear in Church maters again.

My Lord please accept my thanks for your kind treatment to me last Monday and believe me to be your effectually Humbled Servent./ [signed] Patrick Walsh.

We trust that this letter did no less for Patrick Walsh than standing barefoot in the snow did for Emperor Henry IV. Nevertheless, the interdict stayed, and new troubles boiled up. The Carthaginians were taken in by a pseudo-priest, and there was murmuring in Redwood against Father Clarke, who wrote to the bishop at the turn of 1862.[85]

In reply to your favour of the 19th of Dec. which came to hand today, asking the truth of a statement made in a letter from a Redwood correspondent, I beg to say that I have taken one Sunday from all the old Churches, that I might thereby be enabled to pay the indebtedness of the New, which I have accomplished sometime ago. [See note 86]

Furthermore, I refused to attend funerals unless they occurred whilst I was in the place. Perhaps this might be the great sin with Mr. Gallagher's influence who has a Dep[u]t[y] Chair Seller in that place. [See note 87]

I remember that Mr. Tass came for me to attend the funeral of a near relative of his, whilst I was engaged in duty at Montague, and I refused him and he left indignant. I saw nothing different at Red[wood] since only this man does not sing. [See note 88] I thought he might feel uncivill so I intend to see you before long and I am sure with regard to Carthage, I think there is a better appearance at present than there has been for some time.

The people are very uneasy and unhappy about their Church [St. James's of Carthage] & I think that it will be given over to them before long. I hear many rumours about the Key asking me what right has such a man with our Key. I tell them I have nothing to say on the matter.

I can see evidently great trouble. Walsh called on Mr. Wynn [a lawyer of Watertown] lately for advice about opening the church, and it appeared then that if it were necessary that the door would be forced in and [that we would] take possession and keep it for the people and then give it over to you. [See note 89] Mr. Wynn told me this on yesterday on my way from the North. We confered together and I told him to write to you for advice.

Those few bad men had a suspended Priest amongst them for a

while offering him five hundred dollars per year. He was very witty [sly?] he said you were very sorry for what you had done at Carthage & would soon revoke the sentence. [See note 90] That you sent him to examine the whole matter and he found them innocent, etc. He received a few dollars and decamped. His name H.H. McDonough here & Father O'Connor in other places, to be certain who he was, I cannot tell. He got drunk on their hands and told that he was a British deserter. They are now very still.

Any directions that you may have to give me regarding the opening the Church I will wait for it. Still I think it well to let them work for a while amongst themselves....

Finally, at a parley between the vicar general, Father John J. Conroy, and the trustees of St. James's, the church and the cathedral made peace. It was a simple arrangement: the promise of a new pastor in exchange for the church key in Father Clarke's hand. According to Middleton, Bishop McCloskey was grudging. He lifted the interdict "mainly at urgence of his vicar general."[91] In any case, it was on, or about, the Sunday of September 7, 1862, that Father Clarke said a mass for the congregation in St. James's. The interdict had lasted a year and nine months.[92]

Lay trusteeism was behind the trouble in Carthage, no doubt about it.[93] What made it worse was that one missioner had the care of a scattering of thousands. The priest's house and the pew rents and a frustrated boomerism were only the smoke puffs of a fire. It was pioneer life that best explains the Gallaghers and the Walshes. For years, in a forest clearing, in a church they had built themselves, without priests for months at a time, with Protestants wooing them off, they had huddled together in prayer, they had taught their children the Creed, they had struggled to keep the Faith, they had managed their church alone,.

Then came the decade of the fifties and the first permanent pastors in the Black River valley. But, ideas were on the wind.[94] Secessionism and republicanism and anticlericalism swirled about. The wind blew strong in Carthage. In 1856, every congregation of the mission had turned over its deeds to the bishop, except St. James's. It would not do so until 1872.[95] The men of Carthage were filled with a new wine. No priest would spend their money against their wish. No pastor would malign them without a lawsuit. They scorned episcopacy. They railed like Know Nothings. They cheered the enemy of Peter. They flaunted their hats before the Crucified.

They became, in the North Country, as notorious as their fourth-century, North African namesakes.⁹⁶

Following the interdict, Father Clarke was sent to Amsterdam, then, in time, to Schenectady, where he died in 1872. His life was marked by the Galilean irony. Outside the village of his youth, he was remembered as a holy priest, and marvelous cures were laid to him.⁹⁷ But the discord in Carthage did not die. In 1874, Bishop Wadhams of the new diocese of Ogdensburg, wearied by a mulish people, turned them over to the Augustinian Fathers. Then, finally, St. James's settled down to a quiet Catholic life.⁹⁸

¹*The Catholic Encyclopedia* (1913), VIII, 73-75.
²McNamara, *Diocese of Rochester,* p. 75, speaks only of the interdict of 1854-1855 on the Church of St. Louis in Buffalo. For the earlier one on that same church in 1843-1844, see Rev. Peter Leo Johnson and Rev. William Nellen (eds.) Letters of the Reverend Adelbert Inama, O. Praem.," *Wisconsin Magazine of History* XI, No. 4 (June 1928), p. 439. St. Patrick's of Rouses Point was interdicted for six months at sometime in 1875-1877. Smith, *Ogdensburg,* p. 169. For the interdict at Norwalk, Ohio, see Rev. John F. Byrne, C.SS.R., *The Redemptorist Centenaries* (Phila.: Dolphin Press, 1932), p. 77.
³Interdicts have differed in their prohibitions. I do not know exactly what took place at St. James's during the interdict, but my description is possible, even probable. *Catholic Encyclopedia,* VIII, 73-75: *New Catholic Encyclopedia* (1967), VII, 567-568.
⁴Smith, *Ogdensburg,* pp. 110-121 and *passim;* Rev. Thomas C. Middleton, O.S.A., "An early Catholic Settlement. The Third Founded in the State of New York, St. James of Carthage. 1785-1818-1898," *Records of the American Catholic Historical Society of Philadelphia,* X (1899), 17-77, 139-195.
⁵*N.Y., Census, 1865,* Table, pp. xlix-lvi.
⁶Michael Edward Clarke to McCloskey, College of Regiopolis, Kingston, Ont., May 12, 1847, Letterbox A24, NY; McFarland to McCloskey, Watertown, Sept. 11, 1847, Letterbox A25, NY; Middleton, "St. James of Carthage," pp. 153, 157.
⁷DeCourcy-Shea, *Catholic Church,* p. 559.
⁸Rev. P.F. (Francis P.) McFarland, "Early Catholic Affairs in Utica, N.Y.," *United States Catholic Historical Magazine* IV, No. 1 (1891-1893), 69. Father McFarland, pastor of St. John's, Utica, wrote this as a letter from Utica, on Feb. 12, 1856, to John Gilmary Shea. Although Shea's name does not appear in the letter, the information turns up in DeCourcy-Shea, *Catholic Church* pp. 473-474, and is credited there to Father McFarland. Father McFarland later became the Bishop of Hartford in 1858.
⁹McFarland, "Early Catholic Affairs," p. 69; Thomas P. Kearnan, "Nicholas Devereux: Model of Catholic Action," U.S. Cath. Hist. Soc., *Historial Records and Studies,* XXV (1935), 157. The Devereux and Father Clarke had a papal audience. They were in the company of Bishop John

Timon of Buffalo, who, as one of the bishops of the Church, had been invited to Rome in celebration of the promulgation of the dogma of the Immaculate Conception. We learn this from a historian who used the papers of the Devereux family but who erred in naming a Father Martin Clarke. Adalbert Callahan, *Medieval Francis in Modern America: The Story of Eighty Years, 1855-1935* (New York: Macmillan, 1936), pp. 31-32.

[10] He was appointed to St. James's on July 20, 1855, and his first entry in the register there was dated Aug. 1, 1855. Middleton, "St. James of Carthage," pp. 152, n., 155. Though Middleton is the best source on the affairs of the Catholics of Carthage, he lost track of Father Clarke between the time he left the village for school and the time he returned as the pastor of St. James's. Middleton was misled by another Rev. Michael Clarke, who served in Indiana in the forties. That Father Clarke appeared in the *Catholic Directory for 1843* to *1847*, as in the diocese of Vincennes. Our Father Clarke is listed in the *Catholic Directory for 1851* on, as in the diocese of Albany. Another source that goes astray, strangely, is Very Rev. James S.M. Lynch, *A Page of Church History in New York: St. John's, Utica* (probably Utica: privately printed, 1893), p. 81, which lists Father Clarke at St. John's from Oct. 28, 1850 to June 15, 1851. What is more puzzling is that *ibid.*, p. 2, shows a photo of a marble wall tablet at St. John's in memory of the dead priests of that church. The engraved dates for Father Clarke are "1850-1851." Now, the best source for the period of Father Clarke's assistantship at St. John's is the letter from Father McFarland to John Gilmary Shea, in McFarland, "Early Catholic Affairs," p. 69. Father McFarland was the pastor of St. John's in 1851-1858, and he also had known Father Clarke at least as early as 1847. Father McFarland said expressly that Father Clarke was the assistant at St. John's from 1851 to 1855, and he said so less than a year after the fact. The *Catholic Directory* for those years confirm the dates.

[11] Middleton, "St. James of Carthage," pp. 152-153, 168. Lynch, *St. John's, Utica*, p. gives the upper half of the same photo shown by Middleton.

[12] Middleton, "St. James of Carthage," p. 155, who used the records at that Church.

[13] Clarke to Rooney, Carthage, Jan. 12, 1856, AA.

[14] Clarke to McCloskey, Carthage, July 28, 1856, AA. Paragraphing is mine.

[15] The trouble over the deed for the church at Belfort, in Lewis Co., was due to the unwillingness of the landlord and patron there to convey the title to what was probably both the land and the church building to the bishop without an assurance that the property would be used for Catholic services. Patrick Somerville Stewart to McCloskey, Carthage, Aug. 7, 1855, AA. Stewart was the agent for Vincent Le Ray de Chaumont, an émigré and a land promoter in the North Country. For Le Ray de Chaumont, see Clarke, *Emigrés, passim*. For the church at Belfort, see Rev. Berard Vogt, O.F.M., *A Historical Monument of Northern New York's Pioneer Days: Souvenir of the Diamond Jubilee of St. Vincent de Paul's Church, Belfort, N.Y.* (n.p.: Privately printed, 1919). The congregation were French Alsatians, who began to worship together around 1832, and the church was built in 1843-1844.

[16] Raymond Walters, Jr., and Philip G. Walters, "David Parish: York State Land Promoter," *New York History*, XXVI, No. 2 (April, 1945), 146-161.

[17]On James Sterling, a local iron manufacturer and land promoter, see Franklin Benjamin Hough, *A History of Jefferson County* (Albany: Joel Munsell, 1854), pp. 217-228.
[18]DeCourcy-Shea, *Catholic Church,* p. 472. It is also quoted in Middleton, "St. James of Carthage," p. 157.
[19]*N.Y. Census, 1855,* pp. 471-473.
[20]Middleton, "St. James of Carthage," pp. 35-36, 143-145, 191-193; Smith, *Ogdensburg,* pp. 110-154.
[21]Hough, *Jefferson County,* pp. 83, 217-228, 299-303.
[22]Middleton, "St. James of Carthage," pp. 182-183.
[23]*N.Y., Census; 1855,* pp. 445-476; Hough, *Jefferson County,* chap. IV.
[24]John Clarke to McCloskey, Carthage, Sept. 20, 1850, Letterbox A24, NY.
[25]Spalding, *Religious Mission of the Irish People, passim,* for the Irish. For the Germans, see Rev. Colman J. Barry, O.S.B., *The Catholic Church and German Americans* (Wash., D.C.: Cath. Univ. Amer. Press, 1953), pp. 24-25. For the belief in the French Canadians as a Chosen People, see Bishop Louis de Goesbriand, *Les Canadiens des Etats-Unis* (a pamphlet, prob. published at St. Albans, Vermont, by the *Protecteur Canadien,* in 1889), p. 10. The parallel between the Diaspora and European Catholic emigration is implicit in Shaughnessy, *Immigrant,* p. 9 and *passim.*
[26]Potter, *Golden Door,* Part I; William V. Shannon, *The American Irish* (New York: Macmillan, 1963), chap. I.
[27]*Freeman's Journal,* July 26, 1851.
[28]When Father F.P. McFarland, the pastor of Watertown, told the bishop in 1850 that Father Michael C. Power, the first resident pastor of St. James's of Carthage, was living there with a "respectable Catholic family," he meant the Gallaghers. McFarland to McCloskey, Watertown, March 20, 1850, Letterbox A25, NY; Middleton, "St. James of Carthage," p. 149.
[29]Gallagher to McCloskey, Carthage, July 12, 1857, AA. Italics are Gallagher's. Paragraphing is mine.
[30]They had done so in 1823. Middleton, "St. James of Carthage," pp. 71-74.
[31]*Ibid.,* p. 185.
[32]In 1960, its population was 4,216. Thompson, *Geography,* p. 513.
[33]Mrs. M.C. Gallagher to McCloskey, Carthage, Sept. 4, 1857, Letterbox A24, NY.
[34]Middleton, "St. James of Carthage," pp. 149, 152-153; Gallagher to McCloskey, Carthage, Sept. 5, 1857, Letterbox A24, NY.
[35]Gallagher to McCloskey, Carthage, July 12, 1857, AA.
[36]Middleton, "St. James of Carthage," p. 158.
[37]*Ibid.,* pp. 157-158.
[38]*Ibid.,* p. 169, n.
[39]Gallagher to McCloskey, Carthage, Sept. 5, 1857, Letterbox A24, NY.
[40]Haberer, likely was the choirmaster whom Gallagher had once advertised for. If so, he was also, probably, a cabinet maker. *Freeman's Journal,* July 26, 1851.
[41]Stewart, as has already been noted herein, was the land agent for Le Ray de Chaumont, the local magnate. Stewart was also a lawyer and a Methodist. Middleton, "St. James of Cathage," p. 33, n.
[42]It was a small, comfortable, frame building, which Father Roche probably

built in 1852, the year he came to Carthage. He later sold it, probably after Father Clarke left Carthage, to the trustees of St. James's. It was then used as the rectory till 1896, when it was torn down to make way for a convent. *Ibid.,* p. 152.

[43]*Ibid.,* 159.

[44]In the archives of the Archdiocese of New York, there are a score of the most vitriolic letters imaginable, written between January of 1848 and June of 1849, by Fathers James Mackey and Hugh Quigley in the course of their feud over the line between their jurisdictions of Ogdensburg and Waddington. Peace came only with the transfer of Father Quigley to Schaghticoke, in Rensselaer Co. Father Mackey remained at St Mary's of Ogdensburg to become the "patriarch of the Diocese of Ogdensburg," until he died in 1883. Walworth, *Wadhams,* pp. 165-166, tells an anecdote about him. When Bishop Edgar P. Wadhams came to Ogdensburg in 1872 with the intention of making St. Mary's his procathedral, Father Mackey, who had been there for 31 years, made an announcement of his arrival, which Father Walworth paraphrases as follows: "God knows I needed help but could not get it. At last a coadjutor has arrived." The old pastor was permitted to rule on at St. Mary's, while the bishop "coadjuted."

[45]Clarke to McCloskey, Carthage, Oct. 23, 1857, AA.

[46]Gallagher to McCloskey, Carthage, Oct. 26, 1857, AA.

[47]Clarke to McCloskey, Carthage, Dec. 8, 1857, AA.

[48]Clarke to McCloskey, Carthage, Jan. 12, 1858, AA.

[49]Father Augustus J. Thebaud, S.J., was the pastor of St. Joseph's, in Troy. Since Carthage was off the beaten path, it is probable that he was sent there by the bishop.

[50]Copy of the Proceedings of the Case, dated Jan. 5, 1858, AA, cited and quoted by Taylor, "Catholicism in Northern New York," pp. 191-192. I have assumed that the trial took place on Jan. 4th and 5th, because they were a Monday and Tuesday.

[51]Middleton, "St. James of Carthage," pp. 27, 34-35, 62-65, 145.

[52]In 1898, Father Power was alive and well in Wappinger's Falls. *Ibid.,* p. 152.

[53]*Ibid.,* pp. 159-160.

[54]*Ibid.,* p. 160.

[55]*Ibid.,* p. 160.

[56]Neary to McCloskey, Carthage, Jan. 30, 1858, Letterbox A25, NY.

[57]Clarke to McCloskey, Carthage, May 30, 1858, Letterbox A24, NY. When Bp. J.J. Conroy came in 1867, there had not been a confirmation in ten or more years. Middleton, "St. James of Carthage," p. 175, n.

[58]In 1853, the Oblate Fathers came from Canada to establish a major mission at St. Peter's, in Plattsburgh, and several mission stations elsewhere in the North Country, incuding one at Redford. They found 100 French Canadian families at Redford in 1853, and built the small church of Our Lady of the Assumption for them in 1854. In 1853-1869, at Redford, they performed 1,425 baptisms and 206 marriages. They attended there once a month, and collected an average of $200 a year. Rev. Gaston Carrière, O.M.I., *Histoire Documentaire de la Congrégation des Missionnaires Oblats de Marie-Immaculée dans L'Est du Canada* (5 vols.; Ottawa: Editions de L'Université D'Ottawa, 1957-1963), IV, 211-213.

[59]Gallagher to McCloskey, Carthage, June 13, 1858, Letterbox A24, NY.
[60]Among the first officers of the "Carthaginian Library" were the Frenchmen (continental), Claudius Silvain Quilliard and John D. Balmat. The library was sold at a public auction on June 14, 1845. That was at the start of the heavy influx of Irish and French Canadians. The sale of the library suggests the wane of belles-lettres in Carthage with the dwindling of the literate first settlers. Middleton, "St. James of Carthage," p., 39, n.
[61]Galleciez to McCloskey, Carthage, Jan. 7, 1859, Letterbox A24, NY.
[62]O'Leary to McCloskey, Carthage, May 25, 1860, AA. On the details of O'Leary's life, see Middleton, "St. James of Carthage," p. 163, n.
[63]Stewart to Clarke, Carthage, Dec. 31, 1860, AA.
[64]Edmund B. Wynn to Clarke, Watertown, April 14, 1864, Letterbox A25, NY. Wynn was the attorney who represented Father Clarke in that case.
[65]Middleton, "St. James of Carthage," p. 160.
[66]Dignan, *Church Property,* pp. 64-66. For the text of the Act, see Appendix V.
[67]Patrick Flynn to McCloskey, Lowville, Jan. 12, 1860 (read 1861), AA.
[68]Middleton, "St. James of Carthage," pp. 160-162.
[69]*Ibid.,* p. 167, n.
[70]*Ibid.,* pp. 160-161.
[71]*Ibid.,* pp. 34, 162, n.; Thomas Brady to McCloskey, Carthage, Jan. 1, 1861, AA.
[72]Middleton, "St. James of Carthage," pp. 46-63.
[73]*Ibid.,* pp. 161-162.
[74]Thomas Brady to McCloskey, Carthage, Jan. 1, 1861; AA; Patrick Flynn to McCloskey, Lowville, Jan. 12, 1860 (read 1861), AA.
[75]Stewart to Clarke, Carthage, Dec. 31, 1860, AA.
[76]Thomas Brady to McCloskey, Carthage, Jan. 1, 1861, AA. Garibaldi was then, perhaps, "the best-known name in the world," as one who made war against the Papal States and who called priests "the scourge of Italy" and the Pope "the negation of God." Christopher Hibbert, *Garibaldi and His Enemies* (Boston: Little, Brown and Co., 1966), p. 354 and *passim.*
[77]"He left the altar with Mass unfinished," says Middleton "St. James of Carthage," p. 162, although after the last communion. His informants recalled this detail after thirty-six years. I cannot believe that the pastor began the proceedings before the *"ite, missa est."*
[78]Stewart to Clarke, Carthage, Dec. 31, 1860, AA.
[79]Thomas Brady to McCloskey, Carthage, Jan. 1, 1861, AA.
[80]Patrick Flynn to McCloskey, Lowville, Jan. 12, 1860 (read 1861), AA. Lowville is fifteen miles south of Carthage.
[81]Taylor, "Catholicism in Northern New York," pp. 189, 195, in the absence of written evidence dating from that period, suggests that there was no interdict, and that the services in St. James's ceased, because the rebels closed the church. But Middleton, "St. James of Carthage,' pp. 70, 168, 186, used the word "interdict" once and the word "schism" twice, and he got his information from about a half-dozen eyewitnesses. Smith, *Ogdensburg,* pp. 111, 118, used the word "interdict" twice, and indicated, here and there in his history, that he too had interviewed many of the old surviving Catholics.
[82]Surely on Richard Gallagher and James Walsh as well. Patrick Walsh to McCloskey, Carthage, July 7, 1861, AA.

[83] Middleton, "St. James of Carthage," pp. 162-163.
[84] Walsh to McCloskey, Carthage, July 7, 1861, AA.
[85] Clarke to McCloskey, Carthage, Jan. 3, 1862, AA.
[86] Father Clarke had many troubles at Redwood, says Middleton, "St. James of Carthage," p. 168, n., but does not say what they were. St. Francis Xavier was built in Redwood around 1849. Hough, *Jefferson County,* p. 84. In 1857, Father Clarke was building churches at Montague and Lewisburgh, in Lewis Co. *Catholic Directory of 1858,* pp. 136-142. It seems from Father Clarke's letter of Jan. 3, 1862, that he took one Sunday collection from the congregations with the older churches, and used the money to pay off the debts on the new churches at Montague and Lewisburgh. This, of course, made for hard feelings at Redwood.
[87] Gallagher manufactured furniture, perhaps just chairs, and had an agent at Redwood. See *Freeman's Journal,* July 26, 1851, for his ad for a cabinet maker and a choir master, which meant a German, in those days. See below, pp. 289-290.
[88] Apparently, Tass, a German, was absenting himself from the choir at Redwood, in pique.
[89] Evidently, Gallagher and his partisans had had possession of St. James's since the Sunday of the fight, when they nailed and locked the church shut. Patrick and James Walsh were now on the side of the pastor and the bishop. Stewart to Clarke, Carthage, Dec. 31, 1860, AA; Walsh to McCloskey, Carthage, July 7, 1861, AA.
[90] What sentence? Here is further proof of an interdict.
[91] Middleton, "St. James of Carthage," p. 164.
[92] The duration is probable. The interdict was in effect on Jan. 3, 1862, with no sign of a near ending. Clarke to McCloskey, Jan. 3, 1862, Carthage, AA. Father Clarke's last entry in the register there was on Sept. 7, 1862, a Sunday, for a marriage. He was promptly transferred when the interdict was lifted. Middleton, "St. James of Carthage," pp. 164, 168. Smith, *Ogdensburg,* p. 118, says that the interdict was not lifted until Rev. Conroy became the bishop in 1865. But reason and the evidence are against him.
[93] Middleton, "St. James of Carthage," pp. 164-167, denies this. Smith, *Ogdensburg,* pp. 116-120, affirms its. Middleton expressly contradicts Smith on this point. He argues that, in Carthage in 1896, there was not a record or a recollection of a trustee meeting or trustee interference in church affairs in the time of trouble. He dismisses, without a word of explanation, his own reference to "side-issues...of semi-economic character." He asserts that the cause of the five years of strife was no more than the aesthetics of the site of the rectory. But, he did not have the use of the Cardinal McCloskey Papers, and could not look behind the scenes, as we have done. Besides that, Middleton, overlooks the significance of the O'Conor Act of 1863, which he himself says was designed as a preventive of similar conflicts between clergy and people. For the relation of that Act to lay trusteeism, and Dignan, *Church Property,* pp. 207-209.
[94] There was not a Catholic congregation that did not have its newspaper readers. Consider the *Freeman's Journal.* Published every Saturday in New York City, for Catholics and the Irish especially, its every issue offered four pages of foreign news, two pages of national and local news, and two pages

of ads. The weekly list of the most recent subscribers with addresses, on page 8, showed an amazing penetration of the diocese. See *Freeman's Journal,* April 2, 1853.

[95] Middleton, "St. James of Carthage," p. 65, n.; "Real Estate Owned by R.C.D.," AA.

[96] Father John Talbot Smith, who was born in Saratoga Springs in 1855, and became the pastor of St. Patrick's of Rouses Point in 1883, had not one good word to say about the "wild tribes of Carthage," whom he identified as Irish. Smith, *Ogdensburg,* pp. 39, 110-121. Father Middleton, an Augustinian, whose order had the mission of the Black River Valley after 1874, writes avowedly to correct Smith's picture, and to shift some of the blame from the Carthaginians to Father Clarke. Middleton, "St. James of Carthage," pp. 165-168, 185-187.

[97] Lynch, *St. John's, Utica,* pp. 82-82. Smith, *Ogdensburg,* p. 39, got the impression from the old inhabitants that he had been eccentric. He was also stubbornly litigious. As late as July of 1863, he was suing a layman of St. James's over a private matter of twenty dollars, and apparently, he was willing to dredge up the past troubles in order to do so. Nor would he heed the request of his successor in Carthage, Rev. J.M. Barry, to drop the suit for the sake of peace. Barry to McCloskey, Carthage, July 20, 1863, AA; William Allen to Clarke, Carthage, April 16, 1864, Letterbox A24, NY. Allen had been Clarke's sexton at Carthage, and was apparently claiming some wages from him.

[98] To be fair to the people of St. James's, it seems that they responded with enthusiasm to the ministry of Father Barry in 1863-1869. Middleton argued that the trouble in Carthage had been due to the personalities of its pastors, especially that of Father Clarke. Middleton, "St. James of Carthage," pp. 168-185.

CHAPTER XIII

A CROWN OF THORNS IN UTICA

In Utica, during the twenty years of turmoil before the Civil War, lay trusteeism was chronic. The Irish and the *Canadiens* were behind it elsewhere, but in that city, it was the turn of the Germans of St. Joseph's. They were the oldest of the congregations of Catholics of their tongue in up-state New York, dating from the thirties.[1] Soon after they bought a church in 1840,[2] the quarreling began amongst them. They had five pastors in the next five years.[3] In 1844, a Benedictine came to them from the Tyrol, the Reverend Florian Schwenninger. Father Florian he was called, because he was a monk. Seventeen months later, St. Joseph's was at it again, as the pastor of St. John's, Father Joseph Stokes, reported to the coadjutor, Bishop McCloskey.[4]

I deferred writing until the German priest, the Rev. Mr. Florian, who has been absent for a week, should return to the City. I asked for Father Martin [See note 5] in this place on a short visit, to see Masseth [a trustee] and others with whom he was acquainted and see to reconcile matters. He did so at my request, and the German priest and the Trustees of his church met and I hope will agree better for the time to come. Had I known the real state of things I should not have consented to the German priest assembling his people in our church. But I was led to believe that violence of the worst kind would have been offered and that the priest's life was in danger. If what I hear now be true, no such danger was to be apprehended. Henceforth the Germans may settle their own differences. I shall not again interfere.

Reverend Mr. Florian has not perhaps been as prudent in his public discourses as he might have been, according to the report of the Germans, but in this respect he will no doubt improve. The priest I find is at liberty to open his church for his people tomorrow. And as this is the case, he shall certainly not be permitted to assemble his congregation in ours....

That a priest was threatened in life and limb, in the United States, in 1845, by his own Catholics, was not so farfetched as it sounds. After all, Father Stokes believed it for a while, and to Father Florian, it was fact. His eyes had been opened to that sort of danger shortly after his coming to America in July of 1844. As a guest of Father Zachary Kunze, the pastor of St. John's, in New York City, Father Florian had heard from his host's own lips about the most recent fray in that congregation between pastor and people. It had happened at Pentecost. Two hundred armed men had tried to storm the priest's house in order to run him out of town. They were from the parish, Father Florian later recollected, although he did not say that some of them might have been non-Catholic. If it had not been for their wives, who had forewarned the priest, and had blocked his doorway with their bodies, who knows the fate that would have befallen Father Kunze. The mob fired at his windows, and the priest was frightened into shooting off his own gun by accident. "I have seen the holes in the wall myself," wrote Father Florian later, who did not doubt the story.[6]

Still, it is likely that Father Florian spoke rashly from the pulpit. A malcontent in the monastery, he found nothing to please him in a world of change. Here, the Stations of the Cross were untraditional. There, the people did not hold their arms correctly in church. He had a rap on the knuckles for all who crossed his path, Jews, women, Irishmen, Americans, priests and bishops. His prior was stingy. Bishop Hughes of New York was inhospitable. But the Tyrolean lavished his gall on the vicar general for the Germans of New York, Father John Stephen Raffeiner, who had recruited him for the diocese. That one was a liar, a cheat and a smuggler.[7]

To Father Florian, the lay trustees were as bad as the nativists, or worse. They stole from their churches. He cited St. Nicholas's of New York City, a German congregation. There, he said, the trustees had once recorded a false expenditure of two hundred dollars to remove the snow from the roof of the church. In an Irish parish, the trustees had done the same, in the amount of one thousand dollars, for Mass wine, which they never bought. That, the Benedictine observed, at a wholesale price of ten cents a bottle, was enough to keep the eight trustees drunk for a year.[8]

How did they get away with it? The missioner explained:[9]

At the end of the year two or more members of the parish are elected to review the accounts. If these two say they find everything in good order then everything is considered settled and that is the end of it. Nothing can be done with the administration. The people in the parish are given only the total amount for expenses and income. Nothing is said about different items. By clever methods in elections they are able to see that only such persons are elected who are in agreement with their system. Often the trustees hold their offices for several years. The books are in the hands of secretary and the treasurer so that even a new trustee does not have a chance to check over previous accounts. Such frauds can be discovered only when the treasurer or secretary are changed, but by that time it is too late. The previous accounts are usually reviewed and declared to be acceptable and consequently the accountants go free. In order to protect them the new accountants keep quiet, or sometimes perhaps they intend to do the same thing themselves.

To the monk from Austria, a land of clerical privilege, lay trusteeism was an abomination. [10]

The trustees think that they are the legal superiors of the priest and therefor have the right to watch over the pastor's actions, his behavior, his work, his housekeeping, etc. However, they cannot do this themselves because they have their own work to do. The most suitable persons therefore are the janitor and the teacher since they are always around the priest. The trustees [feel] that the janitor and the teacher should never be too friendly with the pastor but should stay on the side of the parish (that is, the trustees) since they are paid by the parish and not by the pastor. The teacher should therefore be a policeman and a spy for the trustees. It was therefore a capital sin on the part of the teacher if he did not inform the trustees about everything that happened in the priest's house ... The whole trustee system is against the Church. It is heretical and dangerous for parishes, a real evil, the greatest source of suffering in the American Church ...

In spite of the fact that the Catholics of St. Nicholas's of New York City had once "lassoed" Father Raffeiner inside the church, and had hauled him out at the end of the rope, Father Florian observed in 1854:[11]

Priests are not persecuted any more in the same way they were during penal days, but by more refined methods such as ridicule, libel, contempt, false witnesses, threats, and unjust lawsuits.

He was remembering his six years in the diocese of Albany.

In 1845, the young city of Utica, with four wards, had a population of 12,190, of whom 1,784 were aliens not yet naturalized, 7,365 were born in New York State, 955 in New England, 3,024 on British soil, 105 in France, and 401 in the several German states. There were 1,054 children in 14 common or public schools, with an average daily attendance of 767, and 951 pupils in 29 private schools, which may, or may not have included the boys' academy and the female seminary. Of businesses, there were 118 retail and 36 wholesale, which probably included the 42 inns and taverns, 2 gristmills, 4 iron works, 3 tanneries, 2 breweries and an oilcloth factory. There were 216 merchants, 41 manufacturers, 1,172 mechanics, 68 lawyers, 29 doctors, and 49 farmers. The farmers had 792 cows that produced 26,852 pounds of butter in that year.

Religion was represented by 4 Baptist churches, 2 Episcopalian, 3 Presbyterian, 1 Congregational, 3 Methodist, 1 Dutch Reformed and 2 Roman Catholic. One of the Presbyterian churches cost $34,450, the Dutch Reformed was valued at $25,200, and St. John's, the Irish Catholic church stood in third place at $20,000. St. Joseph's, the German Catholic Church, was worth $1,150 plus $200 for the land.

To judge by the New York Census of 1845,[12] the clergyman's lot was not a wealthy one. Of the 25 of them reported as residing in the city,[13] 22 reported salaries that totaled $9,280. Although this did not include their perquisites and housing, probably, it reveals an average cash income, in that year, of $421, which was far less than the $600 that was fixed for the Catholic priests, but that they often did not get.[14]

From this canal port in central New York, in September of 1846, Father Florian, a Benedictine monk turned missioner, wrote a long letter to his abbot in the Tyrolean Alps.[15] "In one year here, I have lived through many years." Here is the substance of the description by Father Florian of his crown of thorns at St. Joseph's during that one year. Nine saloon keepers, some of them trustees of the church, made his life miserable day after day. It was not only over the affairs of the church, but also because Father Florian was preaching against their sale of hard liquor and their doing it on Sunday.[16] Their ringleader was Joseph Masseth, a rich revolutionary from Alsace.[17] He and the others had already driven away two priests from St.

Joseph's, and now it was Father Florian's turn.

On June 4, 1845, a pastoral letter came from Bishop Hughes, who wished the pastors to see to it that the trustees were worthy and that the management of church monies was careful.[18] The bishop told Father Florian, in a personal note, that the pastoral applied to St. Joseph's. The saloon keepers rushed to defend their authority as trustees, and the congregation split into "sheep" and "goats." One hundred and twenty families of "sheep" followed the pastor, while the sixty families of "goats," or "riff-raff," at the heels of Masseth, reminded Father Florian of the mob that had once shouted: "Let him be crucified!" So things stood in November of 1845.

Since the term of office of the trustees[19] was to end on Easter Sunday, that is, April 12, 1846, the shepherd and his "sheep" were willing to bide their time. But the "goats" campaigned for re-election. They schemed to force out Father Florian, and, if the bishop did not give them another priest, they were going to sell the church and divide the money. The trustees broke their oaths of office; violence became their habit; the "goats" threatened bloodshed in the church. Twice, Father Florian had to say Mass in the Irish church of St. John's. So the monk wrote his abbot.

The trustees also tried to starve him out. For three months, he did not get a penny from them. He finally told this to the congregation, and, after that, they gave their contributions directly to him. The "goats" attacked his house at night. They sent him letters, which he tore up unread. They threatened him with death. "I had to flee to the house of the Irish priest." The "sheep" then mounted a twenty-four-hour guard on him for weeks. "O, topsy-turvy world!"

Next, the trustees locked the church. Between November 24 and December 13, in 1845, and again between January 29 and March 18, in 1846, Father Florian said Mass in his schoolroom, with the permission of the bishop. Then, the trustees served the pastor, in January of 1846, with "a decree of dismissal" by an attendant of the civil court.[20] But the pastor stayed put. Finally, they filed an information against him before the justice of the peace that he had stolen $100 in church goods. The story behind that was that they had placed in his hands a monstrance, a chalice and a ciborium, which they now wanted back, but he was not about to give up. He had to appear in court on March 13, 1846. On his side were most of the Germans of St. Joseph's, the Irish of St. John's, the entire city, the bishop, and, last but not least, God Himself. Thus wrote the monk.

Now, God reached out His hand. Already, in March of 1845, one of the "goats" had hanged himself. Next, three of the trustees fell ill. Then, the man who had threatened the pastor with death died himself, three weeks after his "conversion." Finally, while the trial was underway, the judge's child sickened and died, and the judge postponed the trial. Right after the adjournment, a fight started at the court house. The "sheep" scattered the "goats" pell-mell, and broke their spirit for a while. As a result, the trustees dropped the charges against the pastor, and handed the church over to him. "With my victory, temperance also won the day." The saloon keepers were prohibited from doing business on Sunday, and from selling hard liquor at any time.[21]

But, when the bishop came for confirmation, and would not give the trustees any satisfaction, they resumed the struggle. They sued the pastor again, on September 7, 1846, "over nothing." Father Florian had to call upon two lawyers to represent him. One was Francis Kernan,[22] a son-in-law of the Catholic magnate and philanthropist of Utica, Nicholas Devereux. The other was a "Yankee" by the name of Wallrath, who asked for prayers instead of a fee.[23] At some point in the course of these events, the trustees tried to sell St. Joseph's back to one of the Methodists from whom they had bought it, but he turned them down. "'Look what honest non-Catholics there are here!"

Now, in September of 1846, Father Florian ended his long letter to the abbot in the Tyrol on a note of triumph.

> The complete victory, the deliverance of our church and congregation, the immunity of the episcopal and priestly rights, the peace of the pastor and the rest that belongs to this quarrel and triumph, must be credited to the Lord.

A year-and-a-half, in March of 1848, Father Florian worte to his abbot again.[24] Now, he bubbled with optimism and jocularity. Through his eyes, we glimpse the dangers to Catholicism in Europe from the "revolutionary Sans-culottes," which he read about in the newspapers. But we hear the note of satisfaction in his remark that the United States had agreed to respect the rights of the Church in the Mexican Cessions.

In central New York, the Faith was prospering. Utica alone had over a thousand German Catholics. The congregation of St. Joseph's had doubled in four years; the church was too small; and he had to binate and preach twice on Sundays and holydays. He was glad to have turned over Constableville (in Lewis County) to two resident pastors, a German and an Irishman. But there were two hundred souls in the east of his territory, whom he had visited only twice in 1847, and was now hoping to treat as a mission station. On the other hand, there were Germans to the north (Lewis County) and to the south (Madison County) whom he simply had no time for.[25]

In 1846, he had formed a congregation at Rome, with the bishop's approval and the support of Father Raffeiner, the vicar general for the Germans, but over the opposition of the Irish priest (Father William Beecham, eventually known as "the Pope of Rome"), who would not let Father Florian make a collection in his preserve. The Tyrolese missioner, however, did not let that stop him. With his own money, he bought the land in 1846, built the church of St. Mary in 1847, already owed one hundred dollars on it, and was expecting the cost to reach two thousand dollars. The lot was 80 by 150, and the church was 40 by 60. "What a joy it was for me, when I was able to celebrate the Mass on the third Sunday in Advent of 1847 for the first time in *my* church." As for the financial burden, he left that to God. Now, the congregation of St. Mary's numbered three hundred, and he attended them once a month.

Father Florian asked his abbot to pass along a word of advice to those who had been writing to ask whether they could make their fortunes in America. It was fine for those who had grown up among Protestants and were firm in the Faith. But America had far too few priests, was filling up with secret societies[26] in the mold of Freemasonry, and the Tyrolese, in particular, might fall away. Another fact of life in America for Catholics was contagion. As immigrants and residents along the waterways, they dwelt in the path of plague. Eleven of Father Florian's congregation in Utica, most of them young, had died of smallpox since the New Year.

But the missioner had his health (he was forty-one), and kept his sense of humor. He jested about democracy in America. "If the people are sovereign, then everybody is an emperor. Good gracious! Ten million emperors and ten million empresses. What a majestic people." Come to think of it, he, Father Florian, was an emperor too, so he sent his regards to his brother, Ferdinand, the emperor of Austria. In sum, things were looking up for the Holy Faith in New York, "praised be Jesus Christ and Mary." So wrote Father Flrian to his abbot.

The snake lingered in the garden of St. Joseph's, however. In 1847, or early 1848, the pastor and the trustees were at each other again — it may have been over the pew rents.[27] — and both sides asked Bishop McCloskey to Utica. He came, with the German pastor of Syracuse, Father Theodore Noethen, as an interpreter. At the hearing, in which the bishop took care to be impartial, the trustees did not make their charges stick. Later, the bishop spoke to the congregation. "Though his appearance was calm, his words were full of fire." He defended the priesthood; he tried to unite the church. Then, he announced a retreat. For three days, ending with a High Mass, three German missioners preached four times a day, filling St. Joseph's in spite of a stormy February. Wrote an unidentified correspondent to the *Freeman's Journal:*"A great many were reconciled with God, their neighbors, and moreover, with their pastor."[28]

But, it was wishful thinking. In June of 1849, Father Joseph Stokes, the Irish pastor of St. John's, Utica, where Father Florian and his "sheep" had once found a sanctuary, wrote to tell the bishop that Father Noethen had gone back to Syracuse after having spelled Father Florian at St. Joseph's for two weeks, and that the Benedictine had now returned to his *via crucis.* "The Germans appear quiet just now. How long they will continue so is uncertain."[29]

A week later, Father Noethen, the pastor of St. Mary's (German) of Syracuse, and the future vicar general for the Germans of the diocese, sent a report to the bishop on St. Joseph's.[30]

Last week I finished my exchange at Utica, and I hope I brought some common sense amongst those who continually persecute the priest; it is however very difficult to manage those fellows, particularly for this following reasons:
1. Masseth is the head of a secret germ[an] society assembled in his house weekly, and all its members are against Father Florian, as Masseth commands them.
2. Masseth & Co. want to govern the church, priest etc. They always say: "We bought the church, and have nothing to say." Besides I may add that those men have had and have yet *Seven Trustees,* in spite of the Bishop and the statutes of the Diocese. [See note 31]
3. This noble compagnie requests *the Bishop to do his duty;* but as he did not do his duty last winter [February, 1848, when the bishop came to Utica], in keeping F[ather] Florian, instead of sending his off, *they will do now what the Bishop did not do;* so they have said publicly; hence the prosecution of the law against F. Florian, and the buying of the judgement.
4. Masseth & Co. want to have a priest (no regular, no Jesuit, no Redemptorist, no Benedictine, etc., friar, but a secular) after their own style. Masseth has a relative in Elsas [Alsace], a

secular priest, à la Roth [Francis X. Roth, at Salina, Syracuse, Manlius, in 1845-1846], whose name is Oster, who would like to come to this country, and be stationed amongst his friends in Utica; as soon as they knew his design, they wrote an invitation to him; he may come, as they would procure a mission for him amongst them, etc; hence the persecution against F. Florian. That priest however does not venture as yet to come *on such terms!*

5. Their character as Christians, if they deserve this name may be marked by the following latin verses:
Colligunt floribus ex venenosis dulce apes mel,
Hi vero venenum, floribus ex melleis;
Omnia subvertunt de his, quae loquitur pastor,
Contraria eligunt, rixas habeant. [See note 32]

6. A particular reason why they cannot be managed, is because they have seats in Revd. Stokes' church [St. John's, Utica], and *still trouble* the German priest and his congregation, middling [meddling] with their affairs, though they properly do not belong any more to the german congregation. If they only kept their seats [at St. Joseph's] and would be quiet, every thing would be in order; no trouble at all would be in the german congregation. This fact was also acknowledged by Revd. Mr. Stokes, who told them not to come any more into his church, as they, having seats in his church, still persecute the german priest, etc. [See note 33]

7. They do not believe in eternal punishment, as several of them had courage enough to make this assertion publicly before me and others; this is, so they say, an invention of priests, as they do not believe it themselves, etc; and still they want to go to confession, in order to escape hell! You see how far they are!

8. This reasons, methink, Monseigneur, are strong enough to convince anybody how bad those men are, and how difficult to be managed; supernatural aid is here required, as no man is capable to change them only one inch from their unchristian life. I ordered, accordingly, during my presence, the prayers of teh whole congregation to implore the Almighty. .He may in his mercy and infinite goodness look upon them, and united them all into one! May God grant us this grace and this our prayer!....

There they were, laid out, some of the thorns in Father Florian's crown, the heresy of universalism and a secret radical society. It would have been miraculous if those Germans had escaped the fashions of forty-eight. They bedevilled their priest with a civil suit to try to force him out. "We bought the church," they said, "and have nothing to say."

In the meantime, Father Florian had the problems that were usual to the mission in those days in upstate New York. For example, two first cousins at St. Mary's, in Rome, wanted to marry each other, and were petitioning for a dispensation, through the pastor, who explained the circumstances to the bishop.[34] Their families had come from the Kingdom of Württemberg, where Catholics were in the minority, where, therefore, mates outside the prohibited degrees of consanguinity were in short supply, and where marriage within the prohibited degrees was common. The situation at St. Mary's, in Rome, was the same. More than that, the male cousin had to support his old and infirm parents in his house as well as a deaf-mute brother of sixteen, and where was the woman who would take that on. The pastor pointed to yet another reason. He had already talked the man out of marrying a Protestant woman, but if he could not take his Catholic cousin to wife, he was sure to wed outside the Church. One girl in the family had already done so. Father Florian closed with: "I invoke Kindness of Your Lordship to have patience with these souls...."

To return to trusteeism, we now hear from Father Noethen, in August of 1849, a surprising bit of news about Father Florian.[35]

I have been for few hours last Tuesday at Utica, and seeing Father Florian about some thing, I heard from him that he will have *regular Trustees* again. He published it last Sunday for the first time. [See note 36]

I told him, he may [must] apply to You for permission in doing so, but I got a negative answer, and as great troubles, and even serious disturbances will certainly occur, I think it my duty, to inform You about it.

He will exclude his opponents from the vote, and this, methink, will be enough, to have a riot, law-suit and what not. [See note 37] The reason why he wants Trustees is, because he lost a law-suit for not having regular Trustees; as soon [as] he will have now Trustees, he will have law-suits without end....

Sure enough, a month later, after the election of the trustees at St. Joseph's, Father Florian was again at bay. Father Noethen was willing to swap missions with him "for the sake of avoiding more scandal."[38] If the Benedictine were in Syracuse, he would have the advice of the two other missioners there, Fathers Michael Heas and Joseph Guerdet, an Irishman and a Frenchman, "who would speak as friends and brothers to him, if he should follow any course, creating disturbance."

Father Theodore Noethen was one of those able, talented and

hard-working priests, who had the makings of a bishop, and who served the diocese as vicar general for the last seven years of his life. Born in Cologne in 1816, he was at the seminary there, when trouble broke out between Archbishop von Droste-Vischering and the Prussian government over mixed marriages.[39] Noethen lost the use of one arm for life in a fight at the seminary to prevent the arrest of the archbishop, and he had to flee his native land himself. Walking most of the way to Rome, he then finished his studies at Propaganda, came to New York in 1841 at Bishop Hughes's invitation, and was ordained in that year, just in time for Christmas. It was at the Church of St. Louis, in Buffalo, one of the hottest spots of trusteeism in all of America, at that very time, that he mounted the ramparts as an assistant. After the pastor withdrew from the field of battle, Father Noethen remained as the only German missioner for years between Buffalo and Rochester. He later fought the trustees in Syracuse at St. Mary's (German), also called the Church of the Assumption, for four long years. In 1850, he became the pastor of the Church of the Holy Cross (German), in Albany, where he stayed until his death in 1879. In the midst of his labors, Father Noethen found the time to publish many writings, polemic, pious and historic. He had the bulldoggedness of a Bishop Hughes, with a greater sense of humor.[40] Now, here he was, in September of 1849, agreeing with Father Stokes, for the second time, that Father Florian was imprudent.

Three days later, the Benedictine, replying to an inquiry from the bishop, sent a long list of his woes.[41]

Right Reverend Bishop!/ Having received Your letter I haste to give a full explanation of the state of St. Josephs Congregation at Utica, praying to excuse my incorrect style and to supply inaccurateness of language by Your kindness.

From February 1848 to May 1849 we enjoyed happy peace and made some progresses. 1. We bought two lots joined to the church and a house for a priests-residence. About 200 dollars are paid. 2. A school-house at rear of the church was built. Its costs about 150 dollars, is paid. 3. The catholic school numbered last winter about 100 scholars, this summer about 60. 4. We agreed arrangements to build a new church. The subscriptions-List exhibits about 1000 dollars. It may be the fourth part of the sum, expected from the congregation. The collection is not finished.

5. A religious society (the confraternity of the scapular

B.V.M.) [of the Brown Scapular] arose since last summer for purpose of piety and benevolence. It numbers now about 60 members. — In general I would be injust, when I did not acknowledge the fervour of my congregation for all good and administring payments, &c. [See note 42]

Besides these advances only one grievance afflicted my heart, that the known enemies remained in their obstinacy, defying the paternal words of the Bishop and of the priests, present last year at the retreat. When [if] this undisciplined part of the congregation were converted, our congregation at Utica would be a singular specimen of a German congregation in this country, having no zizania [tares]. Pooh! Who would expect it? [See note 43] There is a great solace when this zizania is the most lesser part than the wheat.

You know, few bad men make a greater noise, than a multitude of good. Taberne-keepers are the most frightful aut[h]ors of nosie among the German people. Our congregation is unlucky to have such in its near [vicinity]. *Masseth* and (since few years) *Keiser* like to see troubles, because they fill their tabernes.

The state of impenitence of these and their fellows was like to peace before storm. They waited for an occasion to renew their troubles, and it was merely inevitable, that they did not find by and by an opportunity. When it was impossible to do a mans will, or when I was needed to give correction to one, such men run to *Masseth* or *Keiser* as to well known enemies to complain of me or to consult against me. — Indeed since last Easter causes and opportunities have been found by the said men and their fellows.

John Leinenger, known to Your Right Reverence as schoolmaster and sexton of our church two years ago, afterwards for the same business at Albany, not attending my counsel and proposals, began since May an opposite school near our church. I kould not consent, knowing his character as unfavourable to priests and therefore as unworthy of confidence. This teacher and his emissaries — two godfathers of the children of L[eininger]. — viz: Ph. Ernenwein & M. Ifrig, with their ladies did all to disturb the school on our church. Both last named *E.* and *If.* insulted me once on a *Sundays afternoon,* that I was needed to flee from my residence. They wished to dispute and litigate. I would not expose myself to their insolence, and fled. For that they were sorry and since enemies against me to now.

At the same time (after Easter) I was involved in another trouble, *but not caused by the congregation.*

Here, Father Florian explained that he had taken a poor family into his house, in charity, and that the family had boarded him, at his table. By and by, the son had become a drunkard, in Masseth's tavern. The pastor had, for that reason, asked the young man to move out, and the family did so. "It is nearly without doubt, that this family has been instigated by Masseth to bring me to law, asking a debt of 100 dollars." The pastor went on to explain, in his clumsy English, that he had paid the family the sum of thirty dollars a month for board, that is, a dollar a day; that they, right after moving out, had sued him for an additional and equal amount of money, or twice what they had agreed on; that he had previously boarded with the family of John Leininger at the rate of twenty-five cents a day for two meals; and that Leininger's successor as schoolmaster and sexton, a man by tne name of Ammenwerth, a bachelor, had boarded at the pastor's table, and had paid the family two dollars a week. What had complicated the arrangement between pastor and family was that the pastor had furnished them with fire wood, the use of his furniture, the vegetables from his garden, and so forth. In court, the family appearing against the pastor,

> the father was accuser, son and daughter wittnesses. I stood alone. For it I refused the service of a lawyer. I was sentenced to pay 95 dollars in all. Quickly *Masseth* took the paper of the sentence, written by the justice, saying it belonged now to him. The family was now totally poor, and I could not more ask from her, what she dues [owed] to me. I need not to say, that is [it] was only a trick to twist me. The same day afternoon *Masseth* sent the sheriff to sequester my books and furnitures on the church at Rome. Few days after a lawyer was sent by *Masseth* to close that church. I hindered it all. [See note 44]

Having come from a monastic cocoon, snug and tight, in the Tyrolean Alps, to Utica where the rough and tumble of the Jacksonian frontier mixed with the radicalism and free-thinking from Germany, the Benedictine now became "'nearly sick." With permission, he exchanged with Father Noethen for two weeks in June of 1849. But that missioner gave one sermon at St. Joseph's that made Father Florian a laughing stock. Before, Father Noethen was a friend. Now, he was a "passionated enemy."[45] So wrote Father Florian to the bishop.

There was another barb between the Benedictine and Father Noethen. The latter did not like regulars. When the bishop was in Utica, in February of 1848, Father Noethen said to him, in Father Florian's presence: "Bishop, I beg of You, let no regular priest nor convents exist in Your diocese." Father Florian rebuked Father Noethen then and there. Later, in April and June of 1848, the two of them crossed swords over the Christian Brothers. In letters to the editor of *Der Wahrheits Freund,* the voice of the see of Cincinnati, Father Noethen criticized the Brothers, and Father Florian defended them.[46] Thus continued Father Florian to the bishop, on September 11, 1849.

Then, what did Father Noethen do, according to Father Florian? He wrote letters to *M. Keiser* and *Masseth,* enemies of our congregation. Encouraged hereby, both tavern-keepers began to collect mobs; public meetings were held in their taverns, attended by Protestants and bad Catholics.

I will mention here only one letter of Rev. Noethen to a person of my congregation, exactely translated. The letter itself is at my hand. Rev. N. wrotes: "Did you read the last number of the Wahrheits-Freund? Is it not abominable done by P. Florian, that he for reason of the simple-minded schoolbrothers blames me, his defensor and friend, so most injustly and vulgarly? But his hour will come soon, because he shall not more find in me a help. Is that my reward, for I have punished those troublemakers? I think now otherwise and say: P. Florian is in fault of all; he merits no better treatment, but is not more worth, than to be transported (banished) from Utica. He shall see me soon, but not as his friend. Oh! I never thought that he would do so against me! But he shall soon receive his reward."

Right Reverend! A priest writes so to a layman of the congregation of his brother-priest! What Rev. Noethen wrote to M. *Keiser,* I heared only by a wittness. From doing such, Rev. N. brought the Germans of Utica, the good as well as the bad, to a state of disturbance since beginning of August past ...

After my letters [to *Der Wahrheits Freund]* no news-paper want to publish a reply of Rev. N. For this reason he is so sorry [hostile] to me; and revenged himself by so unpriestly doing, as I mentioned. That, that and not an election of trustees caused the troubles. Rev. N. promised to my enemies since beginning of August, that he will try to discharge me from Utica within 3 weeks; and running around to M. *Keiser* and *Masseth* on 10 Aug., he visited me, and said the same....

The point of reestablishing trustees on our church is a composition of *falshoods* and *misrepresentations. Neither myself, nor the congregation, that is, the persons living as true catholics and paying to the church, wish to have trustees. We neither wish nor attempt to alter anything, being in accordance to the rules of this dioecese about the churchs-administration. But, besides of the churchs-committees, only for businesses before law, pro tempore et casu to have legal trustees, I never thought wrong neither for myself, nor for the congregation.* [See note 46A] I explain it. 1846 Our church was closed by *bad trustees*. The good part of the congregation elected 2. Febr. 1846 Trustees, only for the business, to obtain the church. As soon as that was done, they neither had nor claimed any right to immixt themselfes in other affairs on administration of the church. — 1848 The congregation would buy two lots and a house. We needed *trustees* for *that* business. It was done up by them, and the office of the trustees was ended. — I never thought it wrong to what we have been forced by an unhappy condition in our country.

You know for the churchs-administration we had no trustees, but committees since 1846. But you know likewise. Masseth and his grocerys-company [See note 47] were not satisfied.

At this point, Father Florian reminded the bishop of his visitation to St. Joseph's in February of 1848. On that occasion, the pastor accused the opposition of wanting to have trustees again. But when the bishop asked Masseth about that, he denied it. The pastor could not back up the charge, because he had forgotten who had brought the rumor to his ears. Father Florian's letter of September 11, 1849, continued:

We heared often, that the old bad trustees claim the right to be the true trustees of our church; we heared, not the congregation were incorporated, but only the body of the trustees (9 years ago) [seven years, in fact]; and that from thence the congregation has no right to possess property; that the property belongs to the body of Trustees [true, under the Act of 1813]; we heared, that Masseth and other old trustees intend to hinder the congregation in building a new church, and that they would not consent, that the congregation moves or sells or touches the now-church, &c.

The pastor and his "sheep" remained in the dark about the truth of these hugger-muggerings in the taverns of Keiser and Masseth, until an incident brought them into the open.

July past a man of the adversary part (A. Seiling) broke the lock of our burying-ground, to bury his dead child, without my consent and without paying. The same struck [broke] windows of my room [house] last January; and is suspected for having done the same in the night of 30 June 1848. For safety of my person and of the congregations-property, the same congregation, admonished by Rev. Noethen to save and defend the priest, brought the cause to law.

But the case had been dismissed. Those who had laid a charge against Seiling had had no standing in court. Only the trustees might have prosecuted, and they had refused to do so. In fact, Masseth, had stood alongside Seiling at his breaking in.

We saw no other help before law, than to oppose against the old bad trustees — new and good trustees, *to act in in the name of the congregation,* but not to administer the churchs-income. We understood, that by doing so 1. the old trustees lose their power totally before the law. 2. that only good men as trustees (pro casu) save the welfare of the congregation. *a.* in the case, when by Your consent, the deeds may be written to Your name. The good part of the congregation wishes it, forseeing, that only by this way may be obtained a solid peace.

By the will of the congregation I published an election of legal trustees.... The convention for election was held on 27 August [a Monday]. *Masseth & Keiser* were followed by their *mob.* The present sheriff had no power to keep order. the *mob* called officers of the election from their part [See note 48]. Neither law, nor rule was observed; the protest of the congregation was not attended. About 70 persons, not belonging to the congregation gave their votes, but members of the congregation were not admitted to vote; and by this way the *mob* obtained a majority of 16 votes. The sheriff himself is wittness of the *unlawfulness* of that election.

The ticket of the mob exhibts following persons: 1. *Jos. Masseth,* one of the old trustees, tavern-keeper; the black side of his character is more known, than the contrary. He is a troublemaker from beginning. 2. *John Weigand,* old trustee; one of those, who discharged me as their pastor three years ago. 3. *Paul Keiser,* tavernkeeper, in whose house a radical society nestles, reading 15 anticatholic news-papers, seducing from faith and morality. 4. *Philipp Rithger,* one, who neglect to exercise religion. These four men are not legal members of the congregation. [See note 49]

5. *Philipp Ernenwein,* named above, as in connexion with the bad minded teacher Leininger. 6. *Michel Ifrig,* named above, likewise not well minded to me for reason of Leininger; drunkard. 7. *Joseph Knobloch,* for an unknown reason unfriendly to me since two months. He spoke as orator in the tavern of Keiser in abusive words. These three last named are new troublemakers, to whom may be added J. Th. Dumminger, known to You as such since two years.

Seeing the mob, I did not partake in the election at all. For a little while an unhappy motion was in the church, afterward on the street. As I have gone out from my house to dispers the mob, using only sweet words, I was insulted by Masseth in abusive words, I were the greatest rogue &c.

I hear a newspaper of Utica tells of a fight or assault, but there is no connexion with the said election at all. One of the combatants or assailant is *N. Miller,* a German, a catholic by baptism, living in a catholic mariage, educating his children in Protestantism, totally unknown to me, for he never belonged to our congregation. This man came to our church to *vote* against the congregation, as one of the mob. *A day after* the election he inflicted a wound by a knife to an American infidel. A poetizing [over-imaginative] writer brought this assault in connexion with the election.

But besides that, scandals enough were given by the *mob;* the whole congregation is afflicted about it. When [if] You, Right Reverend! ask: Who is in fault of the new troubles and scandals at Utica? that [is], who stirred up, or that [is], who had no power to hinder? I answer: When [if] the first will be acknowledged, then is it *Leininger, Rev. Noethen, Masseth,* etc. But in the latter case: I myself & my whole congregation. Rev. *Noethen* wrote his stirring letters to *Keiser* and *Masseth* weeks before we intended to elect trustees ...

Saturday past (Sept. 8) at evening two of the *mob trustees* P. *Ernenwein* and *M. Ifrig* came in my house to demand of me to give now account of my administration, and to exhibit the books. Knowing such asking as wrong, I refused to do it. [See note 50] They sayd, they would come again next Friday Sept. 14) for the same purpose. Yes, Right Reverend! That is the true reason of all our troubles. The bad part will not consent, that the priest with the committees keep the churchsadministration; they try and try to obtain it again. For that the mob has sent both said men to me. But I and the congregation will resist against such anticatholic attempt.

Pastor and congregation had petitioned a civil court to set aside the election on account of the irregularities of the mob, and had obtained an injunction that forbade the mob-trustees to take office before a deeper judicial look into the matter. At the moment of writing, on September 11, Father Florian and his supporters were hoping that the civil court would declare their seven candidates as the winners.

The 7 men, proposed as trustees of our congregation (for a short time) *promised* publicly and by writting, only to act to Your Right Reverence will and wishes, and never to immix themselves in the churchs-administration, and to lay down their office as quick as You or the priest wished it, or when the business in [is] done, for what they are appointed etc. [See Note 51] By means of such precautions I believed not to injure the catholic cause.

Finally I annex only my wishes and prayers to Your Right Reverence: 1. Please not to esteem, that my adversary part on the said mob be good catholics. It were conducible for honour of the holy church, that they never belonged to it. As long as Germans immigrate in this country, the number of the bad as well as of the good will increase. God may grant, that the majority may be good, as it is indeed. [See Note 52]

2. Please never to acknowledge the above named *Mob-trustees*, who have sent the inclosed letter to You; they are lusting after the churchs-administration. [See Note 53]

3. After such scandals I needed by duty to show my detestation of it publicly, and remarked that the four headmen of this troubles are unworthy of sacraments, untill they desist from their uncatholic attempts.

The four headmen and their public faults and scandals are as follows: 1. *Jos. Knobloch,* the above named mob-trustee. For his scandalous harangue at the tavern of Keiser. 2. *J. [or I.] Th. Dumminger,* by his mouth the headman of the rioters.

3. *P. Ernenwein,* a mob-trustee; chairman of the scandalous convention, saying: "I am parish-priest this day, etc. etc."

4. *M. Ifrig,* a mob-trustee; for fighting in the church and breaking pews, etc.

Other points of their fault are mentioned above. Right Reverend! Please to consent for my declaration about these four men, untill the[y] desist from their attempt, to rob the churchs-administration from the priests hand. Other headmen of the mob do not take care of religion, it is merely a superfl[u]ous undertaking to punish them.

Farther I beg of Your Right Reverence, that You in this matter may not give a full confidence to Rev. Noethen. He is passionated since two months.

I beg of You, that You may favour with paternal love the catholic Germans at Utica, about 2000 souls, of whom only about 100 are implicated in the troubles, as seduced by some troublemakers. Do not punish a multitude of innocents for reason of few seductors. [See Note 54]

Concerning my person, do, what You please. Your disposition may show me, what I shall do. There is no matter about myself, but about the congregation.

I will not attempt to give counsel to Your Right Reverence, but I will only say my meaning and thinking about the affairs, troubles and scandals on my congregation: There is no hope for a solid peace, as long as the deeds do not belong to the Bishop....

It appears, then, that the lay trusteeism at St. Joseph's had many facets: the sale and use of hard liquor by some of the congregation, their inobservance of the Sabbath, the control of church, school and graveyard, the appointment and dismissal of the pastor, the payment of the pew rents, and the election of the trustees. Add to that list the issue of whether the pastor was to be a regular or a secular. It is evident that the trustees had had their fill of regulars, what with a Redemptorist, a Franciscan, a Premonstratensian and a Benedictine, one after the other. They favored a secular, no doubt, because they believed that he would be pliant without the backing of an order. To Father Florian, this was a sore point, and it explains his ill will for Father Noethen. The Benedictine was still brooding over it five years later.[55]

The election of lay trustees was like a civil election of the time. At St. Joseph's, there was caucusing in the taverns and violence at the poll, that is, in the church. And, just as there was, in civil affairs, some fraud in voting, which turned on residence, and citizenship, and so forth, so St. Joseph's had the problem of deciding who belonged. It was a Gordian knot. Did it depend on a money offering, and how much, or on attendance at church, and when, or on the acceptance of doctrines, and which, or on the site of one's home, and where, or on the identity of one's relatives, and who, or on one's mother tongue, and what about the children, or even on the right of a missioner, who might be here today and gone tomorrow, to bar an old resident from the sacraments? In particular, what about the German trustees of St. Joseph's who had been attending the Irish church of St. John's? The canonists and the civil lawyers have not been able to define membership in a church any better than membership in the Church.[56]

The nature of the feud at St. Joseph's was highlighted by certain statements. Said Philipp Ernenwein, who supervised the election on August 27: "I am parish-priest this day." Said Father Florian of his adversaries: "They are lusting after the churchs-administration." Again, he said: "There is no hope for a solid peace, as long as the deeds do not belong to the Bishop." Well, the deeds of St. Joseph's did not belong to the bishop until 1862.[57]

Other circumstances there were, of a general sort, that helped to roil the congregation. Trustees were often men with no skill in business or social affairs. Many of them belonged to secret clubs of freethinkers, which bred in the ferment of the forties, and which turned heads against the Church.[58] There was also the crazy quilt of ethnicities. Said Father Adelbert Inama, who preceded Father Florian at St. Joseph's:[59]

> The Germans here are not, like the Irish, peas from the same pod. But, in the same place, there will be people from Lorraine, Alsace, the Palatine, Baden, Prussia, Franconia, etc. It is difficult to bring so many heads together under one roof.

Two of the men in the junto against the Benedictine are known to us in some detail. One was Paul Keiser. He may have been a tavern keeper in the time of trouble, but he later became an alderman in the city government and an owner of the *Deutsche Zeitung* [the *German News*]. When he died in 1874, the Utica *Morning Herald* gave him a eulogy.[60]

Andreas Kleespies was the other one. (This is from Father Florian.)[61] Kleespies was among the seven Germans who bought the building for St. Joseph's in 1840. A popular man, he became one of the first trustees. He had been a school teacher in Bavaria, but he started life in Utica with a tavern. When he went bankrupt, he opened a butcher shop. In 1844, his wife died, and he wanted to marry his sister-in-law. Father Inama, who was the pastor them, warned him that he needed a dispensation. But, he retorted that "Father Inama talked too much and that he did not care if he got a dispensation or not." If the pastor did not officiate, said Kleespies, then he would find another priest. Father Inama refused to officiate, so the couple went to Rome, where they were married by Father William Beecham, an Irish priest. (Here, Father Florian's words turned sharp at what he eyed as an act of poaching.)[62] The Irish priest officiated without a question. He just collected five dollars. Afterwards, Kleespies bragged how he had fooled the two priests, the Irish one and the German. Father Inama declared the marriage void. He barred the couple from the sacraments until they got a dispensation. But Kleespies laughed if off. As far as he was concerned, the priest had dispensed him from the sacraments. After Father Florian came, the butcher continued stubborn. His business went downhill, and he faced bankruptcy again. "On the first Sunday of Lent, 1845," wrote Father Florian, "he was found in his butcher shop where he had hanged himself."

The name of Keiser was prominent enough to find a place in the genealogy of northern New York,[63] which bares an interesting German connection and another insight into lay trusteeism. Paul Keiser must have been related to the George Keiser who immigrated from Alsace to Utica in 1838 with a wife and a clutch of a dozen children. One of the girls, Julianna, married a Henry Haberer of Carthage. In that small Catholic-German-American world, the wedding took place in St. Joseph's of Utica in 1845. Father Florian officiated. Haberer, a cabinetmaker, had come from Bavaria to Utica in 1841 at the age of twenty. Later, he moved to Carthage to work for a furniture manufacturer by the name of Gallagher, and then went into business for himself with a furniture store and an undertaking parlor.[64] Haberer enlisted in 1861, fought at Bull Run, Antietam and Fredericksburg, was honorably discharged in 1864, re-enlisted, and saw action again in several battles. After the war, he returned to his businesses. He moved to Lowville, in Lewis County, in 1876, where he died in 1887. He is remembered as a solid citizen and a charter member of the Lowville post of the Grand Army of the Republic. He was, of course, the man who played an ambiguous role in the trouble at St. James's of Carthage.[65]

Henry Haberer and Julianna Keiser Haberer had six children. Two of them were John Edward (1851-1908) and George Joseph (1853-1907). They were educated in the public schools of Carthage, learned cabinetmaking in that village as apprentices to Gallagher, and later moved to Lowville, where Haberer Brothers became one of the largest manufacturers of furniture in northern New York, with a factory that covered acres, a payroll of near a hundred men, and a business that was nation-wide. Rich and active in civic affairs, they remained staunch Catholics, and gave generously to Church and charities. John Edward was a charter member and the first Grand Knight of the Lowville council of the Knights of Columbus. In short, some of the families behind lay trusteeism, were, in the economic and social sense, the backbone of Church and country.

Few at St. Joseph's lent support to the trustees, or shared the attitude of Kleespies, or were so far gone as to think of harming their pastor and burning their church.[66] Most, in fact, were good Catholics, docile and zealous, in spite of their early years without a missioner and among proselytizing Protestants. In storm, they filled their pews; in moderate circumstances, they gave their offerings;[67] in faction, they venerated the Mother of God.[68] It was the quarreling of the trustees and the shepherd that confused some of the sheep.[69]

In November of 1849, Father Florian was transferred to St. Mary's[70] (German), in Syracuse, where he spent the next ten months.[71]

I, Florian Schweninger, of the Order of St. Benedict, a
Tyrolese, previously pastor of Utica, have taken charge of the
souls of this place on the 1st of November, 1849. Pious Reader!
remember me, whether dead or alive, in thy sacred functions!

But the trouble at St. Joseph's did not abate. Nor did Father Florian disentangle himself from it. In Syracuse, he replaced Father Noethen, who went to Albany to organize a German congregation there, and, in Utica, Father Florian was replaced by a Father J. Arnold, who had apparently just come from Germany.[72]

The account of the prolongation of the feud among the German Catholics of Utica comes to us mainly through the letters of Father Florian, in Syracuse, and of his partisans in Utica.[73] According to that version, Father Arnold, before the transfer, had spent a while with Father Noethen at St. Mary's, in Syracuse. There, the one secular priest had picked up from the other secular priest an animus against regulars, in general, and a grudge against Father Florian, in particular. When Father Arnold came to St. Joseph's, and was there for a time with Father Florian, he swallowed the lies of Masseth and Keiser, and treated Father Florian with scorn. No sooner did the Benedictine leave for Syracuse, than Father Arnold began to change everything around. He turned out Joseph Ammenwerth, who was Father Florian's schoolmaster, and replaced him with John Leininger, whom Father Florian looked upon as an anticlericalist and an archenemy. He also dismissed the committee, which now stood in the place of the old board of trustees, and which Father Florian had left behind, and appointed a new one that reflected not only his views but those of Masseth and Keiser. All of this he did shortly after his arrival.

The wail of the Florian party, of the Confraternity of the Blessed Virgin, reached from Utica to Syracuse. The Benedictine replied as any priest might to a "beloved former congregation." He told them to obey their new pastor, to suffer humiliation for the sake of Christ, and he promised to pray for them. But they were not satisfied. They thought of secession. They withheld their pew rents. After dropping the idea of building a new church for themselves,[74] they looked into buying an Episcopal church. Some of them went to Albany to see the bishop about it, but not finding him at home, they consulted with Father Noethen. They also wrote to Father Florian.

The Benedictine liked the idea. The Episcopal church was in the center of town, and the price was a bargain. He offered to contribute to the purchase fund, if the bishop approved. Father Arnold heard about the letters that were going back and forth between Utica and Syracuse. He attacked Father Florian in a Sunday sermon on November 25, just three weeks after the transfer of the pastors. He complained to the bishop, and sent him an ultimatum: "Mark this. Either I or Florian must leave your diocese, because I shall not have any peace as long as that wolf is on the prowl in Syracuse."[75]

Father Florian denied to the bishop that he had anything to do with a rebellion at St. Joseph's, or that he was scheming to return to Utica. He did favor the acquisition of an Episcopal church, but he insisted that his offer of a contribution was based on the bishop's approval. And, he made counter-accusations. Ever since he had bested Father Noethen in a public dispute over the Christian Brothers, that secular priest, with an aversion for regulars, had been thirsting for revenge. That was why Father Noethen had joined forces with Masseth and Keiser, and had drawn Father Arnold into the same plot, to banish the Benedictine monk from Utica, and to humiliate him among his parishioners. And, that was why they were now persecuting him, as the trustees of St. Joseph's had once persecuted Fathers Prost and Inama, a Redemptorist and a Premonstratensian, before him.[76] The trouble at St. Joseph's was all now a vendetta against him. When Father Arnold had used the pulpit in that church, on November 25, to vent his malice on its former pastor, some of the people walked out in disgust. That, said Father Florian, was the beginning of the secession. And, now he was tired of the whole tedious and loathsome business of having to defend himself against a pack of lies. "I thought that I would get some desired peace in Syracuse, but in vain ... In the middle of the explanation, I put away my pen."[77] And so he did. There is not another word from Father Florian among the papers of Cardinal McCloskey. But, sad to tell, his life and departure at St. Mary's, in Syracuse, was of a piece with his misery at St. Joseph's.[78] It will add nothing to this story of sin at the foot of Sinai.

At St. Joseph's, with the board of trustees gone, the persevering Germans turned their attention to the school to stoke up a tired fire. Father Arnold dismissed Joseph Ammenwerth, who was a Father Florian man, and replaced him with John Leininger, who stood with Masseth and Keiser. Although the purpose of this change may have been compromise, or spite, or it may have been a sort of spoils system (we do not know), Ammenwerth opened another school for twenty-five families of Florianites. When Father Arnold barred them all from the sacraments until they returned to Leininger, they appealed to the bishop for justice. The ending lies behind a veil.[79]

Father Florian resigned from the diocese in the summer of 1850, and received his *exeat* after an episcopal visitation to Syracuse. He said his last Sunday Mass at St. Mary's on September 1. Then, after wrangling for a week or more with the committee (no longer trustees) and the new pastor, Father Simon Saenderl over his (Father Florian's) salary, his furniture and his housekeeper, whose residence in the priest's house so scandalized Father Saenderl that he used the slur of "strumpet," Father Florian left St. Mary's of Syracuse. But he did not leave the diocese. Instead, he went back to Utica, where he ministered to his partisans for a while, without faculties. He used the two Irish churches there, until they shut their doors to him. Then he left the diocese.[80]

Because the trouble at St. Joseph's would not die down,[81] Bishop McCloskey, in 1859, promulgated the "Rules of Administration for St. Joseph's German Catholic Church of Utica":[82]

    1st. The Trustees shall be chosen from among the members of the congregation, who have a seat in the church, and have paid the rent due thereon for the past year. And any person belonging to a secret society or who has not made his Easter Communion cannot be chosen.

    2nd. The Trustees shall be required half-yearly to present to the congregation an account of the receipts and expenditures, but to the Bishop at the expiration of the year. The Bishop retains the power to examine as often as he shall think proper the Books of Administration, and the special permission of the Bishop shall be required for every expense exceeding $300.

3rd. The pastor shall be present Ex Officio at the session of the trustees for the transactions of Church-business, and should he lay his Veto on any question and will not withdraw it therefrom it shall be decided by the Bishop.

4th. The pastor shall appoint persons for the Church service, as, Organist, Sachristan [sic], and Schoolmaster, however he shall first consult the trustees and should they disagree the question shall be decided by the Bishop.

5th. The congregation shall be incorporated under the above Rules of Administration; and never shall one cent belonging to St. Joseph's congregation be expended for any other purpose than for St. Joseph's church and congregation.

Given Albany November 28th 1859.

[signed by a secretary] John Bishop of Albany

In that year, too, the Franciscan Fathers Conventual accepted the care of the German souls of Utica, and, like the rain from heaven after a summer of drought, peace came to St. Joseph's.[83]

Justice asks an epilogue for Father Florian. After Utica and sickness and inactivity, he became an assistant for a year in Paterson, New Jersey. Then, he labored for the rest of his life on the mission in the gold fields of California. In 1854, he wrote to his brethren in the Tyrol about his adventures. He had given up the quietude of the Alps for the sake of his countrymen in America. In Utica, he had found the cross that he had forseen in a vision, one spring morning on the Georgenberg.

But California was different. In five northern counties between the Pacific and the Sierras, over twenty thousand square miles of mountain, he made his way, on mule or afoot, from mining camp to mining camp, bearing the body of Christ. He did it for sixteen years. At times, he lay sick and alone in a hut. At times, he journeyed 130 miles to make his own confession. He built a church with his own hands. He carved wooden markers for the graves that he blessed. He taught the guitar. To those who knew him and loved him , he was "the Padre of Paradise Flat." In 1866, broken down in body, he became the assistant at the cathedral in Marysville. And, there, on July 28, 1868, at sixty years of age, he died, his sorrowing bishop beside him. A crabbed monk, he had served God and man as he was able. Today, in the cemetery of the Cathedral of St. Joseph, his gravestone, old and tilting, begs us to "pray for Father Florian."[84]

[1] Germans first came to Utica in 1821. In 1837, those of them at St. Johns, in the midst of an Irish majority, welcomed Father John Lewis Warrath or Wariath, a *landsmann,* who came to serve them, as assistant to Father Walter J. Quarter. Hewitt, *Diocese of Syracuse,* pp. 28-29. In 1839, the German Catholics of Utica organized the Utica German Sick-Aid Society and the St. Joseph's Society. Presumably, they were still using St. John's Church. On the other hand, there is the possibility that they had had a separate place of worship as early as 1835. It might have been, say, a rented loft, as was common then. Rev. Maurice Imhoff, O.M.C., "Notes on the Early History of St. Joseph's Parish at Utica, N.Y., " *Central Blatt and Social Justice,* XXX, No. 11 (Feb., 1938), 349-350.

[2] On Oct. 15, 1840, they bought the First Methodist Episcopal Church, bell, lot and building, for $1,050. Purchasers of record were John M. Lanzer, Joseph Masseth, Matthias Fritz, John Oster, Ignatius Meyer, John Paul and Andreas Kleespies. St. Joseph's Church of Utica was incorporated on March 28, 1842. Meyer, Fritz, Lanzer, Paul and Masseth are identified as the first board of trustees. *Ibid.*

[3] Rev. Francis Guth, occasionally, in 1841. *Catholic Directory for 1842,* pp. 148-151. Rev. Joseph Prost. C.SS.R., in 1842, Rev. Ivo Leviz, O.F.M., in 1843, Rev. Adelbert Inama, O. Praem., in 1844, Rev. Florian Schwenninger, O.S.B., in 1844-1849. Hewitt, *Diocese of Syracuse,* p. 233.

[4] Stokes to McCloskey, Utica, Dec. 13, 1845, Letterbox A23, NY.

[5] Rev. Thomas Martin, O.P., pastor of St. John's, Utica, 1841-1844.

[6] Rev. Gunther R. Rolfson, O.S.B, (ed.), "The Schwenninger Memorial," *The American Benedictine Review,* XI, Nos. 1-2 (March-June, 1960), 154-155.

[7] *Ibid.,* X, Nos. 1-2 (March-June, 1959), 107-135, 245-265, XI, Nos. 1-2 (March-June, 1960), 154-178. For praise of Raffeiner, see Johnson, "Letters of Adelbert Inama," XI, No. 1 (Sept., 1927), 89-91.

[8] Rolfson, "Schwenninger Memorial," X, Nos. 1-2 (March-June, 1959), 259. I have not been able to find any more on these two cases.

[9] *Ibid.,* Father Florian errs here. See Appendix V, section X.

[10] *Ibid.,* p. 255.

[11] *Ibid.,* XI, Nos. 1-2 (March-June, 1960), p. 160.

[12] Table 31, unpaginated.

[13] As there were only 16 churches in the city, we must suppose that some who reported themselves as clergymen were not active, or were assistants.

[14] Father John J. Conroy, pastor, was paid $150 a quarter and an additional $100 in one year for rent. His assistant, Father Thomas Daley, received $100 a quarter with no indication of anything for house rent. Financial Statement for St. Joseph's, Albany, for the period of Jan. 1, 1850-Jan. 1, 1851, Letterbox A25, NY. On the other hand, Father Patrick Phelan, at Potsdam and Waddington, had to pay off the church debt on St. Mary's of Waddington out of his own pocket, and he complained: "I have to pay $60 a year house rent, purchase firewood and hay and grain for the support of my horse," Phelan to McCloskey, Waddington, April 22, 1851, Letterbox A25, NY.

[15] Schweinninger to the Abbot, St. George's Abbey, Fiecht, Austria, from Utica, N.Y., Sept. 26, 1846. A copy of this letter is in the archives of St. John's Abbey and University, Collegeville, Minnesota, and was sent to me by the Rev. Gunther R. Rolfson, O.S.B.

[16] It was a time of crusading for temperance and a respect for Sunday, See Alice Felt Tyler, *Freedom's Ferment* (New York: Harper & Row, 1962, originally 1944), chap. III, "The Temperance Crusade." For sabbatarianism, see Anson Phelps Stokes, *Church and State in the United States* (3 vols., New York: Harper & Bros., 1950), II, chap. XIV.

[17] He was a trustee and one of the owners of St. Joseph's, under civil law. Imhoff, "St. Joseph's, Utica," pp. 349-350. On freethinking among the German immigrants then, see A.E. Zucker (ed.), The *Forty-Eighters* (New York: Russell & Russell, 1966, originally 1950), chap. I-II.

[18] The letter was no doubt a copy of the pastoral issued by Bp. Hughes on Sept. 8, 1842, on the administration of the sacraments, on secret societies and on the "trustee system." Bp. Hughes was then coadjutor to Bp. John Dubois and administrator of the diocese of New York. For the text of the pastoral, see Kehoe, *Works of Bishop Hughes*, I, 314-327. For Bp. Hughes's fight against lay trusteeism in the forties, when the diocese covered all of New York and the eastern half of New Jersey, see John R.G. Hassard, *Life of the Most Reverend John Hughes* (New York: D. Appleton, 1866), chap. XV.

[19] See Appendix V, the Act of 1813, Section VI.

[20] It must have been a cease and desist order against trespass, or against disturbing the peace. Father Florian's English was poor, having been in America not two years.

[21] Father Florian said nothing in the letter about a city ordinance or an election of trustees at the church.

[22] After becoming a lawyer in 1840, Francis Kernan was one of the most prominent Catholics in the public affairs of the state of New York. He defeated Roscoe Conkling in 1862 for a seat in the House of Representatives. In 1867-1868, he was a delegate-at-large at the New York Constitutional Convention. He served as a state senator in 1875-1881. M.M. Bagg (ed.), *Memorial History of Utica, N.Y.* (2 vols.; Syracuse: D. Mason, 1892), II, Part II, pp. 36-37.

[23] Father Florian says nothing about the outcome of the case.

[24] Schwenninger to Abbot, St. George's Abbey, Fiecht, Austria, from Utica, N.Y., March, 1848. Copy is in archives of St. John's Abbey and University, Collegeville, Minnesota, and was sent to me by courtesy of Father Rolfson.

[25] While at Utica, Father Florian attended Constableville, West Turin, Hamilton, Salina (Syracuse), Manlius, etc. His limits had a diameter of about sixty miles and covered counties of Oneida, Madison, Lewis and Onondaga. *Catholic Directory* for years 1846-1851.

[26] Rev. Fergus Macdonald, C.P., *The Catholic Church and the Secret Societies in the United States* (New York: U.S. Cath. Hist. Soc., 1946), chap. I. See text of pastoral letter, Sept. 8, 1842, by Bp. Hughes, "In Regard to the Adminsitration of the Sacraments, Secret Societies, and the 'Trustee System' ", Kehoe, *Works of Bishop Hughes*, I, 314-327. Bp. Hughes, after issuing this pastoral, explained that he had not been thinking of the Freemasons and the Odd Fellows, as the Protestants suspected, but of the Irish societies of "Corkonians," "Connaught Men," etc., who fought and killed each other over jobs and old rivalries, as do the "Mafia families," or "Pistol Unions," today. They would not even hear Mass under the same roof. Hassard, *Life of Bishop Hughes*, pp. 258-259.

[27] In 1845-1846, when the trustees locked out Father Florian from St. Joseph's, and tried to use a civil process to get rid of him, they also withheld the pew rents. Schwenninger to McCloskey, Syracuse, Jan. 2, 1850, Letterbox A25, NY. I guess the rent pews, because they were payable by quarters, and the third quarter ended soon after Christmas, that is, three months before Easter.

[28] "A Subscriber" to the Editor, Syracuse, March 6, 1848, in the *Freeman's Journal*, March 25, 1848. I think the writer was Father Noethen

[29] Stokes to McCloskey, Utica, June 22, 1849, Letterbox A25, NY. Fathers Noethen and Florian exchanged the two Sundays of June 10 and 17. Schwenninger to McCloskey, Utica, Sept. 11, 1849, Letterbox A25, NY.

[30] Noethen to McCloskey, Syracuse, June 28, 1849, Letterbox A25, NY. Italics are Father Noethen's.

[31] Bp. Hughes was willing to tolerate lay trustees where they already existed. But, in 1845, he published his "Rules for the administration of the churches without trustees." Hassard, *Life of Bishop Hughes*, p. 264. Father Noethen indicates here that Bp. McCloskey had the same policy.

[32] Prof. Julian G. Plante, the Curator of the Monastic Manuscript Microfilm Library of St. John's University, Collegeville, Minnesota, has kindly made a literal translation for me. I trust that he will not take offense, if I, knowing the situation at St. Joseph's, Utica, which Father Noethen had in mind, make some change in Prof. Plante's translation, in order to versify as follows:

Bees sip honey from deadly flowers.
Trustees wring venom from sacred hours.
They will twist whatever the priest may say.
They foul his path, they gloom his day.

[33] In those days, the missioners were jealous of their revenues and their jurisdictions, as they had to be, not only for the sake of their maintenance, but also for the enforcement of episcopal rules and canon law. Since Father Florian did not complain, in his many letters to the Bishop, about the attendance of the German trustees, their families, and, presumably, some of their partisans, at St. John's, it may be that the arrangement had the acquiescence of the bishop and the German pastor.

[34] Schwenninger to McCloskey, Utica, Jan. 24, 1849, Letterbox A24, NY.

[35] Noethen to McCloskey, Syracuse, Aug. 10, 1849, Letterbox A25, NY.

[36] Evidently, the trustees had either resigned, or ceased to function, and their term of office had expired. So, the pastor gave the fifteen-day notice of election as required by the Act, of 1813. He gave it on Aug. 5.

[37] If his opponents had been members of St. Joseph's, Father Florian would have been in violation of the Act of 1813. But, it is possible that Father Florian viewed them as members of St. John's. In any case, Father Florian was poking a nest of hornets. See Appendix V, Act of 1813, sections VI-VIII, on trustees elections.

[38] Noethen to McCloskey, Syracuse, Sept. 8, 1849, Letterbox A25, NY.

[39] Rev. James MacCaffrey, *History of the Catholic Church in the Nineteenth Century* (2 vols; 2d ed.; Dublin: M.H. Gill, 1910), I, 93-101.

[40] Corrigan, "Register," II, Part II (1902), 261-262. There are twenty-nine letters in the archives of the Archdiocese of New York from Father Noethen to Bp. McCloskey, dating from 1847 to 1857.

[41] Schwenninger to McCloskey, Utica, Sept. 11, 1849, Letterbox A25, NY. The paragraphing is mine. Italics are his.

[42] In Letterbox A25, NY, there is a large printed broadside, undated, in French, on the Scapular of the Immaculate Conception, or of the Blessed Virgin. There are seventeen such confraternities, each related to a religious order, and each with its indulgenced scapular. Donald Attawater (ed.), *A Catholic Dictionary* (New York: Macmillan, 1942), p. 476.

[43] Who would expect to find a German American congregation without troublemakers?

[44] It is not clear how Father Florian hindered a sheriff's sale of St. Mary's, in Rome. We know the following facts. He purchased the lot for St. Mary's in 1846, and began to build on it in 1847, doing both with his own money. But he had to go into debt to finish the church. See above, pp. 264-265. In 1849, one Elijah Brush conveyed unidentified real estate at Rome to Father Florian, who, in the same year, conveyed unidentified real estate at Rome to Bp. McCloskey. "Real Estate Owned by R.C.D.," AA. My guess is that the real estate was the church of St. Mary's. A church lot in those days cost about $150 or $200, which Father Florian could have paid, cash on the barrelhead. Elijah Brush was probably the builder of the church. As was usual at that time, he probably passed title to the pastor, when the bills were settled. But, as we have already seen, a judge issued an attachment on St. Mary's, as the personal property of Father Florian. The only way Father Florian could have conveyed the church to Bp. McCloskey was to get rid of the lien first. That that happened, and that Bp. McCloskey probably paid off the debt, is evident from a letter of George Murphy to McCloskey, Utica, Jan. 4, 1850, Letterbox A25, NY, as follows:

> Mr. Masseth wishes me to write you a note in relation to a judgment against the Rev. L. Sweininger [sic.]. And I would say that Mr. Masseth has not control whatever over that judgment, as it belongs to a gentleman named Lee. I was the att[orney] who obtained the judgment against Mr. Florian, and he informed me you would rather pay than have the church sold. The sheriff has informed me that Mr. Lee has written several times to Sweininger in Syracuse & he pays no attention to the matter whatever.

[45] Thereafter, Father Florian sounded paranoiac about Father Noethen, while the latter showed no ill will at all in his many letters to the bishop.

[46] I am waiting to receive photocopies of those letters from the Catholic Central Union of America, in St. Louis, the only listed depository for that weekly newspaper of that year.

[46a] I have never come across any general set of rules of Bp. McCloskey for the administration of the temporalities of his churches. He did issue rules for St. Joseph's, which appear towards the end of the chapter. I suppose that Father Florian, in his letter of Sept. 11, was referring to Bp. Hughes's "Rules for the administration of churches without trustees," which were published in 1845, and remained in effect for years. Hassard, *Life of Archbishop Hughes,* pp. 264-265. Those rules applied to central and northern New York in 1845, of course, and presumably were continued by Bp. McCloskey after 1847. Accordingly every pastor had to name two men of the congregation to help him with the temporalities. It goes without saying that, wherever a board of

trustees already existed, under the Act of 1813, the rules of Bp. Hughes depended on the willingness of the trustees to retire, and the willingness of the congregation to cease to replenish the board by elections. This was their option under the Act of 1813, by implication. Under the rules of Bp. Hughes, the pastor had the full control of the temporalities with the help of the two men, whom he could discharge at will. However, in the case of St. Joseph's, it seems that, for reasons which appear below, Father Florian and the congregation saw fit to revive the board of trustees after it had ceased to act. It also seems that some of the trustees still claimed authority under the Act of 1813, especially, and presumably, if their term of office, which was three years, had not yet ended. In order to understand what followed in Father Florian's letter, that is, his explanation of the subsequent events at St. Joseph's, we must bear in mind that, under the Act of 1813, only the trustees were recognized by the civil law. We must also bear in mind that the trustees, if obedient to pastor and bishop in the Catholic sense, were an advantage in safeguarding the property of the congregation, and that Bp. Hughes, in trying to prevent the election of any more trustees, was going from a great evil to a lesser evil, in his judgement. We presume that Bp. McCloskey felt the same way. On the other hand, we will see that Father Florian had good reason for wanting to revive his board of trustees *"pro tempore et casu,"* even though Father Noethen thought that he was opening Pandora's Box. See Appendix V, for the text of the Act of 1813, and see Dignan, *Church Property,* chaps. III-VII. I add here that when Father Florian spoke of a church-committee, he meant the two men as mentioned above in this note.

[47] Grocers sold liquor, and groceries were taverns.

[48] At such an election, two of the church elders, wardens, or trustees, or in the absence of them, two members of the congregation, to be named then and there by the electors, were to preside, by receiving, counting and validating the votes. See Appendix V, Act of 1813, section III.

[49] They had been attending St. John's, the Irish church. See above, p. 269.

[50] Ernenwein and Ifrig, as trustees, were within their civil rights. See Appendix V. Act of 1813, sections IV and X. But, Father Florian was following canon law and episcopal rule.

[51] To build a new church, to dispose of the old, to safeguard the burial ground, and so on.

[52] When Bp. Hughes organized his Church Debt Assoc. in 1842 in order to rid his ten churches of debt, the three congregation that refused to join were German. Hassard, *Life of Archbishop Hughes,* p. 256.

[53] I have not found the "inclosed letter."

[54] I have the feeling that, when Father Florian wrote these words, he was thinking of the Korite rebellion and the words of Moses and Aaron: "O God...if one man sins, wilt thou be angry with the whole community?" Numbers, XVI:22. It is another of many clues in Father Florian's letters that he was Yahwistic, that is, that he thought of God and His priests as demanding absolute obedience. If so, it was probably one reason for his troubles as a pastor of Germans, many of whom were libertarians. For Father Florian's contempt for the "irreligious ex-revolutionaries" from Italy and German in America, see Rev. John B. McGloin, S.J., "A California

Gold Rush Padre: New Light on the 'Padre of Paradise Flat'," *California Historical Society Quarterly*, XL, No. 1 (March, 1961), pp. 56-64.

[55] In the letter to his abbot in 1854, Father Florian listed eight reasons why regulars were better than seculars. He began with the statement that "religious priests are on the average less selfish and are therefore more loved by the people." For that reason, he said, most American bishops favored the "religious priests are on the average less selfish and are therefore more loved by the people." For that reason, he said, most American bishops favored the religious orders, and many priests on the American mission were regulars. Conventuals, 8 Augustinians, 2 Benedictines, 12 Redemptorists, 2 Dominicans, and 1 Third Order Franciscan, among a total of 263 priests, or 83 regulars and 180 seculars. When regulars do pastoral work, the problem may arise of jurisdiction. Are they to be under the rule of the ordinary or of their superior general? See Byrne, *Redemptorist Centenaries*, pp. 52-60, for a clash in the 1830's between Bp. Frederick Rese of Detroit and Redemptorists.

[56] Bachofen, *Catholic Parishes*, pp. 242-248, 314-315; Zollman, *Civil Church Law*, pp. 367-368; Charles M. Scanlan, *The Law of Church and Grave* (New York: Benziger Bros., 1909), chap. IX; Charles Z. Lincoln, *The Civil Law and the Church* (New York: Abingdon Press, 1916), pp. 868-873. The civil courts favored a definition of church membership based on attendance and financial support. Canonists add baptism, Easter duty, and so on. For a definition of a Catholic, see Attwater, *Catholic Dictionary*, p. 87.

[57] "Real Estate Owned by R.C.D.," AA; D. Gilmore to McCloskey, Utica, April 3, 1850, Letterbox A24, NY. Gilmore was a lawyer.

[58] Salzbacher, *Reise*, pp. 335-340; Macdonald, *Secret Societies*, chap. I.

[59] In Utica, in 1843, the Germans were from Alsace, Baden, Franconia, Lorraine, Rhenish Prussia, Rhenish Bavaria and Württemberg. Johnson, "Letters of Adelbert Inama," XI, No. 2 (Dec. 1927), 200, 214-215. Incidentally, there was a small German Lutheran congregation from 1842 and a German Methodist congregation from 1849. Bagg, *Memorial History of Utica*, I, 430, 436. In 1845, Oneida Co. had 1,220 Germans. *N.Y., Census, 1845*, Recapitulation Table No. 1.

[60] Imhoff, "St. Joseph's, Utica," p. 350.

[61] Rolfson, "Schwenninger Memorial," XI, Nos. 1-2 (March-June, 1960), 172-173.

[62] Germans had to be married by German pastors. Abp. Michael A. Corrigan (ed.), *Synodorum Archidioeceseos Neo-Eboracensis Collectio* (Neo-Eboraci: Typis Bibliothecae Cathedralis, 1901). p. 14.

[63] William Richard Cutter, *Genealogical and Family Record of Northern New York* (3 vols.; New York: Lewis Historical Publishing Co., 1910), II, 673-675.

[64] Perhaps he did so in 1851, because Richard Gallagher advertised then for cabinetmakers. *Freeman's Journal*, July 26, 1851.

[65] See above, pp. 220, 247.

[66] "The former pastor was hardly sure of his life, nor the church from fire." So wrote Father Adelbert Inama in 1843 from St. Joseph's to the *Katholischen Blätter* in the Tyrol. Johnson, "Letters of Adelbert Inama," XI, No. 2 (Dec., 1927), 212.

[67] In 1843, they were about 90 families, or 400-500 persons, about one-third of whom were farmers. All gave generously and willingly to the church. *Ibid.,* XI, No. 2 (Dec., 1927), 199, 205.

[68] Her cult was popular among the Germans. As we already know, there was a Confraternity of the Blessed Virgin at St. Joseph's with 60 members. Father Joseph Prost, C.SS.R., established the Confraternity of the Brown Scapular in Buffalo in 1836. Byrne, *Redemptorist Centenaries,* p. 61.

[69] Laity of St. Joseph's to McCloskey, Utica, Jan. 12, and another letter around April, 1850, Letterbox A25, NY.

[70] Some sources refer to it as the Church of the Assumption. But the *Catholic Directory* for the years 1850-1854, lists it as St. Mary's.

[71] He signed in, in the register, on Nov. 1, 1849, and signed out on Sept. 15, 1850. His first entry was quoted by Hewitt, *Diocese of Syracuse,* p. 128.

[72] He wrote to the bishop in Latin. I have not been able to determine his first name, or to trace him before and after Utica. He was at St. Joseph's in Oct. 20, 1849-Dec. 10, 1854. *Ibid.,* p. 233. It is possible that that experience told him all that he wanted to know about martyrdom, and he went back to Europe, as so many missioners did.

[73] Schwenninger to McCloskey, Syracuse, Dec.30, 1849, Jan. 1, 2, 4, and 5, 1850, Letterbox A25, NY; Unidentified laymen to McCloskey, Utica, Jan. 12, 1850, Letterbox A25, NY; Petition with 25 signatures to McCloskey Utica, c. April, 1850, Letterbox A25, NY; Joseph Ammenwerth to McCloskey, Utica, April 16, 1850, Letterbox A24, NY.

[74] The number of German-born in the diocese of Albany went from 2,067 in 1845 to 10,482 in 1855, and St. Joseph's was overcrowded. See above, pp. 131, 319. At that very time, St. Joseph's was being enlarged. McCloskey to the Prince Archbishop of Vienna, Albany, Jan. 21, 1850, *Berichte der Leopoldinen-Stiftung,* XXIII (1851), 51-54. A division of the congregation at that time of great expense would have been dangerous. But, it did not take place.

[75] Arnold to McCloskey, Utica, Jan. 4, 1850, Letterbox A24, NY.

[76] There is no evidence that Father Noethen had any wish but to separate the Benedictine monk from a scandalous situation for his own good and the good of the Church. More, Father Noethen was willing to change places with Father Florian. Noethen to McCloskey, Syracuse, Sept. 8, 1849, Letterbox A25, NY. Although Father Florian had a paranoia about Fathers Noethen and Arnold, yet there was a basis in fact for the antipathy between seculars and regulars in the same missionary diocese. It was due to a friction over jurisdiction sometimes. To whom were the regulars subject, to the bishop or the superior general? Such a dispute could destroy or cripple a mission. For an example, involving Bp. Frederick Rese of Detroit versus the Redemptorists, in the 1830's, in which Father Prost was directly concerned, see Byrne, *Redemptorist Centenaries ,* pp. 52-60. While we are on the subject of Father Florian's paranoia, we ought to be aware, in fairness to his memory, that his tribulations among the German Catholics may have been partly to blame. One Redemptorist historian speaks of the "particularly strong German brand" of lay trusteeism, which harassed Father Prost in New York, Ohio and Pennsylvania, in 1835-1843. Father Prost himself has left some some hair-raising encounters with German Catholics in America.

One woman, caught between a stubborn Protestant husband and Father Prost, who insisted on a Catholic upbringing for her children, plotted with the husband to cry "rape" in the confessional, but did not go through with it. Rev. Joseph Prost, C.SS.R., "Relationes," *Annales Congregationis SS, Redemptoris Provinciae Americanae: Supplementum ad Volumina I, II, III, Pars I,* ed. Rev. Joseph Wuest, C.SS.R. (Ilchestriae, Md.: Typis Congregationis Sanctissimi Redemptoris, 1903), pp. 56-75. Father Prost said expressly that German trustees made more trouble than the Irish ones, and quotes Bp. Hughes as saying the same thing. The reason was that German trustees had often been bureaucrats in the homeland. But, we ought to bear in mind that Irish and French Canadian missioners thought as strongly about their lay trustees and mixed marriages. Remember what Father "Mad Phil" O'Reilly had to say about the Irish. See above, p. 116.

[77]Schwenninger to McCloskey, Syracuse, Jan. 5, 1850, Letterbox A25, NY. This letter was translated for me from the Latin by Prof. J.G. Plante, as already noted, and by Miss Claire Murray, of White Plains.

[78]Rev. Joseph Guerdet to McCloskey, Salina, Sept. 8, 10, 11, 1850, Letterbox A24, NY; Rev. Simon Saenderl to McCloskey, Syracuse, Sept. 9, 11, Oct. 4, 1850, Letterbox A25, NY. By the way, Father Guerdet, a Frenchman, stationed next to Syracuse, had nothing nice to say about Father Noethen or about his former congregation of St. Mary's, Syracuse, or about some of the Irish of his own Church of St. John's, Salina, who were threatening a "split," becuase they could not have their own way. Guerdet to McCloskey, Salina, Feb. 12, March 14, 1850, Letterbox A24, NY.

[79]Undentifiable Laity to McCloskey, Utica, Jan. 12, 1850; Petition with 25 German signatures to McCloskey, c. April, 1850, Utica; both in Letterbox A25, NY; Joseph Ammenwerth to McCloskey, Utica, April 16, 1850, Letterbox A24, NY. I take this opportunity to correct a small error that has been published on the history of St. Joseph's school. Rev. Maurice Imhoff, O.M.C., "Notes on the First Parochial School in Utica," *Central-Blatt and Social Justice,* XXX, No. 12 (March, 1938), p. 387, dated its first year as 1851 and named its first teacher as John B. Jost. But Father Florian who came to St. Joseph's in 1845, spoke of a schoolroom there as early as November of that year, and of a teacher coming in September of 1846. The teacher's name was John Leininger. The school had 100 pupils in the winter of 1848-1849 and 60 in the summer of 1849. Schwenninger to Abbot, St. George's Abbey, Fiecht, Austria, from Utica, N.Y., Sept. 26, 1846, and March 23, 1848. Copies of these two letters are in the archives of St. John's Abbey, Collegeville, Minnesota.

[80]He was in Utica from Sept. 15 till at least Sept. 28, 1850, and probably longer. Arnold to McCloskey, Utica, Sept. 28, 1850, Letterbox A24, NY.

[81]Michael Albrekt to McCloskey, Utica, April 14, 1854; Fanny Homberger to McCloskey Utica, Jan. 11, 1859; both in Letterbox A24, NY; Martin Stadler and Others to McCloskey, Utica, Jan. 11, 1859, Letterbox A25, NY. In 1870, some of the German families of St. Joseph's, who were living in east Utica, in a section called "Corn Hill", received permission from Bp. John J. Conroy to form a new congregation. They did so in that year under the incorporated title of "St. Mary's of the Immaculate Conception." That was the first swarming from St. Joseph's with episcopal approval. Hewitt,

Diocese of Syracuse, p. 243. Hewitt here says that "Michael Albrecht and Jacob Geist were the first lay trustees" of the new church. But he may be using a misnomer. See text and note immediately below.

[82] The trustee system under the Act of 1813 was not mandatory. Bp. McCloskey and the congregation of St. Joseph's were not using a committee of laymen, who were sometimes called trustees, out of habit, but were appointed by the pastor, and had no hold on the temporalities. Archives of the Diocese of Albany has a copy of the "Rules."

[83] Hewitt, *Diocese of Syracuse,* p. 232.

[84] Rolfson, "Schwenninger Memorial", X, Nos. 1-2 (March-June, 1959), 107-119, XI, Nos. 1-2 (March-June, 1960), 91, 176-178; Rev. John B. McGloin, S.J., "A California Gold Rush Padre: New Light on the 'Padre of Paradise Flat'," *California Historical Society Quarterly,* XL,, No. 1 *(March, 1961), 49-67;* Rev. Henry L. Walsh, S.J., *Hallowed Were the Gold Dust Trails* (Santa Clara: Univ. Santa Clara Press, 1946), pp. 263-269, 327-330, 410-418, and *passim,* and miscellaneous information from the archives of St. Vincent's Archabbey, Latrobe, Penn.

CHAPTER XIV

THE ROOTS OF THE TREE

The few Catholics in the young United States had no organization to speak of. They lived in insalutary neglect. As immigrants, amidst impiety and proselytism, they groped in a confusion of cultures. Slowly, deliberately, Holy Mother Church, as Catholics once were wont to say, came looking for her strays. But, they were chasing isms. In religion, they had lay trustees. As the *fabriques d'église* of France and the *marguilliers* of Canada,[1] those elected officials found a welcome in the Church, so long as they minded her law. But, under an American sky, there were those who kicked against the goad. Schism and heresy met interdict and excommunication. Like falling stars in September, the apostates left the Church.

The lay trustees are silhouetted in their own frame of time. From a Europe in revolution, they came to an America in reform. The Garibaldis in the Old World were matched by the John Browns in the New. Everything, everywhere, was changing. In upstate New York, some Catholics threatened to kill their priests and burn their churches. They cursed their bishops. They desecrated their altars. But, in the end, as Patrick Walsh of Carthage, the most of them repented, and remained in the faith of Peter. Were they worse than Father Rooney in scandal, or Bishop Dubois in the management of property? Did they diffffer from Protestants, who also fought in their churches, and rioted against their ministers, and broke up their Sunday services?[2]

Still, it is good for the children to ponder the sins of their fathers, for which they are paying, yea, unto the fourth generation and we may no more pass over those misdeeds than an astronaut can ignore the dark side of the moon. At Belleville, in Jefferson County, in 1845, Father Philip Gillick told the congregation that he would rather be the master of a dog kennel than the pastor of their church.

It was also alleged that he had threatened to shoot two of their number, if they did not dismiss their trustees.³ The congregation of Manlius, in Onondaga County, in 1848, paid Father Theodore Noethen the sum of four shillings, that is, a half-dollar, for his expense on two visits to them from Syracuse. And, they promised him the bonus of a beating if he came again. When the bishop asked how it happened that he was the first missioner to make such a complaint of them, he replied: "They cursed me, because I signed the deed of the land in Your name."⁴

At Malone, in Franklin County, in 1849, Father Bernard McCabe of St. Joseph's barred a few men from the sacraments until they admitted before the congregation that they had spread lies about him. He gasconaded from the altar that his enemies "would get one leg drawn thro' the other."⁵ Father Daniel Cull dragged a man from a pew in the Church of St. John's, Schenectady, in 1849, becuase he had not paid his pew rent, probably, and then called off the Mass. But, later in the day, he said Mass for a few dozen of his friends, and afterwards "prayed that his curse & the curse of God might fall on John Keely & Patk Keyes." The complainant added: "This makes the third time that he has pronounced this dreadful malediction."⁶ At Keeseville, in Essex County, in 1849, at the Church of the Immaculate Conception, the enemies of Father Michael A. McDonnell became so fed up with his tyranny, as they petitioned the bishop, that "an open war is anticipated in the church."⁷

At Constableville, in Lewis County, in 1850, some of the people cried out to the bishop for relief from Father Francis J. Kapp, who had nagged them into buying a farm for his thriftier support, which they could ill afford. "Many a man has not bread one half of the time over night for his children."⁸ The trustees of St. Mary's, in Potsdam, in 1851, accused Father James Mackey of receiving more money for the church than he recorded.⁹ The members of St. John's of Schenectady, in 1851, quarreled with Father Anthony McGeough over their right to send their children to the public school without being excommunicated. That case is special, because it bared a viper in the bosom of the Church, that is, nativism among Catholics. Wrote a layman to the bishop.¹⁰

> Now as a Native born American Citizen I cannot conscienciously submit to have my & my children's rights usurped by a Foreign subject of a Monarchy...for the Rev. Gentleman is not even an adopted Citizen.

At Little Falls, in Herkimer County, in 1858, the trustees of St.

Mary's made a contract with Father Bartholomew McLaughlin to divide the income of the church in a certain way between them, and to give the trustees the right to hire and to pay the schoolteacher. Later on, they complained to the bishop that the pastor was reneging. "We want our rights, nothing more or less."[11] The trustees of the Church of Saints Peter and Paul, at Dayansville, in Lewis County, in 1859, accused Father Anthony Heimo, a Franciscan Conventual of perjury in a civil suit between them. But the judge in the case came to the friar's defense before the grand jury, and he was not indicted.[12]

The hydra-heads of lay trusteeism, which begat bloodshed at the altar, discord in the courts, and rancor at the side of the grave, were all attached to the same body. It was the spirit of localism and individualism, which lives in every Catholic congregation, ready to roar when conditions are ripe. So it was, that at Troy and Utica, at Carthage and Oswego, at Potsdam and Malone, at Croghan and Rosiers, at Albany and Florence, at Chateaugay and Rouses Point, at Manlius and Little Falls, at Plattsburgh and Ogdensburg, at Watertown, West Turin and Waddington, at Syracuse, Schenectady and Saratoga Springs, at Keeseville, Belleville Danville and Constableville, the many-throated populism of the Catholics of the diocese of Albany rumbled for a generation before the Civil War, and afterwards, in the post-war period, here and there, for years, like thunder on the horizon, after the storm has passed.[13]

Nevertheless, the diocese grew. Its Catholics multiplied in the period of 1790-1865 from 2,500 to 134,100,[14] and its priests, who were at first as rare as comets, were 95 in the end. At the close of the Civil War, the see of Albany had an inventory of 120 churches, 8 chapels, 60 mission stations, 3 academies for boys, 2 for girls, 6 orphanages, and parochial schools for more than a dozen congregations. Its religious orders in residence were, of males, the Augustinians, the Oblates, the Jesuits, the Brothers of the Christian Schools, the Franciscan Conventuals and the Brothers of the Third Order of St. Francis. Of females, they were the Sisters of Charity, the Sisters of Mercy, the Sisters of St. Joseph of Carondelet, the Sisters of the Third Order of St. Francis, the Sisters of Charity from Montreal (Grey Nuns), and the Ladies of the Sacred Heart. Not the least of Bishop McCloskey's assets were his twenty young men at the Provincial Seminary in Troy, in that bright and bygone day.[15]

Immigration goes far to explain the growth. There were 1,442,200 Catholics who entered the port of New York in 1847-1864.[16] It was a new Diaspora. Said Bishop Louis de Goesbriand of Burlington: "We believe these emigrants are called by God to cooperate in the conversion of America."[17] But, it was more than immigration. In spite of weak bishops, bad priests, stiffnecked laymen, apostates, Know Nothings, poverty, ignorance, sin, of dizzying democracy itself, it was the steadfastness of the immigrant in the Faith that built the Church in America and in New York. In 1838, when the spirit of nativism was on the rise, a German in Erie, Pennsylvania, described an instance of it.[18] It had been the custom there, at funerals, to process to the cemetery in silence. In deference to it, the Catholic priest had performed the service for the dead in the home of the deceased, and had then removed his vestments in order to join the laity in the procession. But, our German, who had just arrived from Rhenish Bavaria, protested to the priest[19] against such a non-Catholic usage. He argued in the name of American religious liberty. Then, another Catholic died.

> When the corpses had been placed in the wagon which served as a hearse, the pastor, still wearing his vestments approached me, asking me to sing the Miserere. There were many people present and I was told by them not to sing, as that would cause disturbance and arouse ridicule. The pastor continued to urge me: Sing, sing! The thought came to me: I may be laughed at in this world (if I sing now) but not in the next. The priest and I walked forward then, side by side, the hearse following us. I started to sing, the pastor joining me as heartily as he could. The procession passed through the city; crowds of people gathered near us, and some followed us to the grave, for they never before had seen or heard anything like this. We had to walk quite a distance to the cemetery, and therefore sang the Miserere twice. But no one laughed at or jeered us. On the contrary: after the burial many told the pastor they had never witnessed such a scene and that they liked it very much, these comments making our pastor very happy.

Behind that staunchness of the immigrant, there lay the organization of the Church. The Holy See ruled the missions, in Rome, through the Congregation for the Propagation of the Faith,[20] and, in America, through the bishops, collectively and severally, in councils, synods and pastoral letters.[21] What held that organization together was the voice of obedience, period! Said Bishop McCloskey: "When the Holy Father speaks, there remains nothing for me but silence. His will in all things to me is law."[22] Said Father Florian to Bishop McCloskey: "Concerning my person, do what you please,"[23] Said three hundred laymen of St. Paul's of Oswego to the bishop, in defense of their *sogarth aroon* and in a rare plea by the semi-literate and silent majority: "We are happy to inform you [Dear Bishop] that the number of such men [adversaries of the pastor] are few and amongst them are the old trustees who we heartily wish to get Rid off & to come under the administration of the Dioces."[24]

Thanks be to the Catholics of Europe for great gifts of money and articles of worship to the Catholics of America. In 1822-1871, the Society for the Propagation of the Faith, in France, sent a total of $4,000,000 and the Leopoldine Association, in Austria, and the Ludwig Missions-Union, in Bavaria, each contributed $500,000.[25] These alms were a response to pleas from the bishops here. In 1830, Bishop Dubois of New York wrote to the Society in Lyons.[26] The money from it to him in 1828 had gone as a loan to St. Mary's, in Albany, and a congregation in Newark, New Jersey, to enlarge their churches, which were overcrowded. Of his visitation in the North Country, he added:

> The fatigues of the body were nothing like the anguish of the spirit which I felt at the sight of this multitude of abandoned souls which I found during my visitation who asked me for pastors, and whom I could answer only through my tears.

In 1852, Bishop McCloskey appealed to the Emperor Francis Joseph of Austria:[27]

> The undersigned, an humble missionary Bishop, having charge over a poor and widely extended flock, presumes to recommend the claims of his poor, among whom are not less than 12,000 Germans, to Your Majesty's kind consideration.

As a result, the diocese of Albany received $43,844 from the Society in 1847-1866,[28] $3,000 from the Association in 1846-1860,[29] and, in the same period, $1,200 from the Missions-Union.[30] Best of all gifts from Europe, in the eyes of some, were the priests.[31]

Thanks be to the relgous orders, too, for contributions of material resources, special skills and the very lives of their men and women. Think of the Redemptorists and the Paulists.[32] When we talk of the mass revivals in America, in the nineteenth century, with their organization, showmanship and emotion, those commandos of Christ must be mentioned. It was they who invented some of the techniques of modern evangelism.[33] After all, the Redemptorists had been giving folk missions for a hundred years before anyone ever heard tell of Charles Grandison Finney and the Burned-over District of upstate New York.[34]

Founded by St. Alphonsus Liguori in 1732 to preach missions from diocese to diocese and parish to parish, at the invitation of bishops and pastors, the Redemptorists, until 1858, and the Redemptorists and the Paulists, separately after that, crisscrossed the continent of North America. In 1851-1861, they preached about 125 missions in English, German and French, in the northeastern quarter of the United States, distributed a quarter-million communions and heard about the same number of confessions. Fourteen of the missions were in the diocese of Albany, as well as thirty thousand of the communions. Add to that a host of conversions, confirmations, vocations, marriages made good, and fires of faith that were stoked up in the cold hearts of every class and conditon of the sons of Adam. Such as "one of the chief forces of the Catholic revival in the nineteenth century."[35]

Picture one of those missions: a large platform, with a ten-foot cross under a white cloth canopy, at the front of the church, built to stage the preacher and to give him leg room, whilst he strove to rouse the throng to tears with blunt and pungent words. It was not a Methodist circuit rider. It was a Paulist Father, brandishing a crucifix and preaching "fire and brimstone." Picture St. Patrick's, in Utica, (where Father Florian had once taken refuge), in 1855, during twelve mornings and evenings of instruction and exhortation, when pastor and people sat like stones. But, then came that last evening. Let one of the Paulists who was there describe it.[36]

> The renewal of the (baptismal) vows made up for all. Never did I hear such answers from men's throats, and at the word *"Farewell"* there was such a burst of grief as I never heard. Some wailed right out...The pastor stood and looked on the scene as much as to say, "What's this fuss about?" All being done we returned to the house. Half an hour afterwards the pastor entered our room with his eyes red from weeping.

Picture St. Peter's, in Troy, in 1852, one of the most beautiful Gothic churches in America, (which Father Philip Mark O'Reilly had helped to build with anguish four years earlier), where, at the end of the two-week mission, the Way of the Cross was solemnly erected and performed, with vestments and acolytes and fourteen little boys, carrying the picture-stations, and fourteen little girls, in white, carrying crosses, and "the aisles were so crowded that it was difficult to pass along."[37]

Picture St. John the Baptist's, in Plattsburgh in 1858, where the traveling mission band reported why they did not mind the necessity of scouring the countryside to collect the well-to-do farmers.[38]
We had here an evidence of the good which the persevering zeal of a faithful priest can effect, for owing to the exertions of the former Pastor, the Rev. Father Rooney, the vice of drunkenness is almost unknown, and in place of its attendant miseries, intelligence and prosperity prevail.

Picture St. Peter's, in Saratoga Springs, in January of 1852, when the snow lay deep, and "the sacred blood froze in the chalice," and the old, wooden church was filled with workingmen at five o'clock in the mornings. Picture St. Joseph's, in Albany, a few weeks later, on the last evening, a spillover crowd, kneeling in the snow, to receive the Papal Benediction. Picture the scenes at other missions: the Negro servant girl, after her baptism, dancing for joy at the gifts of a cruxifix and a prayer book, and, afterwards, converting an Irish girl from Ulster; an old Catholic, dashing his Masonic badge to the floor; a bulging church saying the rosary, and sounding, in the street, like the roaring of the surf; the ex-jailbird, confessing, after thirty years; the couple, in twenty-three years of concubinage, being maried and going off happily; the workmen at a blast furnace, escorting the mission fathers to the railroad train, and saying "God be with you"; the consecration to Our Lady of a church full of men; the old man, fasting on one meatless meal a day; a notorious nativist, "beside himself with rage"; the whiskey sellers, knocking the bungs from their barrels; four hundred children at their communion, singing sweetly; the Irishman, killing pigs in a slaughterhouse, and taking a minute to baptize his friend there, validly; a bunch of men and women, dragging a sinner to confession, an old woman, trudging the thirteen miles to a mission, across the ice of the St. Lawrence River; a young Catholic wife, whose tears could not wheedle an absolution, until her Protestant husband made the promise about the rearing of their children; the Protestant quartet, singing a High Mass; the Catholics of a far-flung country mission, all together for the first time, and feeling the strength of their numbers;[39] and, in the price of all that salvation, the Redemptorists in cold confessionals, in the cellar of a church, for ten hours a day, and not long thereafter, their names in a marble slab, before the high altar of the Church of the Most Holy Redeemer, in New York City, all dead before their time, all "martyrs of the confessional.[40]

One thing remains to be said about the importance of those missions. It was not only that they were flung, like a defiance, into the teeth of the Know Nothings, who fumed in futile protest. And it was not that they also made converts, who were publicized by Catholic editors in the same way that Crazy Horse later counted coups. But the importance of those missions is bared by the statistics.

In 1858-1862, there were 154 converts and 106,880 communions.[41] After years without priests, the Catholics had to be habituated by the missions to the sacraments.

In spite of the divisions among Catholics and of apostasy and nativism, Catholic life flourished in the diocese of Albany in the early nineteenth century on account of the natural resources and the improvements of man, which made New York the Empire State, the organization of the Church and its religious orders, immigration, the European mission aid societies, the steadfastness of priests and people on the frontier in the Faith, and the friendly help of some Protestants. There have been those too, who believe with Father Florian that "the spreading of our faith and the extension of the Holy Church of Christ is not the work of man, but one of the great deeds of God.[42]

[1] Dignan, *Church Property,* pp. 67-70.
[2] Joel Munsell, *The Annals of Albany* (10 vols.; 2d ed.; Albany: Joel Munsell, 1869-1871), VII, 338, 349-350, IX, 241, 343.
[3] Michael Kearney to McCloskey, Belleville, Jan. 4, 1845, Letterbox A23, NY.
[4] Noethen to McCloskey, Syracuse, March 18, 21, 1848, Jan. 17, 1849, Letterbox A25, NY. Manlius had lay trustee trouble on and off, at least until 1880, and probably until 1901. Hewitt, *Diocese of Syracuse,* pp. 130-137.
[5] Charles Carlisle to Father James Rooney, Malone, March 28, 1849. Letterbox A25, NY.
[6] Dennis Haugh to McCloskey, Schenectady, Dec. 17, 1849, Letterbox A24, NY. See also C. Martin to McCloskey, Schenectady, Jan. 5, 1850. Letterbox A25, NY, in defense of Father Cull. The trouble was over the deed to the priest's house.
[7] Petition from 76 Laymen to McCloskey, Keeseville, prob. 1849, Letterbox A24, NY. The bishop was scheduled to visit Keeseville on July 11, 1849. Wm. Henry Hoyt to McCloskey, St. Albans, Vt., July 6, 1849. AA.
[8] Jacob F. Brest and Others to McCloskey, Constableville, March 20, 1850, Letterbox A24, NY.
[9] Rev. Patrick Phelan to McCloskey, Waddington, April 22, 1851, Letterbox A25, NY.
[10] Ferdinand J. Myers to McCloskey, Schenectady March 23, 1851. Letterbox A25, NY. See also Rev. Daniel Falvey to McCloskey, Schenectady, Nov. 30, 1859, AA.
[11] M. Reddy to McCloskey, Little Falls, Dec. 30, 1858, Jan. 27, 1859, Jan.

18, 1860, AA, Jan. 15, 1859, Letterbox A25, NY.

[12]William R. Wadsworth to McCloskey, Constableville, Sept. 17, 1859, AA. Wadsworth was the judge.

[13]I list villages about which the sources do not expressly use the word "trustee," but imply it. See Vincent Le Ray de Chaumont to McCloskey, New York City, July 2, 1852, AA; Rev. Michael Guth to McCloskey, Rosiere, Jan. 24, 1849, Letterbox A24, NY; Bp. Hughes to Coadjutor McCloskey, New York City, June 3, 1844, Letterbox A22, NY; Rev. Joseph Stokes to McCloskey, Utica, July 4, 1849, Letterbox A25, NY; Rev. James Agidius Moschall to McCloskey, West Turin, Feb. 11, 1851, Letterbox A25, NY; Rev. J.M. Barry to McCloskey, Saratoga Springs, June 1, 1863, Letterbox A24, NY. After the O'Conor Act of 1863 (see above, p. 183), the Church of Notre Dame in Ogdensburg had four trustees in 1864 in contravention of that act, and the trustees were active there at least till 1878. Garand, *History of Ogdensburg,* pp. 257-267, 277-284. At St. Peter's in Plattsburgh, there was a threat of a lawsuit between the congregation and the Oblate Fathers in 1869, and Bp. Conroy in that year had to insist that the pastors conform to the O'Conor Act by reducing the number of trustees, presumably. There was trouble there as late as 1881, and in 1889, the lay trustees seem to have been in legal possession of St. Peter's. Hogue, *St. Peter's,* pp. 40-48, 55. See also "Real Estate, R.C.D.," AA. St. John's, Utica, had trouble till 1882, and St. Mary's, Manlius, until 1901. Hewitt, *Diocese of Syracuse,* pp. 131-137, 222-223. Also Smith, *Ogdensburg, passim.*

[14]See Appendix II, and p. 43.

[15]*Catholic Directory* for 1848-1865, annually, *passim.*

[16]That includes only the Irish, German, English and Scotch Catholics. See Appendix II. The total immigration at Quebec and Montreal was 531,477 in 1847-1864, and 72% of it went on to the U.S. See above, p. 129.

[17]Quoted in Wade, "Survivance," p. 173.

[18]Rev. George Timpe (ed.), "An Emigrant's Letter of 1838," *Central- Blatt and Social Justice, XXIX, No. 12 (March, 1937),* 385-387.

[19]It was Bernard McCabe. He served in the dio. of Albany in 1844-1857.*Ibid.: Catholic Directory,* 1845-1858.

[20]For the papal documents on America, see Shearer, *Pontificia Americana.* For a discussion of the activity of the Congregation in North America, see Rev. Raymond Corrigan, *Die Kongregation De Propaganda Fide und ihre Tätigkeit in Nord-Amerika* (München: E. Joergen, 1928). For the published records of the Congregation, see Ionnes Dominicus Mansi (ed.); *Sacrorum Conciliorum Nova et Amplissima Collectio* (53 vols.: Paris and Leipzig: Hubert Welti, 1903-1927, Kraus Reprint, 1964), XLIV, XLVII-XLVIII, *passim;* Presbyteris S.J.E. Domo B.V.M. Sive Labe Conceptae ad Lacum, *Acta et Decreta Sacrorum Conciliorum Recentiorum Collectio Lacensis* (7 vols.; Freiburg im Breisgau: Sumtibus Herder, 1870-1890), III, *passim;* Raphaelis de Martinis, *Iuris Pontificii de Propaganda Fide, Pars Prima* (2 vols.; Roma: Ex Typographia Polyglotta, S.C. De Propaganda Fide, 1888-1897), VI, 25, gives the bull that erected the diocese of Albany.

[21]Baltimore was first the metropolitan and then the primatial see of the U.S. in the 19th century. For a discussion of its councils, provincial and plenary

(national), and a resume of their legislation, see Guilday, *Councils of Baltimore.* For the texts of the pastoral letters from those councils, see Rev. Peter Guilday, *The National Pastorals of the American Hierarchy (1792-1919)* (Wash., D.C.: National Catholic Welfare Council, 1923). For a discussion of the diocesan synods and provincial councils of New York, see Rev. John J. Considine, "The History of Canonical Legislation in the Diocese and Province of New York, 1842-1861," (Unpublished MA Dissertation Catholic Univ. of Amer., 1937). For the texts of that legislation see Corrigan, *Synodorum.* Bp. McCloskey covened one synod for the diocese of Albany on Sunday, Oct. 7, 1855. Shea, *Church,* IV, 479. An agenda, in his hand, gives the following rubrics: impediments of marriage, mixed marriage, confessionals, mass in private houses, sanctuary, sacred vessels, vestments, church accounts, theological studies, preparation of sermons, conferences, clerical deportment, schools, Peter Pence, clerical fund, and so on. No date, Letterbox, A38, NY.

[22] He was asking not to be considered for the vacant metropolitan see of New York. McCloskey to Cardinal de Reisach, Albany, Jan. 26, 1864, Letterbox A38, NY. This is a copy of a letter in the archives of Propaganda in Rome.

[23] Schwenninger to McCloskey, Utica, Sept. 11, 1849, Letterbox A25, NY.

[24] Members of the congregation of St. Paul's of Oswego to McCloskey, Oswego, Feb. 5, 1846, Letterbox A23, NY.

[25] Rev. Theodore Roemer, O.F.M., *Ten Decades of Alms* (St. Louis: B. Herder, 1942), pp. 221-222.

[26] Dubois to the Society, Rome, Italy, March 16, 1830, *Annales,* IV, No. 22 (Oct. 1830), 447-465.

[27] McCloskey to the Emperor, Albany, prob. 1851, or 1852, Letterbox A38, NY. This is a draft.

[28] Rev. Edward John Hickey, *The Society for the Propagation of the Faith* (Wash., D.C.: Catholic Univ. of Amer., 1922), p. 188.

[29] Rev. Benjamin J. Blied, *Austrian Aid to American Catholics,* 1830-1860 (Milwaukee: Author, 1944), pp. 26-27.

[30] Rev. Theodore Roemer, "The Ludwig-Missionsverein and the Church in the United States (1838-1918)," *Franciscan Studies* No. 12 (Aug., 1933), p. 105. Some have seen as much of nationalism as of Christianity in these gifts. In fact, it is believed that Bp. McCloskey received no more from the Missions-Union of Bavaria than is above-stated, because of complaints that he was slighting his Germans, *Ibid.,* p. 105; Blied, *Austrian Aid,* pp. 29-32.

[31] Before 1847, when Bp. McCloskey came to Albany, most of them in the diocese were foreign-born; afterwards, many of them.

[32] I single out these two orders, only because space will not let me dilate on the others. The Paulists separated from the Redemptorists in 1858, on account of a call to the English-speaking peoples of America. For the Redemptorists, see Byrne, *Redemptorist Centenaries,* and Curley, *Provincial Story.* For the Paulists, see Rev. Vincent F. Holden, C.S.P., *The Yankee Paul: Isaac Thomas Hecker* (Milwaukee: Bruce Publishing Co., 1958). For the work of both together, see Archives of the Paulist Fathers, "Chronicle of Missions," MS., 2 vols. This is a copy of the original in the archives of the Redemptorists.

[33]"Chronicle of Missions," I, *passim;* Byrne, *Redemptorist Centenaries,* chap. XI; Curley, *Provincial Story,* chap. VI; Holden, *Yankee Paul,* chaps. VIII-IX.

[34]For Protestant revivalism in the region of the diocese of Albany and elsewhere see Bernard A. Weisberger, *They Gathered at the River* (Chicago: Quadrangle Books, 1966, originally 1958); Timothy L. Smith, *Revivalism and Social Reform* (New York: Harper & Row, 1965, originally 1957); Whitney R. Cross, *The Burned-Over District* (New York: Harper & Row, 1965, originally 1950), all *passim.*

[35]In Europe and America, Byrne, *Redemptorist Centenaries,* p. 260. In Europe, the Redemptorists were persecuted and expelled by the revolutionaries and liberals of 1848. *Ibid.,* p. 261. Bavarian legislators called them "Jesuits in masks." *Freeman's Journal,* Aug. 14, 1847. Most of the detail on the American missions of the Redemptorists and Paulists comes from the "Chronicle of Missions," I, *passim.*

[36]"Chronicle of Missions," I, 74.

[37]*Ibid.,* I, 28.

[38]*Ibid.,* I, 151.

[39]*Ibid.,* I, *passim.* Where in the world did Weisberger, *They Gathered at the River,* p. 140, get the idea that "Catholicism had no room for the revival"?

[40]Byrne, *Redemptorist Centenaries,* pp. 272-273. While the Americans preached above, the Europeans heard confessions below. The Americans founded the Paulists. Curley, *Provincial Story,* p. 117.

[41]"Chronicle of Missions," I, 298. For 1840-1931, the Redemptorists of the Baltimore Province (all of U.S. and Canada till 1875, thereafter east of Chicago) count 32,048 missions, 13,497 converts, 6,923 catechumens, and 21,478,909 confessions. Byrne, *Redemptorist Centenaries,* p. 278.

[42]Rolfson, "Schwenninger Memorial," XI, Nos. 1-2 '(March-June 1960), 176.

APPENDIX I

The statistics for the Catholic Church in the United States, 1847-1864, are stated in the order of diminishing reliability. They suffer from the same crudity of compilation as that of the statistics for the entire Church. The reasons were the inchoate nature of the Church in the U.S. then, the difficulty of getting information, owing to the Civil War, and the bar arithmetic of the compilers. Ciangetti, pp. 57-70; the *Catholic Directory for 1848*, p. 273; the *Catholic Directory for 1865*, pp. 51-256. (The *Directory for 1865* gives no tabular summary, as the others do.) Since there were no episcopal returns from the big sees of New York, New Orleans and Baltimore in 1864, the actual number of priests and churches must have exceeded those that were reported for that year, and that are given here. The numbers of the communicants, which I give, need explaining. Shaughnessy, *Immigrant* p. 189, gives the Catholics in the U.S. as 663,000 in 1840, 1,606,000 in 1850, 3,103,-000 in 1860 and 4,504,000 in 1870. Since these figures of his depend on his estimates of the numbers of Catholic immigrants to the U.S. every year, and since the numbers of immigrants rose and fell erratically from year to year, I could not extrapolate from Shaughnessy's four figures, above-given, to those for the two years of 1847 and 1864. What I did was to set up a numerical series, which pivots on Shaughnessy's four figures, and, at the same time, reflects the annual tide of Catholic immigration to the U.S. for 1847-1864. For the whole annual immigration to the U.S., by countries of origin, I used the U.S., Bureau of Census, *Historical Statistics of the United States, 1789-1945* (Wash., D.C.: U.S. Govt. Print Off., 1949), p. 34. For the Catholic percentages among the immigrants, by countries of origin, I used Shaughnessy, *Immigrant*, p. 112, for the Irish and Germans. For the English and Scotch, I used James E. Handley, *The Irish in Scotland, 1789-1845* (Cork: Cork Univ. Press, 1945), pp. 108, 110, 91. Handley corrects Shaughnessy on those two ethnic groups. There are no official figures for immigration to the U.S. from Canada for that period. The Irish, Germans, English and Scotch provided most of the Catholics in the U.S. then. For an idea of what the numerical series, aforementioned, looks like, see Appendix II.

APPENDIX II

The Catholic population of the diocese, from year to year, made a numerical series that I can display by beginning with three fairly fixed points, viz., the N.Y. censal figures for 1845, 1855 and 1865. See *N.Y., Cen-*

APPENDICES

sus, 1875, p. 2. The numerical series that I am after must correlate with another numerical series, which is the one that shows the numbers of Catholic immigrants to the port of New York, year by year, in the same period. New York City's port was the chief source of Catholics in the diocese. See pp. 129-130. I have distilled this latter series from the U.S., Scty. of State, "Report of Passenger Arrivals," annually, 1846-1848, in the *U.S. Govt. Documents Serial Set*, Vols. 500, 518 and 538; Kapp, *Immigration*, pp. 232-233; William Forbes Adams, *Ireland and the Irish Emigration to the New World from 1815 to the Famine* (New Haven: Yale Univ. Press, 1932), pp. 413-414; with the aid of the Catholic percentages from Shaughnessy, *Immigrant*, p. 112, and Handley, *Irish*, pp. 91, 108 and 110. Thus we get the following:

year	Catholics to Port of N.Y. (rounded)	Catholics in the Diocese (rounded)
1845	38,300	69,200
6	54,800	72,800
7	60,800	76,700
8	97,200	83,000
9	110,700	90,200
1850	109,900	97,300
1	151,700	107,200
2	131,900	115,800
3	127,900	124,200
4	121,700	132,100
1855	52,000	138,200
6	54,200	137,700
7	72,000	137,200
8	30,600	137,000
9	35,200	136,700
1860	49,500	136,300
1	29,300	136,100
2	34,600	135,800
3	83,300	135,200
4	89,700	134,500
1865	84,100	134,100
6	90,700	134,700

"Catholics to Port of N.Y." means only German, English, Scotch and Irish." Catholics in the Diocese" means only the foreign-born groups that are itemized at the end of Appendix III, and does not include native Americans. Bp. McCloskey estimated the Catholics in his diocese only as follows: 60,000 in 1848, 60,000-70,000 in 1849, 80,000 in 1850, 80,000 in 1851 and 120,000 in 1852. His successor, Bp. John Joseph Conroy, estimated over 230,000 for 1866. *Catholic Directory for 1849,* annually, to that *for 1867,* sections on the Albany diocese. Since my estimates are based partly on the New York census reports, I believe that they are more accurate than these episcopal estimates. Bp. McCloskey's under-estimates are understandable, in view of the famine stampede after 1847. But I cannot explain Bp. Conroy's huge overestimate.

A contemporary observer in 1864 believed that "there must be a fixed ratio between the growth of the flocks [of Catholics] and the multiplication of pastors." E. Rameau, "The Progress of the Church in the United States," *The Catholic World,* I, No. 1 (April, 1865), pp. 7-9. The article appeared originally as "Du Mouvement Catholique aux Etats-Unis," *Le Correspondant* (Paris), LXIII (Sept.-Dec., 1864), 689-716. The author suggested the ratio of 2,000 or more Catholics to every priest, as applicable not only to the entire U.S., but apparently to every diocese there as well. Shaughnessy, *Immigrant,* p. 262, prints a table that shows a tight ratio of about 1,100 Catholics to every priest in the U.S., throughout 1790-1920, although in the text, he speaks only of the probability of such a ratio over decades on the frontier. *Ibid.,* p. 258. But Shaughnessy's figures are defective. For example, in the above-mentioned table, he gives 1,800 priests for the U.S. in 1850, whereas the *Catholic Directory for 1851,* p. 224, gives only 1,303.

In spite of Rameau's hocus-pocus of reasoning, to my mind, I tested his theory for 1855. Based on the numbers of Catholics, which were estimated by the bishops from year to year, and the number of "priests on the mission," the numbers of Catholics per priest in the several dioceses were as follows; Baltimore 1,714; Philadelphia 1,346; Pittsburgh 714; New York 3,-309; Buffalo 1,282; Hartford 1,410; Burlington 2,500; Cincinnati 1,100; Detroit 2,656; and Cleveland 1,041. The *Catholic Directory for 1856,* p. 308, gives the data for these calculations. In the diocese of Albany, the like numbers fluctuated as follows: 1,964 in 1847, 1,442 in 1850, 1,791 in 1853 and 1,292 in 1864. See *Directories,* 1848-1865. There was even less chance of a fixed ratio between the numbers of Catholics and the dollar value of church property in that day of flux and makeshift, when the Holy Sacrifice of the Mass was commonly celebrated in upper rooms, as it were, of one sort or another. Rameau's ratio typified the 19th-century quest for a natural law of mathematical form to express human relations.

APPENDIX III

(a) The New York, Scty. of State, *Census of the State of New York for 1845* (Albany: Carroll & Cook, 1846), Recapitulation Table No. 1 [no pagination; at back of book], in sorting the population by "place or origin," assigns 93,949 persons to "Great Britain and Possessions." That lump covered every British acre from Bombay west to Vancouver Island. To break it open, I assume that the ratio of Irish to British in the diocese was the same as the ratio of Irish to British among the immigrants to the ports of Quebec and New York. At Quebec, in 1829-1845, the ratiowas 71.5%. Cowan, *Emigration,* p. 289; Adams, *Irish Emigration,* pp. 413-414. At New York, in 1829-1845, the ratio was 58.7% U.S., Scty. of State, "Report of Passenger Arrivals," 1830-1846, annually, in the *United States Government Documents Serial Set,* Vols. 209, 221, 235, 257, 275, 291, 304, 331, 340, 369, 378, 404, 422, 463, 486, and 500; Bromwell, *Immigration,* p. 86. The combined ratio at the two ports was 65.1%. That Irish part of 93,949 was 61,161. Shaughnessy, *Immigrant,* p. 112, suggests 81% as the Catholic part of the Irish then. So, the Catholic Irish in the diocese in 1845 were 49,540.

(b) This is 79% of 114,566. Shaughnessy, *Immigrant,* p. 112, and the *N.Y., Census, 1855,* pp. 168-177, which now begins to distinguish the immigrants from Ireland.

(c) This is 77% of 104,138. New York, Supt. of the Census, *Census of the State of New York for 1865* (Albany: Chas. Van Benthuysen & Sons, 1867), pp. 183-194; Shaughnessy, *Immigrant,* p. 112. The foreign-born population in the state, during the Civil War, lost 80,987 persons. *N.Y., Census 1875,* p. 8. Immigration to the port of New York plummeted. See Appendix II and Kapp, *Immigration,* pp. 232-233.

(d) This is 30% of 6,889. *N.Y. Census, 1845,* Recapitulation Table No. 1; Shaughnessy, *Immigrant,* p. 112.

(e) This is 31% of 33,815. *N.Y., Census, 1855,* pp. 168-177; Shaughnessy, *Immigrant,* p. 112. In 1850, Bp. McCloskey said that his Germans numbered 10,000. Rev.Emmet H.Rothan, O.F.M., *The German Catholic Immigrant in the United States (1830-1860)* (Wash., D.C.: Cath. Univ.Amer., 1946), p. 20.

(f) This is 34% of 32,296. *N.Y. Census, 1865,* pp. 183-194; Shaughnessy, *Immigrant,* p. 112.

(g) This number hides in "Great Britain and Possession," and defies exposure. *N.Y. Census, 1845,* Recapitulation Table No. 1. Canada has never counted her emigrants to the U.S. M.C. Urquhart, *Historical Statistics of Canada* (Cambridge: Univ. Press, 1965), p. 3. The U.S. did not count immigrants from Canada till 1894. U.S., *Historical Statistics,* p. 19. We can back into an idea of the number of Canadian-born Catholics in the diocese of Albany in 1845, if we list all of the other Catholic ethnicities there and then, and subtract their sum from the estimated total of Catholics there and then, using the *N.Y. Census, 1845,* Recapitulation Table No. 1, and Shaughnessy, *Immigrant,* p. 112. Thus, we get: Irish 49,540; Germans 2,067; European French 2,327; Swiss, very few; Dutch, very few; and Polish, very few. The total of these is 53,934. Subtracting that number from 69,200 (see Appendix II) leaves 15,266.

Now we face the problem of separating the French Canadians from those of English, Scotch and Welsh lineage from both the British Isles and the British North American Provinces. There are some guidelines to help us. For instance, there is an indication of the small numbers of French

Canadians in the diocese before the Papineau Rebellion of 1837, in Nell Jane Barnet Sullivan and David Kendall Martin, *A History of the Town of Chazy, Clinton County, New York* (Burlington, Vt.: George Little Pess, 1970), chap. 23, "Settlement after 1804." The town or township of Chazy as well as the village of Chazy within it lay a few miles south of Rouses Point, which was one of the chief entrances from Canada to the U.S. Using the manuscript census returns for Clinton County, the authors say that, in 1810, the town had 234 families in residence, of whom only 18 had French names, and contained 102 members. In 1820, the town had 2,313 inhabitants, of whom 16 families with French names contained 58 persons.

But after 1837, there sprang up a heavy immigration from Canada, owing to economic and political troubles there. The Canadian government took alarm, and appointed two committees to investigate, one in the late forties, and the second, about ten years later. They reported, among other facts, that the French were anywhere from 50% to 90% of the emigrants. Canada, Parliament, *Report of the Select Committee* (1849), pp. 5-10; Canada, Parliament, *Rapport Du Comité Spécial Sur L'Emigration* (Toronto: J. Lovell, 1857), p. 5. It seems probable, however, that that percentage was 90% if not more. The reason is that the people came from the thickly French-speaking counties near New York, where the population was as high as 99% French-speaking and Catholic. Canada, Dominion Bureau of Statistics, *Analysis of the Stages in the Growth of Population in Canada* (Ottawa: Dominion Bureau of Statistics, 1935), pp. 17-21; Canada, Dept. of Agriculture, *Census of Canada, 1870-71* (4 vols.; Ottawa: I.B. Taylor, 1873-6), Vol. IV: *Censuses of Canada, 1665 to 1871: Statistics of Canada, passim.* Therefore, I assume that 90% of the Canadian immigrants were French. Applying this as a touchstone to the 15,266, aforementioned, we get 13,739, or a round 13,740 French Canadian Catholics in the diocese in 1845.

This leaves a remainder of 1,526 Catholics, who were Scotch, English and Welsh. Probably, most of them were Scotch at that time, owing to the fact that some of the Canadian immigration came from Glengarry County, in Ontario, just across the river from Ogdensburg. In 1861, the heavy Scotch population in that county and its vicinity was 51% Catholic. Canada, Board of Registration and Statistics, *Census of the Canadas, 1860-61,* Vol. I: *Personal Census* (2 vols.; Quebec: S.B. Foote, 1863), p. 158. Those from Scotland contained about 7.5% of Catholics, owing to a heavy Irish immigration to Scotland after the Napoleonic Wars. Handley, *Irish in Scotland,* pp. 91, 108, 110. (Shaughnessy, *Immigrant,* p. 112, had assumed only 3%).

(h) This is 90% of 33,317. The *N.Y. Census, 1855,* pp. 168-177, now begins to distinguish the Canadian-born. For the 90% see above, this note, part (g). By the way, I am not using Shaughnessy, *Immigrant,* p. 112, to reckon the Catholics among the Canadian-born. He is wide of the mark, here. He suggests 25% without citing any authority. He apparently did not see the documents that I have used.

(i) This is 90% of 40,761. *N.Y. Census, 1865,* pp. 183-194; above, this note, part (g).

APPENDICES

In summary, the foreign-born Catholics in the diocese of Albany then may be displayed in this way, by land of birth or origin:

	1845	1855	1865
Irish	49,540	90,507	80,186
French Canadian	13,740	29,895	36,685
German	2,067	10,482	10,980
Scotch & English	1,526	2,635	2,423
Welsh	"	187	152
French (Eur.)	2,327	3,893	3,226
Swiss	?	320	303
Dutch	?	209	177
Polish	?	264	195
Total	69,200	138,392	134,327

APPENDIX IV

Here are the statistics to show the growth of the entire population of the state of New York (N.Y.), of the region of the diocese of Albany (ALB), and of its three sub-regions, to wit, the Hudson-Mohawk Corridor (HMC), the North Country (NC), and the Southern Tier (ST), first in absolute numbers, then in percents of gain, by decades. See New York, Supt. of the Census (Franklin B. Hough), *Census of the State of New York for 1865*, (Albany: Charles Van Benthuysen & Sons, 1867), pp. xlii-xliii, or *N.Y. Census, 1875*. p. 2.

	NY	ALB	NC	ST	HMC
1790	340,120	148,139	1,614	?	?
1800	573,175	290,546	17,304	70,235	203,007
1810	960,052	525,944	49,747	136,085	340,112
1820	1,372,824	658,128	87,536	176,693	420,899
1830	1,919,403	895,858	149,867	220,419	525,572
1840	2,428,921	1,054,032	203,829	235,558	614,645
1850	3,097,394	1,229,573	257,631	251,257	720,685
1860	3,880,735	1,349,521	286,880	262,155	800,486
1865	3,827,818	1,333,137	277,748	256,425	798,964
1790-1800	62.5	96.1	972.0	0	0
1800-1810	67.4	81.0	187.4	93.7	67.5
1810-1820	42.9	25.1	75.9	29.8	23.7
1820-1830	39.8	36.1	71.2	24.7	24.8
1830-1840	26.5	17.6	36.0	6.8	16.9
1840-1850	27.5	16.6	26.3	6.6	17.2
1850-1860	25.2	9.7	11.3	4.3	11.0
1860-1865	-1.4	-1.2	-3.1	-2.1	-0.1

(Owing to the undifferentiation of the counties, I cannot reckon a figure, where I place a question mark.)

APPENDIX V

"An Act to provide for the Incorporation of Religious Societies," which replaced an act of 1784, was passed on April 5, 1813. Source is the *Laws of the State of New York, Revised and Passed at the Thirty-Sixth Session of the Legislature,* ed. William P. Van Ness and John Woodworth (2 vols.; rev.; Albany: H.C. Southwick, 1813), II, 212-219. After dealing with the Protestant Episcopal and Dutch Reformed congregations, the Act went on:

III. *And be it further enacted.* That it shall be lawful for the male person of full age, belonging to any other church, congregation or religious society, now or hereafter to be established in this state, and not already incorporated, to assemble at the church meeting-house, or other place where they statedly attend for divine worship, and, by plurality of voices, to elect any number of discreet persons of their church, congregation or society, not less than three, nor exceeding nine in number, as trustees, to take the charge of the estate and property belonging thereto and to transact all affairs relative to the temporalities thereof; and that at such election every male person of full age, who has statedly worshipped with such church, congregation or society, and has formerly been considered as belonging thereto, shall be entitled to vote, and the said election shall be conducted as follows: the minister of such church, congregation or society, or in case of his death or absence, one of the elders ordeacons, church wardens or vestrymen thereof, and for want of such officers, any other person being a member or a stated hearer in such church, congregation or society, shall publicly notify the congregation of the time when and place where, the said election shall be held at least fifteen days before the day of election; that the said notification shall be given for two successive sabbaths or days on which such church, congregation or society, shall statedly meet for public worship, preceding the day of election; that on the said day of election, two of the elders or church wardens, and if there be no such officers, then two of the members of the said church, congregation or society, to be nominated by a majority of the members present, shall preside at such election, receive the votes of the electors, the judges of the qualifications of such electors, and the officers to return the names of the persons who, by plurality of voices, shall be elected to serve as trustees for the said church, congregation or society; and the said returning officers shall immediately thereafter certify, under their hands and seals, the names of the persons elected to serve as trustees for such church, congregation or society, in which certificate the name or title by which the said trustees and their successors shall be forever thereafter called and known, shall be particularly mentioned and described; which said certificate,(being duly acknowledged or proved by one or more of the subscribing witnesses, before the chancellor or one of the judges of the supreme court, or one of the judges of the court of common pleas of the county, where such church or place of worship of such congregation shall be situated, shall be recorded by the clerk of such county in a book to be by him provided for that purpose]; and such trustees and their successors shall also thereupon, by virtue of this act, be a body corporate, by the name or title expressed in such certificate; and the clerk of every county for recording every certificate of incorporation by virtue of the act, shall be entitled to seventy-five cents, and no more.

IV. *And be it further enacted,* That the trustees of every church, congregation or society, herein above mentioned, and their successors, shall respectively have and use a common seal, and may renew and alter the same at their pleasure, and are hereby authorised and empowered to take into their possession and custody all the temporalities belonging to such church, congregation or society, whether the same consist of real or personal estate, and whether the same shall have been given, granted or devised, directly to such church, congregation or society, or to any other person for their use; and also, by their corporate name or title, to sue and be sued in all courts of law or equity, and to recover, hold and enjoy all the debts, demands, rights and privileges, and all churches, meeting-houses, parsonages and burying places, with the appurtenances, and all estates belonging to such church, congregation or society, in whatsoever manner the same may have been acquired, or in whose name soever the same may be held, as fully and amply as if the right or title thereto had originally be vested in the said trustees; and also to purchase and hold other real and personal estate, and to demise, lease and improve the same, for the use of such church, congregation or society, or other pious uses, so as the whole real and personal estate of any such church, congregation or society, other than the corporation of the minister, elders and deacons of the Reformed Protestant Dutch church of the city of New York, and the first Presbyterian church of the city of New York, and the rector, church wardens and vestrymen of St. George's church in the city of New York, and of the minister, elders and deacons of the Reformed Dutch church in the City of Albany, shall not exceed the annual value or income of three thousand dollars; and of the said corporation of the minister, elders and deacons of the Reformed Protestant Dutch church of the city of New York, the annual value or income of nine thousand dollars; and of the said first Presbyterian church of the city of New York, the annual value or income of six thousand dollars; and of the said rector, church wardens and vestrymen of St. George's church, in the city of New York, the annual value or income of six thousand dollars; and of the minister, elders and deacons of the Reformed Dutch church in the city of Albany, the annual value or income of ten thousand dollars; and also to repair and alter their churches or meeting houses, and to erect others if necessary, and to erect dwelling-houses for the use of their ministers, and school-houses and other buildings for the use of such church, congregation or society; and such trustees shall also have power to make rules and orders for managing the temporal affairs of such church, congregation or society, and to dispose of all monies belonging thereto, and to regulate and order the renting the pews in their churches and meeting-houses, and the perquisites for the breaking of the ground in the cemetery or church yards, and in the said churches and meeting-houses for burying the dead, and all other matters relating to the temporal concerns and revenues of such church, congregation or society; and to appoint a clerk and treasurer of their board, and a collector to collect and receive the said rents and revenues, and to regulate the fees to be allowed to such clerk, treasurer and collector, and them or either of them to remove at pleasure, and appoint others in their stead; and such clerk shall enter all rules and orders made by such trustees, and payments ordered by them, in a book to be provided by them for that purpose.

V. *And be it further enacted,* That it shall be lawful for any two of such trustees...or their successors, at any time to call a meeting of such trustees,and that a majority of the trustees...being lawfully convened, shall be competent to do and perform all matters and things which such trustees are authorized or required to do and perform, and that all questions arising at any such meetings shall be determined by a majority of the trustees present, and in case of an equal division, the presiding trustee shall have a casting vote.

VI. *And be it further enacted,* That the trustees first chosen according to the third section of this act, shall continue in office for three years from the day of their election, and immediately after such election the said trustees shall be divided by lot into three classes, numbered one, two and three, and the seats of the members of the first class shall be vacated at the expiration of the first year, of the members of the second class at the expiration of the second year, and the members of the third class at the expiration of the third year, to the end that the third part of the whole number of trustees, as nearly as possible, may be annually chosen, and the said trustees, or a majority of them shall, at least one month before the expiration of the office of any of the said trustees, notify the same in writing to the minister, or in case of his death or absence, to the elders or church wardens, and in case there shall be no elders or church wardens, then to the deacons or vestrymen of any such church, congregation or society, specifying the names of the trustees, whose times will expire, and the said minister, or in case of his death or absence, one of the said elders or church wardens, or deacons or vestrymen shall, in manner aforesaid, proceed to notify the members of the said church, congregation or society of such vacancies, and appoint the time and place for the election of new trustees to fill up the same, which election shall be held at least six days before such vacancies shall happen, and all such subsequent elections shall be held and conducted by the same persons, and in the manner above directed, and the result thereof certified by them, and such certificate shall entitle the persons elected to act as trustees, and in case any trustee shall die or refuse to act, or remove within the year, notice thereof shall be given by the trustees as aforesaid, and a new election appointed and held, and another trustee be elected in his stead, in manner aforesaid.

VII. *And be it futher enacted,* That no person belonging to any church, congregation or society, intended by the third section of this act, shall be entitled to vote at any election succeeding the first, until he shall have been a stated attendant on divine worship in the said church, congregation or society, at least one year before such election, and shall have contributed to the support of the said church, congregation or society, according to the usages and customs thereof, and that the clerk to the said trustees shall keep a register of the names of all such persons as shall desire to become stated hearers in the said church, congregation or society, and shall therein note the time when such request was made, and the said clerk shall attend all such subsequent elections, in order to test the qualifffcations of such electors, in case the same shall be questioned.

VIII. *And be it further enacted,* That nothing in this act contained shall be construed or taken to give any trustee of any church, congregation or society, the power to fix or ascertain any salary to be paid to any minister thereof, but the same shall be ascertained by a majority of persons entitled to elect trustees, at a meeting to be called for that purpose, and such salaries, when fixed, shall be ratified by the said trustees, or a majority of them, by an instrument in writing under their common seal, which salary shall thereupon be paid by the said trustees out of the revenues of such church, congregation or society.

IX. *And be it further enacted,* That whenever any religious corporation within this state, other than the chartered corporations, shall deem it necessary and for the interest of such religious corporation to reduce their number of trustees, that it shall and may be lawful for any such religious corporation to reduce their number of trustees at any annual meeting: *Provided,* That such reduction shall not be such as have a less number than three trustees....

X. *And be it further enacted,* That the treasurer of every religious corporation, singly, or the trustees or persons entrusted with the care and management of the temporalities of any church, congregation or religious society already incorporated, by virtue of any act of the legislature or which may hereafter be incorporated in the city of New York, Albany, or Schenectady, or a majority of them respectively, shall once in every three years, and between the first day of January and the first day of April triennially, to be computed from the first day of January last, exhibit upon oath to the chancellor, or to one of the justices of the supreme court, or any of the judges of the court of common pleas in the county where such church, congregation or society shall be situated, an account and inventory of all the estate, both real and personal, belonging at the time of making such oath to the church, congregation or society, for which they respectively are trustees or managers as aforesaid, together with an account of the annual revenue arising therefrom; and if any such trustees or person entrusted as aforesaid, shall neglect to exhibit such account and inventory for the space of six years, after the expiration of every three years as aforesaid, and shall not then exhibit the same, and procure a certificate to be endorsed thereon by the chancellor or judge, that he is satisfied that the annual revenue arising from the real and personal estate of such corporation does not, nor has not for the six preceding years, exceeded the sum which by law it is allowed to receive, then such trustees or persons entrusted as aforesaid, shall cease to be a body corporate: And in every case where it shall appear from such account and inventory, that the annual revenue of any church, congregation, or religious society in either of the said cities, exceeds the sum which by virtue of any charter or law they may or can respectively hold and enjoy, it shall be the duty of the chancellor, justice or judge before whom the same shall be so exhibited, to report the same, together with such account and inventory, to the legislature at their next meeting.

XI. *And be it further enacted,* That it shall be lawful for the chancellor of this state, upon the application of any religious corporation in case he shall deem it proper, to make an order for the sale of any real estate belonging to such corporation, and to direct the application of the monies arising therefrom by the said corporation to such uses as the same corporation, with the consent and approbation of the chancellor, shall conceive to be most for the interest of the society to which the real estate so sold did belong: *Provided,* That this act shall not extend to any of the lands granted by this state for the support of the gospel.

XIII. *And be it further enacted,* That every corporation of any church, congregation or religious society heretofore made in pursuance of any law of this state, and in conformity to the directions contained in this act, shall be, and the same is hereby established and confirmed and such corporation shall be deemed to have commenced from the time of recording such certificate as aforesaid; and in case of the dissolution of any such corporation, or of any corporation hereafter to be formed in pursuance of this act, by reason of a non-compliance with the directions herein contained, the same may be re-incorporated in the manner prescribed in this act, at any time within six years after such dissolution, and thereupon all the estate real and personal formerly belonging to the same, shall vest in such corporation, as if the same had not been dissolved: *Provided,* That in such case the said account and inventory required to be exhibited by such corporation in the cities of New York, Albany and Schenectady, shall be exhibited within one month after such re-incorporation, and triennially thereafter, as above directed.

....

XV. *And be it further enacted,* That no religious corporation shall be deemed to be dissolved for any neglect hitherto, to exhibit an account or inventory of its real or personal estate, and the annual income thereof, nor for having held or hereafter holding elections of church officers on days before or after any moveable feast observed by such church, the intervening time between such elections being more than a solar year: *Provided,* That such account or inventory shall be exhibited within two years after the passing of this act, and that previous public notice be given to the congregation of the time and place of holding such elections.

XVI. *And be it further enacted,* That whenever any religious corporation shall be dissolved by means of any non-user or neglect to exercise any of the powers necessary for its preservation, it shall be lawful for the religious society which was connected with such corporation to re-incorporate itself in the mode prescribed by this act, and that thereupon all the real and personal property which did belong to such dissolved corporation at the time of its dissolution, shall vest in such new corporation for the said society.

[The only significant differences in the first general act to incorporate religious societies, which was passed on April 6, 1784, was its statement that the purpose of the act was to prevent the misappropriation of property that had been contributed to the support of religion, and, further, the provision that the judicial officer who received the triennial account of the yearly income of a congregation had to report the same to the legislature, if the yearly income was more than twelve hundred pounds, and, further, the provision that any board of trustees that did not exhibit its accounts for a space of four years would lost its status of incorporation. The Act of 1813 provided for a loss of incorporation in case of a failure to exhibit accounts for a space of nine years. Be it also noted that the Act of 1784, section XI, provided "that nothing herein contained shall be construed...in the least to alter or change the religious Constitutions or Governments of either of the said Churches...so far as respects, or in any wise concerns the Doctrines,

Discipline or Worship thereof." But the Act of 1813 did not have such a disclaimer. See *ibid.*, and also the *Laws of the State of New York, Comprising the Constitution and the Acts of the Legislature since the Revolution from the First to the Twelfth Session, inclusive,* ed. Samuel Jones and Richard Varick (2 vols.; New York: Hugh Gaine, 1789), I, 104-110.]

BIBLIOGRAPHY

Archives

Archdiocese of Montreal, Montreal, Canada
Archdiocese of New York, Yonkers, New York
Diocese of Albany, Albany, New York
Diocese of St. Jean de Quebec, Longueuil, Canada
Dominican Province of St. Joseph, Washington, D.C.
Paulist Fathers, New York, New York
Redemptorist Fathers (Baltimore Province), Brooklyn New York
St. John's Abbey and University (Benedictine), Collegeville, Minnesota
St. Vincent's Archabbey (Benedictine), Latrobe, Pennsylvania

Primary Sources:
Unpublished Manuscripts

"Chronicle of Missions," 2 vols. Archives of the Paulist Fathers

Papers of Ignace Bourget, Bishop of Montreal, Archives of the Archdiocese of Montreal

Papers of Michael Augustine Corrigun, Archbishop of New York, Archives of the Archdiocese of New York

Papers of John Joseph Hughes, Archbishop of New York, Archives of the Archdiocese of New York

Papers of John Cardinal McCloskey, Archbishop of New York, Archives of the Archdiocese of New York and of the Diocese of Albany

Papers of the Abbé Pierre-Marie Mignault, Archives of the Diocese of St. Jean de Quebec

"Real Estate Owned by R.C.D. (Roman Catholic Diocese) (before the Erection of Syracuse and Ogdensburg)," Archives of the Diocese of Albany

Theses and Dissertations:
Unpublished

Considine, Rev. John J. "The History of Canonical Legislation in the Diocese and Province of New York, 1842-1861."Unpublished M.A. Dissertation, Catholic University of America, 1937.

Fingerhut, Eugene R. "Immigrants in Colonial New York, 1770-1775." Unpublished M.A. Thesis, Columbia University, 1957.

Holland, Rev. Timothy J., S.S.J. "The Catholic Church and the Negro in the United States Prior to the Civil War." Unpublished Ph.D. Dissertation, Fordham University, 1950.

Howley, William Esmond. "Albany: A Tale of Two Cities, 1820-1880." Unpubished Ph.D. Dissertation, Dept. of History, Harvard University, 1967.

Taylor, Sister Mary Christine, S.S.J. "A History of the Foundations of Catholicism in Northern New York." Unpublished Ph.D. Dissertation, Dept. of American Studies, St. Louis University, 1967.

Reference Works

Attwater, Donald (ed.). *A Catholic Directory*. New York: Macmillan, 1942.

The Catholic Encyclopedia (1913).

Code, Rev.Joseph Bernard. *Dictionary of the American Hierarchy*. New York: Longmans, Green, 1940.

Dictionary of American Biography.

New Catholic Encyclopedia (1967).

Story, Norah (ed.). *The Oxford Companion to Canadian History and Literature*. New York: Oxford University Press, 1967.

Primary Sources:
Published

"The Church in Albany: Letters of Thomas Barry to Bishop Carroll (1802-1807)," *Records of the American Catholic Historical Society of Philadelphia*, XXIII (1912), 175-179.

Eaton, Deacon M. (Missionary of the American Bethel Soceity). *Five Years on the Erie Canal*. Utica: Bennett,Backus & Hawley, 1845.

Grassi, Rev. John S.J. "The Catholic Religion in the United States in 1818," *The Woodstock Letters*, XI, No. 3 (1882), 229-246.

Hale, Edward Everett. *Letters on Irish Emigration*. Boston: Phillips, Sampson & Co., 1852.

Johnson, Rev. Peter Leo and Nellen, Rev. William (eds.). "Letters of the Reverend Adelbert Inama, O. Praem." *Wisconsin Magazine of History*, XI, No. 1 (Sept., 1927), 77-95, No. 2 (Dec., 1927), 196-217, No. 3 (March, 1928), 328-354, No. 4 (June, 1928), 437-458, XII, No. 1 (Sept., 1928), 58-96.

Kehoe, Lawrence (ed.). *Complete Works of the Most Rev. John Hughes, D.D., Archbishop of New York*. 2 vols. in one. New York: Catholic Publishing House, 1864.

McDonald, Capt. Alexander. "Letterbook of Captain Alexander McDonald of the Royal Highland Emigrants, 1775-1779," *New York Historical Society, Collections for the Year 1882* (Vol. XV).

McFarland, Rev.Francis P. "Early Catholic Affairs in Utica, N.Y.," *United States Catholic Historical Magazine*, IV (1891-1893), 64-69.

Maréchal, Ambrose, Archbishop of Baltimore. "Unpublished Letters (1820's)," *Records of the American Catholic Historical Society of Philadelphia*, X (1899), 229.

Plessis, Joseph-Octave, Bishop of Quebec. *Journal des Visites Pastorales de*

1815 et 1816. Qu'ebec: Imprimerie Franciscaine Missionaire, 1903.

Reed, William. *Life on the Border, Sixty Years Ago.* Fall River, Mass.: Adams, 1882.

Rolfson, Rev. Gunther R., O.S.B. "The Schwenninger Memorial," *The American Benedictine Review,* X, Nos. 1-2 (March-June, 1959), 107-135, 245-265, XI, Nos. 1-2 (March-June, 1960), 154-178.

Salzbacher, Rev. Dr. Joseph. *Meine Reise nach Nord-Amerika im Jahre 1842.* Wien: Wimmer, Schmidt & Leo, 1845.

F.E.T. (trans. and ed.). *Diary and Visitation Record of the Rt. Rev. Francis Patrick Kenrick, Administrator and Bishop of Philadelphia, 1830-1851.* Lancaster, Pa.: Wickersham Printing Comp., 1916.

Timon, John, Bishop of Buffalo, *Missions in Western New York and Church History of the Diocese of Buffalo.* Buffalo: Catholic Sentinel Press, 1862.

Timpe, Rev. George (ed.). "An Emigrant's Letter of 1838," *Central-Blatt and Social Justice,* XXIX, No. 12 (March, 1937), 385-387.

Weninger, Rev. Franz Xavier, S.J., Missionär der Gesellschaft Jesu. *Errinerungen aus Meinem Leben in Europa und Amerika durch Achtzig Jahre — 1805 bis 1885.* Columbus, Ohio: J.J. Lessing, 1886.

White, Sister Mary Teresa. "Reminiscences," *Records of the American Catholic Historical Society of Philadelphia,* XII (1901), 61-66.

Documents and Statistics:
Civil

Canada, Board of Registration and Statistics. *Census of the Canadas, 1860-1861. Vol. I: Personal Census.* 2 vols. Quebec: S.B. Foote, 1863.

Canada, Dept. of Agriculture. *Census of Canada, 1870-71. Vol. IV: Censuses of Canada, 1665 to 1871: Statistics of Canada.* 4 vols. Ottawa: I.B. Taylor, 1873-6.

Canada, Dominion Bureau of Statistics (M.C. Maclean). *Analysis of the Stages in the Growth of Population in Canada.* Ottawa: Dominion Bureau of Statistics, 1935.

Canada, Parliament. *Rapport Du Comité Spécial Sur L'Emigration,* Toronto: J. Lovell, 1857.

Canada, Parliament. *Report of the Select Committee of the Legislative Assembly Appointed to Inquire into the Causes and Importance of the Emigration, which Takes Place Annually from Lower Canada to the United States.* Montreal: Rollo Campbell, 1849.

Clinton, Governor George. *Public Papers of George Clinton, First Governor of New York, 1777-1795-1801-1804.* 10 vols. Albany: State Printers, 1899-1914.

Manning, William Ray (ed.). *Diplomatic Corresponence of the United States: Canadian Relations, 1784-1860. Vol. I: 1784-1820.* 3 vols. Washington, D.C.: Carnegie Endowment for International Peace, 1940-1943.

New York, Canal Commissioners, *Annual Reports,* 1818-1820.

New York, Commissioners of Emigration, *Reports* (annual), 1847-1865.

New York. *Laws of the State of New York, Comprising The Constitution and The Acts of the Legislature since the Revolution from the First to the Twelfth Session, inclusive.* Edited by Samuel Jones and Richard Varick. 2 vols. New York: Hugh Gaine, 1789.

New York. *Laws of the State of New York, Revised and Passed at the Thirty-Sixth Session of the Legislature.* Edited by William P. Van Ness and John Woodworth. 2 vols. Revised edition.Albany: H.C. Southwick, 1813.

New York. *Laws of the State of New York, Passed at the Seventy-Eighth Session of the Legislature.* Albany: Van Benthuysen, 1855.

New York. *Laws of the State of New York Passed at the Eighty-Sixth Session of the Legislature.* Albany: Weed, Parsons, 1863.

New York, Secretary of State. "Report of the Secretary of State giving the Census of the Several Congressional Districts in 1820, 1825, and 1830," *New York Senate Documents, Fifty-fifth Session (1832),* Vol. I, Doc. No. 65.

New York, Secretary of State. *Census of the State of New York for 1835.* Albany: Croswell, Van Benthuysen and Burt, 1836.

New York, Secretary of State. *Census of the State of New York for 1845.* Albany: Carroll & Cook, 1846.

New York, Secretary of State. *Census of the State of New York for 1855.* Albany: Weed, Parson, 1856.

New York, Superintendent of the Census. *Census of the State of New York for 1865.* Albany: Charles Van Benthuysen & Sons, 1867.

New York, Superintendent of the Census. *Census of the State of New York for 1875.* Albany: Weed, Parsons, 1877.

O'Callaghan, E.B. (ed.). *The Documentary History of the State of New York.* 4 vols. Albany: Weed, Parsons, 1849-1851.

O'Callaghan, E.B. (ed.). *Documents Relative to the Colonial History of the State of New York.* 15 vols. Albany: Weed, Parsons, 1856-1887.

Urquhart, M.C. (ed.). *Historical Statistics of Canada.* Cambridge: University Press, 1965.

U.S., Bureau of the Census. *A Century of Population Growth.* Washington, D.C.: Government Printing Office, 1909. Reprint by the Baltimore Genealogical Publishing Co., 1967.

U.S., Bureau of the Census. *Heads of Families...Census...1790, New York.* Washington, D.C.: Government Printing Office, 1908.

U.S., Bureau of the Census. *Historical Statistics of the United States, 1789-1945.* Washington, D.C.: Government Printing Office, 1949.

U.S., Bureau of the Census. *The Seventh Census of the United States: 1850.* Washington, D.C.: Robert Armstrong, Public Printer, 1853.

U.S., Bureau of the Census. *The Seventh Census, Report of the Superintendent of the Census for Dec. 1, 1852 (and for) Dec. 1, 1851.* Washington, D.C. Robert Armstrong, Public Printer, 1853.

U.S., Bureau of the Census. *Agriculture of the United States in 1860: The Eighth Census.* Washington, D.C.: Government Printing Office, 1864.

U.S., Bureau of the Census. *Eighth Census: 1860, Manufactures.* Washington, D.C.: Government Printing Office, 1864.

U.S., Bureau of the Census. *Preliminary Report on the Eighth Census, 1860.* Washington, D.C. Government Printing Office, 1862.

U.S., Bureau of the Census. *Statistics of the United States in 1860: The Eighth Census.* Washington, D.C.: Government Printing Office, 1866.

U.S., Twenty-ninth Congress, First Session (1846). "Surgeons on Packet Boats," *House Executive Documents,* VI, No.182, in *U.S. Govt. Docs.* Serial Set, Vol. 485.

U.S. Postal Service, *Directory of Post Offices.* Washington, D.C.: Government Printing Office, 1971.

U.S., Secretary of State. "Report of Passenger Arrivals," annually, 1821-1848.

U.S., Senate. *Report of the Select Committee of the Senate of the United States on the Sickness and Mortality on Board Emigrant Ships,* August 2, 1854. Washington, D.C.: Beverly Tucker, Senate Printer, 1854.

Documents: Ecclesiastic

Congregatio de Propaganda Fide. *Iuris Pontificii de Propaganda Fide, Pars Prima.* Cura ac Studio Raphaelis De Martinis. 7 vols. in 5. Romae: Typographia Polyglotta, S.C. De Propaganda Fide, 1888-1897. VI.

Corrigan, Michael Augustine, Archbishop of New York. *Synodorum Archdioceseos Neo-Eboracensis Collectio.* Neo-Eboraci: Typis Bibliothecae Cathedralis, 1901.

Henry Rev. Hugh T. (ed.). "Papers Relating to the Church in America, From the Portfolios of the Irish College at Rome," *Records of the American Catholic Historical Society of Philadelphia,* VII (1896), 283-388, 454-492, VIII (1897), 195-240, 294-329, 450-512, IX (1898), 1-34.

Kenneally, Rev. Finbar, O.F.M. (ed.). *United States Documents in the Propaganda Archives: A Calendar.* First Series. Volume Two. Washington, D.C.:Academy of American Franciscan History, 1968.

Mansi, Ionnes Dominicus (ed.). *Sacrorum Conciliorum Nova et Amplissima Collectio.* 53 vols. Paris and Leipzig: Hunberti Welti, 1903-1927, Kraus Reprint, 1964. XLIV, XLVII-XLVIII.

Presbyteris, S.J.E. Domo B.V.M. Sive Labe Conceptae ad Lacum. *Acta et Decreta Sacrorum Conciliorum Recentiorum Collectio Lacensis,* 7 vols. Freiburg im Breisgau: Sumtibus Herder, 1870-1890. III.

Shearer, Rev. Donald C. *Pontificia Americana: A Documentary History of the Catholic Church in the United States* (1784-1884). Washington, D.C.: Catholic University of America, 1933.

Serial Publications

Annales de L'Association de la Propagation de la Foi (Lyons and Paris). I. (1827)-XXXVII (1865). The English edition, Vol. 1, appeared from 1840 on.

Annuario Pontificio (Roma). 1864.

Berichte der Leopoldinen-Stiftung im Kaiserthume Oesterreich zur Unterstützung der katholischen Missionen in Amerika (Vienna). I (1830) XXXV (1865). 2 reels of microfilm at the Catholic University of America in Washington, D.C.

Bottoming Out. This was a quarterly of the Canal Society of New York State, and was published from 1956 to 1965.

Catholic Directory. Appearing first in 1817, this annual has been issued under different titles by different publishers. Today, it is the *Official Catholic Directory.*

Central-Blatt and Social Justice. Since 1941, this has been issued under the title of the *Social Justice Review.* The publisher is the Central Bureau of the Catholic Central Verein of America, in St. Louis, Missouri.

La Civiltà Cattolica (Roma). Serie VI, II (1865).

Einsiedler Kalender für 1864 für Amerika.

The Freeman's Journal and Catholic Register (New York).

The Statesman's Yearbook for the Year 1865.

United States Catholic Historical Magazine. (Baltimore).

Secondary Sources:
Books

Abbott, Edith. *Historical Aspects of the Immigration Problem: Selected Documents.* Chicago: University of Chicago Press, 1926.

Abbott, Edith. *Immigration: Select Documents and Case Records.* Chicago: University of Chicago Press, 1924.

Adams, William Forbes. *Ireland and Irish Emigration to the New World from 1815 to the Famine.* New Haven: Yale University Press, 1932.

Albion, Robert G. *The Rise of New York Port (1815-1860).* New York: Charles Scribner's Sons, 1939.

Allaire, Abbé J.-B.-A. *Dictionnaire biographique du Clergé-canadien.* 6 vols. Montreal: various publishers, 1908-1934.

(Bachofen), Rev. Charles Augustine. *The Canonical and Civil Status of Catholic Parishes in the United States.* St. Louis: B. Herder, 1926.

Bagg, M.M. (ed.). *Memorial History of Utica, N.Y.* Syracuse: D. Mason, 1892.

Baird, Rev. Robert *Religion in America.* New York: Harper Bros., 1844.

Bannan, Theresa. *Pioneer Irish of Onondaga.* New York: G.P. Putnam's Sons, 1911.

Barber, John Warner and Howe, Henry. *Historical Collections of the State of New York.* New York: S. Tuttle, 1845.

Barck, Oscar T., Jr. and Lefler, Hugh T. *Colonial America.* New York: Macmillan, 1959, reprint 1964.

Barry, Rev. Colman, J., O.S.B. *The Catholic Church and German Americans,* Washington, D.C.: Catholic University of America Press, 1953.

Bayley, James Roosevelt, Archbishop of Baltimore. *History of the Catholic Church on the Island of New York.* New York: Catholic Publication Society, 1870.

BIBLIOGRAPHY

Bennett, WilliamHarper. *Catholic Footsteps in Old New York.* New York: Kirwin and Fauss, 1909.
Billington, Ray Allen. *The Protestant Crusade, 1800-1860.* Chicago: Quadrangle Books, 1964, originally 1938.
Bishop, J.Leander. *A History of American Manufactures from 1608 to 1860.* 3 vols. 3rd ed. Philadelphia: Edward Young & Co., 1868.
Blied, Rev. Benjamin J. *Austrian Aid to American Catholics, 1830-1860.* Milwaukee: Author, 1944.
Bromwell, W.J. *History of Immigration into the United States.* New York: Redfield, 1856.
Buckman, David Lear. *Old Steamboat Days on the Hudson River.* New York: Grafton Press, 1907.
Burt, Alfred Leroy. *The United States, Great Britain and British North America.* New Haven: Yale University Press, 1940.
Byrne, Rev. John F., C.SS.R. *The Redemptorist Centenaries,* Philadelphia: Dolphin Press, 1932.
Campbell, Rev. Thomas J., S.J. *The Jesuits, 1534-1921.* 2 vols. New York: Encyclopedia Press, 1921.
Callahan, Adalbert. *Medieval Francis in Modern America: The Story of Eighty Years, 1855-1935.* New York: Macmillan, 1936.
Carriére, Rev. Gaston, O.M.I. *Histoire Documentaire de la Congrégation des Missionnaires Oblats de Marie-Immaculée dans L'Est du Canada.* 5 vols. Ottawa: Editions de L'Université D'Ottawa, 1957-1963.
Carrothers, W.A. *Emigration from the British Isles.* New York: Augustus M. Kelley, 1966, originally 1929.
Champlain Transportation Co. *The Steamboats on Lake Champlain, 1809-1930.* Albany: Champlain Transportation Co., 1930.
Childs, Frances Sergeant. *French Refugee Life in the United States, 1790-1800.* Baltimore: Johns Hopkins Press, 1940.
"Father Chiniquy" (Rev. Charles Pascal Chiniquy). *Fifty Years in the Church of Rome.* 12th ed. Chicago: Adam Craig, 1888.
"Father Chiniquy" (Rev. Charles Pascal Chiniquy). *The Priest, The Woman and The Confessional.* 36th ed. Chicago: Adam Craig, 1890.
Clark, Victor S. *History of Manufacturers in the United States.* 3 vols. New York: McGraw-Hill Book Co., 1929.
Clarke, Richard H. *Lives of the Deceased Bishops of the Catholic Church in the United States.* 3 vols. New York: Author, 1888.
Clark, T. Wood. *Emigres in the Wilderness.* Port Washington, N.Y.: Ira J. Friedman, 1967, originally 1941.
Corrigan, Rev.Raymond. *Die Kongregation De Propaganda Fide und ihre Tätigkeit in Nord-Amerika.* München: E. Joergen, 1928.
Cowan, Helen I. *British Emigration to British North America.* Revised and enlarged. Toronto: University Toronto Press, 1961.
Crouse, Nellis M. "The White Man's Discoveries and Explorations," *History of the State of New York.* Edited by Alexander C. Flick. 10

vols. in 5. Port Washington, N.Y.: Ira J. Friedman, 1962, originally 1933-1935. Vol. I, chap. V.

Curley, Rev. Michael J., C.SS.R. *The Provincial Story.* New York: Redemptorist Fathers, Baltimore Province, 1963.

Curran, Rev. Francis X., S.J. *Catholics in Colonial Law.* Chicago: Loyola University Press, 1963.

Daniel-Rops, H. *History of the Church of Christ. VIII: The Church in an Age of Revolution, 1789-1870.* New York: E.P. Dutton, 1965.

DeCourcy, Henry. *The Catholic Church in the United States.* Translated and enlarged by John Gilmary Shea. New York: Edward Dunigan and Bros., 1856.

De Goesbriand, Louis, Bishop of Burlington. *Les Canadiens des Etats-Unis.* St.Albans, Vermont: The Protecteur Canadien, 1889.

Dignan, Rev. Patrick J. *A History of the Legal Incorporation of Catholic Church Property in the United States (1784-1932).* New York: P.J. Kenedy & Sons, 1935.

Dion, J.O. *Souvenir du Réverend Pierre Marie Migneault.* Montreal: Des Presses A Vapeur de la Minerve, 1868.

Eccles, W.J. *The Canadian Frontier, 1534-1760.* New York: Holt, Rinehart and Winston, 1969.

Ellis, David M. and Others. *A History of New York State.* Revised edition. Ithaca:Cornell University Press, 1967.

Ellis, David M. and Others. *A Short History of New York State.* Ithaca: Cornell University Press, 1957.

Ellis, Franklin, *History of Columbia County.* Philadelphia: Everts & Ensign, 1878.

Ellis, Rev. John Tracy. *Catholics in Colonial America.* Baltimore: Helicon Press, 1965.

Flexner, James Thomas. *Mohawk Baronet: Sir William Johnson of New York.* New York: Harper & Row, 1959.

Frazier, E.Franklin. *The Negro Church in America.* New York: Schocken Books, 1963.

French, John Homer. *Gazetteer of the State of New York.* N.P.: Author, 1860.

French, John Homer, *Gazetteer of the State of New York.* 10th ed. Syracuse: R.P. Smith, 1861.

Frost, James Arthur. *Life on the Upper Susquehanna, 1783-1860.* New York: King's Crown Press, Columbia University, 1951.

Garand, Rev. Philias S. *The History of the City of Ogdensburg.* Ogdensburg: Rev. Manuel J.Belleville, 1927.

Glazebrook, G.P. deT. *A History of Transportation in Canada.* 2 vols. Toronto: McClelland and Stewart, 1964.

Griffin, Martin I.J. *Catholics and the American Revolution.* 3 vols. Ridley Park, Penn.: Author, 1907-1911.

Guilday, Rev. Peter. *A History of the Councils of Baltimore (1791-1884).*

New York: Macmillan, 1932.
Guilday, Rev. Peter. *The Life and Times of John Carroll.* Westminster, Md.: Newman Press, 1954, originally 1922.
Guilday, Rev. Peter. *The National Pastorals of the American Hierarchy (1792-1919).* Washington, D.C.: National Catholic Welfare Council, 1923.
Guillet, Edwin C. *The Great Migration,* 2d ed. Toronto: Toronto University Press, 1963, originally 1937.
Halsey, Francis Whiting. *The Old Frontier.* New York: Scribner's Sons, 1901.
Handley, Rev. Dr. James E. *The Irish in Scotland, 1789-1845.* Cork, Ireland: Cork University Press, 1945.
Handlin, Oscar. *Boston's Immigrants.* Revised ed. Cambridge, Mass.: Belknap Press, 1959.
Handlin, Oscar. *The Uprooted.* New York: Grosset & Dunlap, n.d., originally 1951.
Hansen, Marcus Lee. *The Mingling of the Canadian and American Peoples.* New Haven: Yale University Press, 1940.
Harlow, Alvin F. *The Road of the Century: The Story of the New York Central.* New York: Creative Age Press, 1947.
Hassard, John R.G. *Life of the Most Reverend John Hughes, D.D., First Archbishop of New York.* New York: D. Appleton, 1866.
Hedrick, Ulysses Prentiss. *A History of Agriculture in the State of New York.* New York: Hill and Wang, 1966, originally 1933.
Heffernan, Rev. Bernard Leo. *Some Cross-Bearers of the Finger Lakes Region.* Chicago: John Anderson, 1925.
Hewitt, William P.H. (ed.). *History of the Diocese of Syracuse.* Syracuse, N.Y.: Catholic Sun Press, 1909.
Hibbert, Christopher. *Garibaldi and His Enemies.* Boston: Little, Brown & Co. 1966.
Hickey, Rev. Edward John. *The Society for the Propagation of the Faith.* Washington, D.C.: Catholic University of America, 1922.
Higgins, Ruth L. *Expansion in New York: With Especial Reference to the Eighteenth Century.* Columbus, Ohio: Ohio State University, 1931.
Hogue, Roswell A. *Centennial, 1853-1953: St. Peter's Roman Catholic Church, Plattsburgh, N.Y.* Plattsburgh: St. Peter's Church, 1953.
Holden, Rev. Vincent F., C.S.P., *The Yankee Paul: Isaac Thomas Hecker.* Milwaukee: Bruce Publishing Co., 1958.
Hough, Franklin Benjamin. *A History of Jefferson County.* Albany: Joel Munsell, 1854.
Hough, Franklin Benjamin. *A History of St. Lawrence and Franklin Counties,* New York. Albany: Little & Co., 1853.
Hughes, Rev. Thomas, S.J. *History of the Society of Jesus in North America:* Text 2 vols. New York: Longmans, Green, 1908-1917.
Hughes, Rev. Vincent Reginald, O.P. *The Right Rev. Richard Luke Con-*

canen, O.P., *First Bishop of New York (1747-1810)*. Freiburg: Studia Friburgensia, 1926.

Hungerford, Edward. *Men of Erie*. New York: Random House, 1946.

Hungerford, Edward. *The Story of the Rome, Watertown and Ogdensburgh Railroad*. New York: Robert M.McBride & Co., 1922.

Hunt, George T. *The Wars of the Iroquois*. Madison, Wisconsin: University of Wisconsin Press, 1940.

Ives, Moss. *The Ark and the Dove*. New York: Longmans, Green, 1936.

Jones, Howard Mumford. *America and French Culture, 1750-1848*. Chapel Hill, North Carolina: University of North Carolina Press, 1927.

Jones, Maldwyn Allen. *American Immigration*. Chicago: University of Chicago Press, 1960.

Kapp, Friedrich. *Immigration and the Commissioners of Emigration of the State of New York*. New York. The Nation Press, 1870.

Keenleyside, Hugh L. and Brown, Gerald S. *Canada and the United States*. New York: Alfred A. Knopf, 1952.

Knittle, Walter Allen. *Early Eighteenth Century Palatine Emigration*. Philadelphia: Dorrance Co., 1937.

Lanctot, Gustave. *Canada and the American Revolution, 1774-1783*. Cambridge, Massachusetts: Harvard University Press, 1967.

Latourette, Kenneth Scott. *Christianity in a Revolutionary Age: A History of Christianity in the Nineteenth and Twentieth Centuries. Vol. I: The Nineteenth Century in Europe: Background and the Roman Catholic Phase*. New York: Harper & Bros., 1958.

Latourette, Kenneth Scott. *A History of the Expansion of Christianity, Vol. IV: The Great Century, A.D. 1800-A.D. 1914*. 7 vols. New York: Harper & Bros., 1937-1945.

Leng, Charles W. and Davis, William T. *Staten Island and Its People*. 5 vols. New York: Lewis Historical Publishing Co., 1930-1933.

Lincoln, Charles Z. *The Civil Law and the Church*. New York: Abingdon Press, 1916.

Lord, Rev. Robert H. and Others. *History of the Archdiocese of Boston*. 3 vols. New York: Sheed & Ward, 1944.

Lynch, Very Rev. James S. M. *A Page of Church History in New York: St. John's, Utica*. Probably Utica, N.Y.: Privately printed, 1893.

McAvoy, Rev.Thomas T. *A History of the Catholic Church in the United States*. Notre Dame, Indiana: Notre Dame University Press, 1969.

MacCaffrey, Rev. James *History of the Catholic Church in the Nineteenth Century*. 2 vols. 2d ed. Dublin, Ireland: M.H.Gill, 1910.

Macdonald, Rev. Fergus, C.P. *The Catholic Church and the Secret Societies in the United States*. New York: United States Catholic Historical Society, 1946.

Macdonald, Norman. *Canada: Immigration and Colonization, 1841-1903*. Aberdeen, Scotland: Aberdeen University Press, 1966.

McNamara, Rev. Robert F. *The Diocese of Rochester, 1868-1968*.

BIBLIOGRAPHY

Rochester, N.Y.: Diocese of Rochester, 1968.

Maginnis, Thomas Hobbs. *The Irish Contribution to America's Independence.* Philadelphia: Doire, 1913.

Maguire, John Francis. *The Irish in America.* New York: D. & J Sadlier, 1868.

Metzger, Rev. Charles H. S.J. *Catholics and the American Revolution.* Chicago: Loyola University Press, 1962.

Meyer, Balthasar Henry (ed.). *History of Transportation in the United States before 1860.* New York: Peter Smith, 1948, originally 1917.

Moody, T.W. and Martin, F.X. *The Course of Irish History.* New York: Weybright and Talley, 1967.

Moore, John Bassett. *History and Digest of the International Arbitrations to which the United States Has Been a Party.* 6 vols. Washington, D.C.: Government Printing Office, 1898.

Moran, Eugene F. and Reid, Louis. *Tugboat: The Moran Story.* New York: Charles Scribner's Sons, 1956.

Munger, William P. *Historical Atlas of New York State.* Phoenix, N.Y.: Frank E. Richards, 1941.

Munsell, Joel. *The Annals of Albany.* 10 vols. 2d ed. Albany: Joel Munsell, 1869-1871.

O'Daniel, Rev. Victor F., O.P. *Dominican Province of St. Joseph.* New York: National Headquarters of the Holy Name Society, 1942.

Philbrick, Thomas. *St. John de Crevecoeur.* New York: Twayne, 1970.

Poor, Henry V. *Manual of the Railroads of the United States for 1868-1869.* New York: H.V. & H.W. Poor, 1868.

Potter, George W. *To the Golden Door.* Boston: Little, Brown and Co., 1960.

Pratt, John Webb. *Religion, Politics and Diversity.* Ithaca: Cornell University Press, 1967.

Reiter, Rev. Ernst Anthony, S.J., *Schematismus der katholischen deutschen Geistlichkeit in den Vereinigten Staaten Nord-Amerika's.* New York: Friedrich Pustet, 1869.

Roemer, Rev. Theodore. "The Ludwig-Missionsverein and the Church in the United States (1838-1918)," *Franciscan Studies,* No. 12 (Aug. 1933).

Roemer, Rev. Theodore. *Ten Decades of Alms.* St. Louis, Mo.: B. Herder, 1942.

Rothan, Rev. Emmett H. O.F.M. *The German Catholic Immigrant in the United States (1830-1860).* Washington, D.C.: Catholic University of America Press, 1946.

Ryan, Leo Raymond. *Old St. Peter's.* New York: United States Catholic Historical Society, 1935.

Scanlan, Charles M. *The Law of Church and Grave.* New York: Benziger Bros., 1909.

Schrott, Rev. Lambert. *Pioneer German Catholics in the American*

Colonies (1734-1784). New York: United States Catholic Historical Society, 1933.

Seaver, Frederick J. *Historical Sketches of Franklin County.* Albany: J.B. Lyon, 1918.

Seward, William Foote (ed.). *Binghamton and Broome County: A History.* 3 vols. New York: Lewis Historical Publishing Co. 1924.

Shannon, William V. *The American Irish.* New York: Macmillan, 1963.

Sharp, Rev. John Kean. *History of the Diocese of Brooklyn, 1853-1953.* 2 vols. New York: Fordham University Press, 1954.

Shaughnessy, Gerald, S.M., Bishop of Seattle. *Has the Immigrant Kept the Faith.* New York: Macmillan, 1925.

Shaw, Ronald E.Erie *Water West: A History of the Erie Canal, 1792-1854.* Lexington, Ky.: University of Kentucky Press, 1966.

Shea, John Gilmary. *The History of the Catholic Church in the United States.* 4 vols. New York: Author, 1886-1892.

Shea, John Gilmary. *History of the Catholic Missions among the Indian Tribes of the United States, 1529-1854.* New York: P.J. Kenedy, 1854.

Smith, Rev. John Talbot. *A History of the Diocese of Ogdensburg.* New York: John W. Lovell, 1884.

Snyder, Charles M. *Oswego: From Buckskins to Bustles.* Port Washington, N.Y.: Ira J.Friedman, 1968.

Spalding, John Lancaster, Bishop of Peoria. *The Religious Mission of the Irish People and Catholic Colonization.* New York: Catholic Publication Society Co., 1880.

Stevens, Frank Walker. *The Beginnings of the New York Central Railroad: A History.* New York: G.P. Putnam's Sons, 1926.

Stokes, Anson Phelps. *Church and State in the United States.* 3 vols. New York: Harper & Bros., 1950.

Stone, William Leete. *Reminiscences of Saratoga and Ballston.* New York: Worthington Co., 1890.

Stover, John F. *American Railroads.* Chicago: University of Chicago Press, 1961.

Sullivan, Nell Jane Barnet and Martin, David Kendal. *A History of the Town of Chazy, Clinton County, New York.* Burlington, Vt.: George Little Press, 1970.

Sweet, William Warren. *Religion on the American Frontier: The Baptists, 1783-1830.* New York: Henry Holt, 1931.

Taft, Donald R. *Human Migration.* New York: Ronald Press,1936.

Taylor, George Rogers. *The Transportation Revolution, 1815-1860.* New York: Holt, Rinehart and Winston, 1951.

Thebaud, Rev. Augustus, Jr., S.J. *Forty Years in the United States (1839-1885).* New York: United States Catholic Historical Society, 1904.

Thompson, Harold W. Body, *Boots and Britches.* New York: J.B. Lippincott, 1940.

Thompson, John H. (ed.). *Geography of New York State.* Syracuse, N.Y.: Syracuse University Press, 1966.

Thompson, Warren S. and Whelpton, P.K. *Population Trends in the United States.* New York: McGraw-Hill, 1933.

Trelease, Allen W. *Indian Affairs in Colonial New York: The Seventeenth Century.* Ithaca, N.Y.: Cornell University Press, 1960.

Trudel, Marcel. *Chiniquy.* Quebec: Editions Du Bien Public, 1955.

Truesdell, Leon Edgar. *The Canadian Born in the United States.* New Haven, Conn.: Yale University Press, 1943.

Tyler, Alice Felt, *Freedom's Ferment,* New York: Harper & Row, 1962, originally 1944.

Villard, Paul. *Up to the Light: The Story of French Protestantism in Canada.* Toronto: Ryerson Press, 1928.

Vogt, Rev. Berard, O.F.M. *A Historical Monument of Northern New York's Pioneer Days: Souvenir of the Diamond Jubilee of St Vincent de Paul's Church, Belfort,N.Y.* N. p.: privately printed, 1919.

Wade, Mason. *The French Canadians, 1760-1945.* Toronto: Macmillan, 1955.

Wager, Daniel E. (ed.). *Our County and Its People.* 2 vols. N.p.: Boston History Co., 1896.

Waggoner, Madeline Sadler. *The Long Haul West: The Great Canal Era, 1817-1850.* New York: G.P. Putnam's Sons, 1958.

Walker, Mack. *Germany and the Emigration, 1816-1885.* Cambridge, Mass.: Harvard University Press, 1964.

Walsh, Rev. Henry L. S.J. *Hallowed Were the Gold Dust Trails.* Santa Clara, Calif.: University of Santa Clara Press, 1946.

Walworth, Rev.Clarence A. *Reminiscences of Edgar P. Wadhams, First Bishop of Ogdensburg.* 2d. ed. New York: Benziger Bros., 1893.

Wätjen, Herman. *Aus der Frühzeit des Nord-Atlantikverkehrs.* Leipzig: Felix Meiner, 1932.

Watson, Winslow C. *The Military and Civil History of the County of Essex, New York.* Albany: J. Munsell, 1869.

Weise, A.J. *History of the City of Troy.* Troy: William H. Young, 1876.

Whitford, Noble E. *History of the Canal System of the State of New York.* 2 vols. Albany: Brandow Printing Co., 1906.

Willcox, Walter F. (ed.). *International Migrations. Vol. I: Statistics.* Compiled by Imre Ferenczi. New York: National Bureau of Economic Research, 1929.

Woodham-Smith, Cecil. *The Great Hunger,* New York: Harper & Ro 1962.

Zimm, Louise H. and Others (eds.). *Southeastern New York.* 3 vols. New York: Lewis Historical Publishing Co., 1946.

Zollman, Carl. *American Civil Church Law.* New York: Columbia University Press, 1917.

Zucker, A.E. (ed.). *The Forty-Eighters.* New York: Russell & Russell, 1966, originally 1950.

Secondary Sources:
Articles

Ciangetti, Rev. Paul P. "A Diocesan Chronology of the Catholic Church in the United States," *Catholic Historical Review*, XXVIII, No. 1 (April, 1942), 57-70.

Coolidge, Guy Omeron. "The French Occupation of the Champlain Valley from 1609 to 1759," *Vermont Historical Society Proceedings (New Series)*, VI, No. 3 (Sept., 1938), 1-309.

Coolidge, Guy Omeron. "Biographical Index to the French Occupation of the Champlain Valley from 1609 to 1759," *Vermont Historical Society Proceedings (New Series)*, VI, No. 3 (Sept., 1938), 1-40. This article immediately follows the above-cited long article by Coolidge, and shows the traffic of personages along the Champlain Road, beginning with St. Isaac Jogues.

Corrigan, Most Rev. Michael Augustine, Archbishop of New York, "Register of the Clergy Laboring in the Archdiocese of New York from Early Missionary Times to 1885," *United States Catholic Historical Society, Historical Records and Studies*, I (1899)-IX (1916). This appears serially in many volumes.

Curran, Rev. Francis X., S.J. "The Jesuit Colony in New York, 1808-1817," *United States Catholic Historical Society, Historical Records and Studies*, XLII (1954), 51-97.

Daley, Rev. John M., S.J. "Pioneer Missionary, Ferdinand Farmer, S.J.: 1720-1786," *The Woodstock Letters*, LXXV, No. 4 (Dec. 1946), 311-321.

Devitt, Rev. Edward I., S.J. (ed.). "Letters of Father Joseph Mosley, 1757-1786," *The Woodstock Letters*, XXXV, No. 1 (1906), 35-55.

"Disguises and Aliases of Early Missionaries," *The Woodstock Letters*, XV, No. 1 (1886), 72-74.

Ellis, David M. "The Yankee Invasion of New York, 1783-1850," *New York History*, XXXII, No. 1 (Jan., 1951), 3-17.

Herberman, Charles G. "The Rt. Rev. John Dubois, D.D., Third Bishop of New York," *United States Catholic Historical Society, Historical Records and Studies*, I, Part II (Jan., 1900), 278-355.

Imhoff, Rv. Maurice, O.M.C., "Notes on the Early History of St. Joseph's Parish at Utica, N.Y.," *Central-Blatt and Social Justice*, XXX, No. 11 (Feb., 1938), 349-350.

Jones, R.L. "French Canadian Agriculture in the St. Lawrence Valley, 1815-1850," *Approaches to Canadian Economic History*. Edited by W.T. Easterbrook and M.H. Watkins. Toronto: McClelland & Stewart, 1967. Pages 110-126.

Jordan, Rev. P.A. S.J., "St. Joseph's Church, Philadelphia," *The Woodstock Letters*, III, No. 2 (1874), 94-98.

Kelly, Rev. Jeremiah, S.J., "Gonzaga College," *The Woodstock Letters*, XIX, No. 2 (1890), 167-178.

Kernan, Thomas P. "Nicholas Devereaux: Model of Catholic Action," *United States Catholic Historical Society, Historical Records and*

Studies, XXV (1935), 149-162.

Lucey, Rev. William, S.J. "The Diocese of Burlington, Vermont: 1853," *Records of the American Catholic Historical Society of Philadelphia,* LXIV, No. 3 (Sept., 1953), 123-154.

Macdonald, Ewen J. "Father Roderick Macdonell Missionary at St. Regis and the Glengarry Catholics," *Catholic Historical Review,* XIX, No. (Oct. 1933), 265-274.

McGloin, Rev. John B., S.J. "A California Gold Rush Padre: New Light on the 'Padre of Paradise Flat'," *California Historical Society Quarterly,* XL, No. 1 (March, 1961), 49-67.

McLellan, Hugh and Charles W. "Index of Names: Inscriptions from Old Graveyards," *The Moorsfield Antiquarian,* I, No. 4 (Feb., 1938), 325-328, II, No. 4 (Feb., 1939), 347-359.

McLellan, Hugh and Charles W. "Peter Dubree & Peter Jonqueray ads. Jaques Rouse," *The Moorsfield Antiquarian,* I, No. 2 (Aug., 1937), 129-134.

McLellan, Hugh and Charles W. "Pierre Huet de la Valiniere, Priest on Lake Champlain, 1790-1791," *The Moorsfield Antiquarian,* I, No. 4 (Feb., 1938) 239-255.

MacMaster, Rev. Mr. Richard K., S.J. "Parish in Arms: A Study of Father John MacKenna and the Mohawk Valley Royalists, 1773-1778," *United States Catholic Historical Society, Historical Records and Studies,* XLV, (1957), 107-125.

McNamara, Rev. Robert F. "Trusteeism in the Atlantic States, 1785-1863," *Catholic Historical Review,* XXX, No.. . 2 (July 1944), 135-154.

Meehan, Thomas F. "Some Pioneer Catholic Laymen in New York — Dominick Lynch and Cornelius Heeney," *United States Catholic Historical Soceity, Historical Records and Studies,* IV, (Oct., 1906), 285-292.

Middleton, Rev. Thomas C., O.S.A., "An Early Catholic Settlement...St. James of Carthage, N.Y., 1785-1818-1898," *Records of the American Catholic Historical Society of Philadelphia,* X (1899), 17-77, 138-195.

Miller, Rev. Norbert H., O.M. Cap. "Pioneer Capuchin Missionaries in the United States (1784-1816), *United States Catholic Historical Society, Historical Records and Studies,* XXI (1932), 170-234.

Moran, Eugene F., Sr. "The Erie Canal As I Have Known It," *Bottoming Out,* III, No. 2 (1959), 2-18.

O'Connor, Rev. Thomas F. "Catholicism in the Fort Stanwix Country," *Records of the American Catholic Historical Society of Philadelphia,* LX, No. 1 (March, 1949), 79-93.

Parson, Rev. Robert A., S.J. "Father Henry Harrison," *The Woodstock Letters,* LXXXII, No. 2 (May, 1953), 118-147.

Rameau, E. "The Progress of the Church in the United States," *The Catholic World,* I, No. 1 (April, 1865), 1-19.

Ryan, Rev. Joseph Paul. "Travel Literature as Source Material for

American Catholic History," *Illinois Catholic Historical Review,* X, No. 3 (Jan., 1928), 179-238, No. 4 (April, 1928), 301-363.

Schaefers, Rev. William, "Growth of Episcopal Sees in America." *The Ecclesiastical Review,* CVII (Nov. 1942), 367-371.

Sharp, Rev. John K. "The Acadian Confessors on Long Island," *United States Catholic Historical Society, Historical Records and Studies,* XXXIII (1944), 57-76.

Shea, John Gilmary. "Caughnawaga and the Rev. Joseph Marcoux, Its Late Missionary," *The Metropolitan* (Baltimore), III, No. 10 (Nov., 1855), 589-594.

Smith, Rev. Sydney F., S.J. "Pastor Chiniquy: An Examination of His 'Fifty Years in the Church of Rome'," *Publications of the Catholic Truth Society, LXXIV (1908),* 1-64.

Smith, Walter B. *"Wage Rates on the Erie Canal, 1828-1881," Journal of Economic History* XXIII (Sept., 1963), 298-311.

Wade, Mason. "The French Parish and Survivance in Nineteenth Century New England," *Catholic Historical Review,* XXXVI, No. 2 (July, 1950), 163-189.

Walters, Raymond, Jr. and Walters, Philip G. "David Parish: York State Land Promoter," *New York History,* XXVI, No. 2 (April, 1945), 146-161.

Weiss, Rev. Arthur A., S.J. "Jesuit Mission Years in New York State, 1654-1879," *The Woodstock Letters,* LXXV, No. 1 (March, 1946), 7-25.

White, Philip L. (ed.). "An Irish Immigrant Housewife on the New York Frontier," *New York History,* XLVIII, No. 2 (April, 1967), 182-188.

Wilson, Rev. Frederick R. "A History of Catholicism in Vermont," *Vermont Quarterly,* XXI, No. 3 (July, 1953), 211-219.

Wyer, J.I. "Later French Settlements in New York State, 1783-1800," *New York State Historical Association, Proceedings,* XV (1916), 176-189.

Zwierlein, Rev. Frederick J. "Catholic Beginnings in the Diocese of Rochester," *Catholic Historical Review,* I, No. 3 (Oct., 1915), 282-298.

Secondary Sources:
Unpublished

White Philip L. "Patterns of American Community Development: The Rural East." A copy of this unpublished typescript, which is dated 1964, is at the North County Historical Research Center, State University College, Plattsburgh, N.Y.

Recent Correspondence

Brown, Harold F. To me. Malone, Sept. 8, 1972. Mr.Brown is the Managing Editor of *The Malone Evening Telegram.*

Swastek, Rev. J.V. To me. Detroit, Jan. 18, 1971. Father Swastek is the Archivist of the Archdiocese of Detroit.